Spatial Boundaries and Social Dynamics

Case Studies from Food-Producing Societies

by
Augustin Holl
&
Thomas E. Levy

INTERNATIONAL MONOGRAPHS IN PREHISTORY

Ethnoarchaeological Series 2

Printed in the United States of America

ISBN 1-879621-04-5 (Paperback)
ISBN 1-879621-05-3 (Hard Cover)

Library of Congress Cataloging-in-Publication Data

Holl, Augustin.
Spatial boundaries and social dynamics : case studies from food-producing societies / by Augustin Holl & Thomas E. Levy.
p. cm. — (Ethnoarchaeological series ; 2)
Includes bibliographical references.
ISBN 1-879621-05-3 (hard cover : acid-free paper). — ISBN 1-879621-04-5 (paperback : acid-free paper)
1. Land settlement patterns—Africa. 2. Agriculture—Social aspects—Africa. 3. Human territoriality—Africa. 5. Africa—Antiquities. I. Levy, Thomas Evan. II. Title. III. Series.
GN645.H63 1993
306.3'49—dc20 93-21778
CIP

This book is printed on acid-free paper. ∞

International Monographs in Prehistory
P.O. Box 1266
Ann Arbor, Michigan 48106-1266
U.S.A.

Tel. (313) 761-9068
Bitnet: USERKØ2K@UMICHUM

Contents

List of Contributors

Kofi E. Agorsah	Department of History, University of West Indies, Mona Campus, Kingston 7, Jamaïca.
Augustin Holl	Départment d'Ethnologie et de Préhistoire, Université de Paris X–Nanterre, 200 Avenue de la République, 92001 Nanterre Cedex, France.
Thomas E. Levy	Department of Anthropology, University of California, San Diego, La Jolla, CA 92093, U.S.A.
Ibrahim Musa	Department of History, University of Benghazi, El Salamani Post Office, P.O.B. 17679, Benghazi, Lybia.
Glenn D. Stone	Department of Anthropology, Columbia University, New York 10027, U.S.A.

List of Contributors

[illegible]

[illegible]

[illegible] Department of Anthropology, Columbia University, New York 10027, USA

1. Introductory Note to Spatial Boundaries and Social Dynamics: Rounds, Recycling, and the Buildup of an Upward Spiral

Augustin Holl

Introduction

The project of this book emerged at Bradford (England) in 1987 during the annual conference of the Theoretical Archaeology Group. Some of the chapters were presented within a symposium which aimed at exploring the nature, characteristics, and effects of forces which generate the spatial patterning of social behavior, how these patterns are retrievable in the material record, and how they may be amenable to archaeological investigation. Following the numerous and interesting ideas presented during the discussions which took place at the symposium, the papers presented were extensively revised, and additional researchers were invited to contribute to the present book.

It is almost commonsense knowledge that space and time are two of the pillars of archaeological research. With the emergence of behavioral concerns in archaeology, researchers now wish to know more about the complex interrelations between societies and space. In varying degrees, spatial concerns have always been present in archaeological discourses, implicitly or explicitly. For example, the use of distribution maps of individual items—types of pottery, stone tool, metal artifact—to trace the routes of migrations of cultural groups, cultural influences, or diffusion of technology. These early conceptions of space were congruent with the research problems faced then by archaeologists. Present-day researchers are not satisfied with this level of spatial analysis. Consequently, they have initiated a wide range of research on the spatial dimensions of human behavior, with rounds of intensive study followed by quieter periods during which ideas are either neglected or evaluated, tested, and recycled, moving from one theoretical construct to another. This process produces something like an upward spiral:

> The great intellectual riddles of humankind are rarely, if ever, resolved, they may disappear from view but do not cease to exist, and in the end are certain to return to our collective attention. They usually resurface after a period of neglect, then fall again from view, not because their problems are resolved, but because intensive study exhausts their appeal, exposing their complexities and highlighting the need for better understanding of other phenomena or other facets of the problem. This recycling of the fundamental queries is costly. The incremental advances that are made in each new round of interest—that make the process an upward spiral, not an endless circle—occur only after a period of rehearsing the discourse and relearning the lessons that faded during the time of neglect. (Turner 1991:133)

As suggested by the quote above, it appears that in the eighties we have entered a new round of interest in spatial analysis in archaeology, characterized by a stronger emphasis on the behavior which generates spatial patterns in the material record of human societies; quantitative methods are now reevaluated and are selected according to their congruence with the research issues at hand. (Cribb 1991; Fiches and Van der Leeuw 1990; Gamble and Boismier 1991; Hillier and Hanson 1984; Kent 1984, 1987, 1991; Kramer 1982; Rapaport 1976; Tobert 1988; Van der Leeuw 1990; Whallon 1984, 1987; etc.).

The Interpretation of Spatial Patterns

In general, there appears to be a consensus among various researchers about the state of the art in the studies of spatial dimensions in human societies, according to which the identification of spatial patterns in the material record basically depends on the care with which an excavation of a site, and/or the mapping of a settlement are carried out. But it is the interpretation of the observed patterns that is much more difficult. This interpretation is hampered by several factors, which depend on the nature of the settlement, the frequency and the duration of occupation, the raw material used to built shelters and facilities, the density of population, and, for archaeological sites, the consequences of post-abandonment processes. Ethnoarchaeological research and studies of site formation processes can be considered as different but complementary attempts to face the difficulties generated by the new emphasis on human behavior. However, there seems to be some misconception that one of the research "protocols"—ethnoarchaeology—will be able to provide rules and procedures which will put archaeological research on sounder "behavioral" foundations (Clark 1968; Binford 1980). According to Clark (1968:280),

> The operation as I see it, is twofold: first obtain this "ethnoarchaeological" data by fieldwork, to apply it to the archaeological evidence with sufficient precision that a reasonable measure of accuracy in reconstruction is ensured.

In this regard, it is worth noting that the scale at which social relations are spatially reproduced far exceeds the extent of ordinary archaeological excavation. Consequently, if archaeologists wish to investigate the behavioral basis for spatial variation, they will have not only to enlarge the size of their usual sample units but also to create new theories and models which will highlight the meanings of the observed patterns. As pointed out by Gamble (1991:13), this dilemma,

> ... led Binford ten years ago to call for a moratorium (1980:242) on excavation and analysis until the exploration, via ethnoarchaeology, of the conceptual frameworks and local variation had reached a position to guide such work.

At first glance, both the research "protocols" mentioned above seem reasonable, but a closer examination shows that they suffer some serious shortcomings. Differences between ethnoarchaeology and archaeology are taken for granted, and effects of site formation processes on the archaeological record are not considered seriously (Schiffer 1987). The second problem lies in the internal dynamics of each field of research—ethnoarchaeological research may generate its own legitimate new problems, methods and standards, for example. Consequently, even if both these protocols were followed, we are afraid that archaeologists may have to wait for an infinite lapse of time. Ethnoarchaeology does not provide a recipe book of spatial behavior, but presents at various scales aspects of spatial organization of human societies (Gamble 1991). It provides a guide to the interpretation of spatial patterns and not general rules to be applied to the archaeological record. Human geography is also a relevant source for spatial models (Chorley and Haggett 1967; Haggett 1973; Lloyd and Dicken 1977).

Depending on the level under investigation, the spatial requirements of activities and their locations relative to each other, according to the distribution of resources, generate modular spatial units which are at the same time, and in varying degrees, constrained by societies' *world views*. The dynamic interrelationships between social systems and processes of spatial patterning characterized by numerous feedback loops, are basically time-dependent. The world views which shape societies' spatial behavior may be based upon kinship, relations of production, symbolic ties with ancestors' shrines, and/or relations of domination.

In food-producing societies, which are studied in this volume, land is a means of production. Consequently, different forms of appropriation develop, and the natural landscape is progressively transformed into a cultural one. Different principles which structure social relations are thus mapped on the ground. The layout of settlement is often organized according to a subtle hierarchy of structuring principles and levels of social integration. At the level of the household, different dwelling units are often located close to each other according to their functional complementarity and gender relations: husband/wife, parents/children, senior/junior, boy/girl, etc. At the level of settlement or communities, depending on the density of population and political organization, there may be a combination of different structuring principles: kinship, relations of production, and relations of domination. The location of households close to each other may be based on kinship, relations of alliance and/or friendship. The existence of a centralized political system may weaken the efficiency of the above set of structuring principles but does not override them. At the regional level, in the case of autonomous and self-sustaining communities, settlements may be located according to the distribution of critical resources and/or historical links with each other, and competition and cooperation may occur between them.

According to Lloyd and Dicken (1977:316-317), all individuals are aware of only a limited part of what might be called "objective" environment. The part of which they are aware may be considered as *behavioral environment, action space,* or *task environment.* Behavioral, action, or task environment is defined as the segment of the "objective" environment about which information signals are received and interpreted. Consequently,

> Only a limited proportion of the information transmitted by the "objective" environment is effectively received, it is this that determines the nature of the individual's behavioral environment, and it is this, and only this, that is relevant to purposive behavior. Insofar as this is the only environment of

> which people are aware, it is for them the real environment. Phenomena, places, or events outside the behavioral environment have no relevance to, and no influence on, conscious decision-making. (Lloyd and Dicken 1977:316)

More limited components, such as individuals' and groups' activity space, are included within the behavioral space, thus suggesting an unquestionable nested hierarchy of spatial units within every society's relationship to the natural landscape.

The tentative model presented above does not aim to be exhaustive, it is simply an abstract of the issues discussed in the chapters presented in this book. The concrete spatial manifestation of the principles which structure social relations at both intra- and inter-settlement levels are subject to variation and fluctuation according to the dynamics of the social and environmental systems, and a bifurcation, that is, a radical change, may occur when a previously dominant structuring principle is altered and superseded by a new one, as is the case when a former small-scale autonomous social system experiences the development of a centralized political system.

Some Structuring Principles of Spatial Behavior

The studies presented in this book explore the structuring principles of the spatial behavior of a wide range of food-producing societies (Rapaport 1976:25), varying from the Chalcolithic societies of the northern Negev in Israel to the Iron Age societies of Central Darfur in western Sudan, the Late Neolithic societies of southeastern Mauritania, the Nchumuru of the Volta basin in northern Ghana, the Kofyar of the Benue valley in Nigeria, and the Kotoko and Arab-Shuwa of northern Cameroon.

Agorsah's ethnoarchaeological study discusses, from an archaeological perspective, the importance of social relations and behavior as crucial factors in the evolution and spatial patterning of settlements, as well as the development, form, or cardinal orientation of residential units such as houses or compounds within the settlements. At the level of the settlement as a whole, ethnoarchaeological data from the northern Volta basin of Ghana in West Africa are used to demonstrate the impact of the social system on the settlement's physical growth and patterning and how these constitute adjustment mechanisms of the societies involved. Using data on the physical evolution of some selected individual houses or compounds with respect to demographic factors, this study explains how the units take form in response to social requirements. The archaeological implications at both levels of settlement are examined critically in the light of the settlement history of the study area. It is concluded that although social systems are not as rigid as those operative in the physical world, they exert substantial pressure on the trend of patterning and form of residential units at various levels of the spatial development of the settlement. The cross-cultural application of this generalization, the Local Rule model, is presented at the end of the chapter, with some useful suggestions for future ethnoarchaeological research.

Stone's study focuses on the forces which generate the spacing of rural settlement among the Kofyar of the Benue valley in Nigeria. In contrast to numerous archaeological studies of the relationship between site spacing and economic interaction, his ethnoarchaeological research on a dispersed agrarian settlement system explores the effects of cooperation and competition in agricultural production. An analysis of labor mobilization shows the importance of supra-household cooperation in meeting the labor bottlenecks that characterize savanna agriculture. This, and the need to maintain a high enough settlement density to protect their tenure against other ethnic groups and wild predators, promotes low intersettlement distance. At the same time, rising population density promotes establishment of settlement (compounds) on intensively cultivated farms. The result is a pattern of dispersed farmsteads with low variation in nearest-neighbor distances.

In his ethnoarchaeological study, Holl discusses the effects of ethnic interaction, which may be characterized as competitive, in the Houlouf region in northern Cameroon. The region is inhabited by six ethnic groups, among which the Kotoko and the Shuwa-Arabs are the most important. This study aims to explore the forces which determine and guide site location strategies and settlement spatial patterning of those two social groups, with their different socioeconomic, political, and symbolic systems. It is argued that their material culture in general, more specifically the particular spatial patterning of their settlements, the system of allocation of space to different socioeconomic activities, the relative weighting of domestic versus community space, and settlement location strategies in the regional territory are structurally responsive to the competitive nature of their mutual interaction and the inequality which characterizes their participation in the regional political decision-making structures. It thus appears that the maintenance, reproduction, and even the revival of their ethnic identities, symbolically expressed in the total range of their material culture and settlement layout, are features with twofold consequences: the pride of being free pastoral-nomads for the Shuwa-Arabs, balanced by the pride of being the owner of land, for the Kotoko, and at the same time, the maintenance at a certain level of systemic complementarity in matters of subsistence, exchanges of craft items, and regional politics.

Levy considers the problem of differential access to craft production and natural resources in the northern Negev region of Israel and discusses the role of copper metallurgy in the development of Chalcolithic societies which entered that area by the late 5th to early 4th millennium B.C. This study shows that space takes on a new meaning for societies when population increases and more sophisticated methods of production develop. The Chalcolithic societies of the northern Negev have witnessed the development of competition over critical resources, such as farm and grazing lands, and its corollary, warfare. The type of dwellings of the pioneer Chalcolithic settlements, with series of interconnected subterranean rooms, now appears to have been an adjustment to this situation of severe competition and warfare. The copper ore procurement system based on accurate geographic knowledge of the distribution of mineral resources seems to have been under exclusive control; it is thus suggested that special trips made by metal workers or special purpose groups were necessary to provide centers of production with raw material. The emergence of sanctuaries and their locations in the regional landscape also suggest that they have played a key role in regulating competition and conflicts between different Chalcolithic cultural groups of the northern Negev, characterized by tightly knit, wadi-based settlement systems.

Musa considers the relationship between iron technology and settlement patterns in central Darfur in western Sudan. Ethnographic observations, the historical record, and archaeological evidence are used to explore the impact of the new technology on the social systems of the study area. The adoption of iron technology appears to have resulted from the combination of several factors: relocation of population following climatic fluctuations in this marginal environment, mass and small-scale migrations, political actions, and functional advantages. Following the adoption of iron technology, some small groups of craft specialists—iron producers—with different ethnic affiliations or backgrounds, were accepted but never integrated within the social systems of their host communities. The location of iron-working facilities on the peripheries of studied settlements and their frequent association with graveyards show the development of spatial and social segregation in which smiths were included in a cast-like endogamous group, characteristic of numerous savanna and sahel societies in Africa. Space was consequently manipulated to implement, maintain, and reinforce the actual social hierarchy.

In his archaeological contribution, Holl examines the buildup of the cultural landscape of the late Neolithic societies of the southeastern Sahara in Mauritania, and develops an approach based on simple measurements of spatial units: their relative spacing from each other at different levels of the settlement system. The meanings of these measurements are evaluated at different levels of spatial patterns observed in the archaeological record, based on an analysis of the imperatives of the subsistence and socioeconomic systems and patterns of social distance. Depending on the location, the size of settlement, the degree of packing and clustering of habitation units, and the chronological framework, three major sequences of settlement expansion are identified as characterizing the main steps of the transformation of the Neolithic political system, which culminate in the emergence of a four-tiered hierarchy of settlements.

Conclusion

As pointed out by Gamble (1991:19), "spatial archaeology should have as its central theme the transformation of landscape and the construction of the human niche." All the contributions in this book aim to provide explanations of the *how* and *why* of the spatial patterns observed in the material record of a sample of food-producing societies. In political terms, some of the case studies presented concern simple, egalitarian, agricultural societies and others stratified or complex societies. The structuring principles of spatial behavior discovered, however, are always in a state of punctuated equilibrium (Eldredge & Gould 1972); variation, fluctuation, and change may occur at the individual, community, and regional levels, initiating a radical transformation, a bifurcation in the process of the buildup of the human niche, which is often irreversible.

References

Binford, L. R.
1980 Willow smoke and dogs' tails: hunter-gatherer settlement systems and archaeological site formation. *American Antiquity* 45:4-20.

Chorley, R. J. & P. Haggett (eds.)
1967 *Models in Geography*. London: Methuen.

Clark, J. D.
1969 Studies of hunter-gatherers as an aid to the interpretation of prehistoric societies. In *Man the hunter*, R. B. Lee & J. DeVore (eds.), 276-280. Chicago: Aldine.

Cribb, R.
1991 *Nomads in Archaeology*. Cambridge: Cambridge University Press.

Eldredge, N. & S. J. Gould
1972 Punctuated equilibrium: an alternative to phyletic gradualism. In *Models in Paleobiology*, T. J. M. Schopf (ed.), 82-115. San Francisco: Freeman Cooper and Co.

Fiches, J.-L. & S. Van der Leeuw (eds.)
1990 *Archéologie et Espace*. Juan les Pins: Centre de Recherches Archéologiques du CNRS, Editions APDCA.

Gamble, C. S.
1991 An Introduction to the living spaces of mobile peoples. In *Ethnoarchaeological Approaches to Mobile Campsites: Hunter-Gatherer and Pastoralist Case Studies*, C. S. Gamble and W. A. Boismier (eds.), 1-23. Ann Arbor: International Monographs in Prehistory.

Gamble, C. S. & W.A. Boismier (eds.)
1991 *Ethnoarchaeological Approaches to Mobile Campsites: Hunter-Gatherer and Pastoralist Case Studies*. Ann Arbor, International Monographs in Prehistory.

Haggett, P.
1973 *L'Analyse Spatiale en Geographie Humaine*. Paris: Armand Colin.

Hillier, B. & J. Hanson
1984 *The Social Logic of Space*. Cambridge: Cambridge University Press.

Kent, S.
1984 *Analyzing Activity Areas: An Ethnoarchaeological Study of the Use of Space*. Albuquerque: University of New Mexico Press.
1987 Understanding the use of space: An ethnoarchaeological approach. In *Method and theory for Activity Area Research: An ethnoarchaeological Approach*, S. Kent (ed.), 1-60. New York: Columbia University Press

Kent, S. (ed.)
1991 *Domestic Architecture and the Use of Space: An Interdisciplinary Cross-cultural Study*. Cambridge: Cambridge University Press.

Kramer, C.
1982 *Village Ethnoarchaeology: Rural Iran in Archaeological Perspective*. New York: Academic Press.

Lloyd, P. E. & P. Dicken
1977 *Location in Space: A theoretical Approach to Economic Geography*. New York: Harper & Row.

Rapaport, A.
1976 Socio-cultural aspects of Man-Environment studies. In *The Mutual Interaction of Peoples and their Built Environment: A Cross-Cultural Perspective*, A. Rapaport (ed.), 7-35. The Hague/Paris: Mouton Publishers.

Schiffer, M. B.
1987 *Formation Processes of the Archaeological Record*. Albuquerque: University of New Mexico Press.

Turner, B. L., II
1991 Thoughts on Linking the Physical and Human Sciences in the Study of global Environmental Change. *Research and Exploration* 7:133-135.

Tobert, N.
1988 *The Ethnoarchaeology of the Zaghawa of Darfur (Sudan) : Settlement and Transcience*. Oxford: British Archaeological Reports.

Van der Leeuw, S.
1990 Rythmes temporels, espaces naturels et espaces vécus. In *Archéologie et Espaces*, J.-L. Fiches and S. Van der Leeuw (eds.), 299-346. Juan les Pins: Centre de Recherches Archéologiques du CNRS, Editions APDCA.

Whallon, R.
1984 Unconstrained clustering for the analysis of spatial distributions in archaeology. In *Intrasite Spatial Analysis in Archaeology*, H. Hietala (ed.), 242-277. Cambridge: Cambridge University Press.
1987 Simple statistics. In *Quantitative Research in Archaeology: Progress and Prospects*, M.S. Aldenderfer (ed.), 135-150. London: Sage Publications.

2. Archaeological Considerations on Social Dynamics and Spatial Pattern Development of Traditional Settlements

Kofi E. Agorsah

Introduction

One fascinating aspect of archaeological analysis is the explanation of the frequency with which material manifestations of man's behaviour are bonded together. The complexity of the interconnections and associations makes it even more challenging and exciting. Areal variations of the relationships between cultural phenomena are so numerous that archaeologists have, over the centuries, looked for regularities or patterning among distributions of these material manifestations. It is not the patterns that are recognised nor the fact that their distribution varies from place to place that is of greatest interest. Rather it is the past behaviour of the society concerned that is of significance to the archaeological analysis. The basic assumption in dealing with patterns consists of convictions related to *recurring modes of human activities or behaviour*. Artifact pattern analysis (South 1977; Armstrong 1987), spatial pattern analysis (Whallon 1973; Clarke 1977; Fletcher 1978; Hillier et al. 1978; Muehrcke 1980; Agorsah 1988; Kuper 1972; Soja 1971), ceramic typology (Soper 1971; Boomert 1980; Crossland 1973), and various kinds of classification in archaeology assume *regularity* in human behaviour.

Throughout history change has been a constant element in human culture. (Social scientists have identified various processes of change such as independent invention, diffusion, acculturation and culture contact.) Without even examining any of these in detail, it is easy and clear to see why one should recognise that human society and all associated modes of behaviour are not static. That is, they are dynamic. As a corollary, spatial pattern can be considered as adapting to this dynamic nature of the social system. Contributing to the social transformation are factors such as the influence of cosmology (Kuper 1972), traditional views of spatial organisation (Agorsah 1988; Holl 1987; Leinhardt 1977) and exploration of space (Sinclair 1985; Tait 1959), concepts of boundaries (Hillier et al. 1978), territoriality and land tenure, perception of the natural environment, as well as folk traditions about ecology and attitudes towards natural resources. In his study of the morphology of County Durham in England, Roberts (1978:291-322) for example, stated as follows:

> A systematic study of Durham villages reveals clear regularities: thus 60% of all plans are variants of local circumstances of the two-row regular village; a further 10% are variants of this type, a single-row plan, while another 10% comprise multi-row plans.

Although Roberts was using these estimates to explain social and structural transformations over a period of one thousand years, he obviously based these on some expectable regularities. The principle of seriation in archaeology (Deetz 1977) uses the frequency or regularity of occurrence of artifacts for chronological schemes. Patterning, therefore, has become and remains a basis for discussing or explaining systems of classification and abstract concepts of human behaviour. Referring to the social sciences or what has been referred to as "sciences of the artificial," Hillier and his colleagues (1978) state: "We cannot understand the flux which constitutes our human experiences unless we realise that it is raised above the futility of infinitude by various successive types of modes of emphasis which generate the active energy of a finite assemblage...." Hillier and his colleagues were also referring to "patterning" of human behaviour.

One of the lessons that archaeologists have come to learn in recent years is the importance of the patterns of social behaviour to which individuals and groups conform in their dealings with one another in space and time (Leach 1976; Keat and Urry 1975). In fact, some scholars have attempted to demonstrate summary mathematical rules which govern social relations between individuals and groups (Cartwright and Harary 1977). Also, objects or artifacts of archaeological significance are considered as behaving within certain rules (Agorsah 1983, 1988) because they were the products of past human social behaviour. Therefore, the study of artifacts is the study of human behaviour (social, economic etc.) that produces them. However, owing to changes in the size and composition and needs of social groups as well as increased development of survival strategies with time, one cannot expect the products of human behaviour to remain static. Similarly, human activities may occur in various places during different times and according to different needs. The structure of the social group also then tends to be affected by the new order. This accounts for the significance of the dynamic nature of the social factor in the explanation of human behaviour.

Spatial Patterns in Archaeology

The consequences of human behaviour in terrestrial space have posed challenges not only to cultural geographers, but to archaeologists, especially when it comes to explanation of the means by which human societies encounter different phenomena in space and time, as well as various ways in which they interrelate. Human groups have, since prehistoric times, faced the reality of space, but the strategy for coping with it is a cultural variable. Similarly, because human settlements are placed in the natural landscape, they reflect in varying degrees the interrelationships established between human factors such as history, social structure, and physical space (Agorsah 1986). The significance of the social factor, with its dynamic nature, for the understanding and explanation of spatial pattern has been demonstrated elsewhere (Agorsah 1988) and emphasises the contribution of the social group as a whole to the matrix of archaeological evidence (Schiffer 1977; Agorsah 1983, 1986). However, it cannot be assumed that societies, especially prehistoric ones, have a concept of spatial pattern equivalent to that of the social scientist or that of the ethnoarchaeologist. The marriage of the "social" to the "spatial" is so indispensable to archaeological interpretation that considerable attention has been given this marriage in recent years (Clarke 1977; Hodder 1976; Hillier et al. 1978; Leach 1976; Fletcher 1978; Agorsah 1985, 1988; Sinclair 1987; Ucko et al. 1972; Chang 1968).

Writing on the "Archaeology of place" Binford (1983) has stated that "The processes which cause site patterning are long-term repetition of patterns in the "positioning" of adaptive systems in geographic space." Site patterning derives from the repetition or lack thereof in the spatial positioning of systems. In addition to attempting to demonstrate the validity and importance of this statement for archaeological reconstruction and interpretation, this chapter attempts to go a little further (Hodder and Horton 1976; Earle 1976). At the same time, it has been recognised that the socio-spatial consequences of human behaviour vary according to the level of human settlement in space at the macro or micro level. In a recent exposition (Agorsah 1988a), a model of spatial behaviour—the "Local Rule" (LR) model—has been proposed that can help determine the trend of development, depending on an assumption about the state of the social system as the dynamic factor that creates the repetitive patterns that accommodate the bulk of the evidence of human spatial behaviour at archaeological sites. Data from the Volta basin of Ghana has been used to illustrate the patterning at various levels of settlement development. Contemporary cultural phenomena are also invoked in this chapter to demonstrate, in dynamic terms, the factors behind the spatial patterning that we often attribute to past societies. This, in essence, is the basis of the ethnoarchaeological enterprise (Atherton 1983; Donnan and Clewlow 1974; Stiles 1979; Agorsah 1985, 1988).

When Binford (1983) discussed his economic zonation of settlements, he emphasised the "home base" as an important factor built on social patterns of relationships. Although not directly indicated, his example of mobility patterning, the results of which are his so-called economic zones, consists of a direct consequence of social relationships between groups in Nunamiut Eskimo society. Binford's study of within- and between-site variability—as well as variability in site utilisation—also supports the view of the dynamic nature of social systems in shaping the use of space.

Environmental features change over time in various ways, the most important being the state of the features as well as in their spatial positions. For example, structures erode away, which creates problems that call for human reaction (social, technological, etc.), some structures disseminate offspring while others are moved by external forces such as humans and animals as means of adaptation. The result of all this is continual environmental change as well as change in the adaptive behaviour patterns of societies. Also, changes in the nature of things and in their positions produce varying rates of change or adaptation, as well as change in patterning. In addition, adaptive trends may be cyclical or non-cyclical. The interrelationship between the continual adaptation of natural and social phenomena creates a complex situation that presents interpretative difficulties to the archaeologists (Shinnie 1985). Understanding and explanation of archaeological material to reflect this complex situation requires methodological approaches that accept and recognise the reality of this dynamic interaction.

The significance of social factors for spatial interpretation in archaeology has been demonstrated by many scholars (Agorsah 1988b; Bailey 1982; Doby

1967; Mills 1985; Leach 1978) and in one case (Agorsah 1986) it was clearly emphasised that the form of spatial relationship within settlements or archaeological sites must be described in terms of the patterns of social behaviour to which individuals and groups conform in their dealings with one another. But because of the impossibility of observing the social behaviour of past societies we have to rely on models drawn from modern social behaviour patterns. It is well known that the conformity of individuals to localised social patterns of behaviour is formulated in rules which in modern societies are recognised as rules of etiquette or moral rules. It is these rules, especially where they are related to man's use of space, that can be utilised to formulate models that can be applied to the prehistoric situation, and which combine both spatial and social factors in one package. Such models have often been related to settlement pattern analysis (Agorsah 1988; Willey 1972; Sinclair 1987; Zubrow 1975; Hodder 1978).

In the definition of "settlement patterns" Gordon Willey (1956) indicated the above link when he wrote that:

> It refers to dwellings, to their arrangement, and to the nature and disposition of other buildings pertaining to community life. These settlements reflect the natural environment, the level of technology on which builders operated, and various social interaction and control which the culture maintained.

The main concern of settlement pattern analyses during and after Willey's Viru valley study up to the early seventies demonstrated an awareness of theoretical and methodological considerations and relied to a large extent on the use of various techniques and approaches such as central place theory (Johnson 1972), point pattern analysis (Hodder and Orton 1976; Thomas 1972), quantification of archaeological distribution maps Hodder and Orton 1976; Laux 1971), Thiessen polygons (Hodder and Hassel 1971; Lösch 1954), nearest neighbour analysis (Earle 1976; Hodder and Orton 1976), behavioural chain analysis (Schiffer 1977), as well as archaeological sampling (Willey 1956; Parsons 1972) and theory of space syntax (Hillier et al. 1978). Many of the studies lacked models in the real sense that places emphasis on the interplay of social and spatial factors.

The most recent developments in settlement pattern studies have more emphasis on the interaction between the two dynamic factors—spatial and social. The Local Rule (LR) model of spatial behaviour (Agorsah 1988) is one of the models that have been recognised as not only considering spatial and social factors in a single package in the reconstruction of settlement pattern development, but also one that has cross-cultural applicability.

The Local Rule Model

This model is based on the conviction that the activities that create the matrix of archaeological features are a result of human societies. Also, it is argued that the location and distribution of structural features in settlements affect human behaviour, that moving them from one place to another makes a difference, that changing the spatial configuration or pattern or social arrangements alters their functions, and that physically separating two interacting objects affects the degree of the interaction. But the strategy in traditional societies (including prehistoric ones) of space and social dynamics is a cultural variable. Also, as noted earlier, the concept of space of the archaeologist in analysing the material may not be equivalent to that of the society being studied. All these lead to a single conclusion that spatial behaviour cannot be understood apart from its social context, because geographical space constitutes a reflection of social meanings about how the space is used (Kuper 1962; Soja 1971; Gonzales 1973). The LR model deals with decisions about the choice of location in space. It explains that social groups locate themselves in space such that they are either close together (clustered) or far apart (dispersed). The decision of human groups to locate in nearby areas is considered to constitute an indication of closer relationship. Members of the group or groups thus recognise that they are able to share the same geographical space without causing deviation from desired goals (Agorsah 1988b). The decision that results is a clustered distribution or positive rule. Conversely, when members of a group or groups are unable or unwilling to share the same space the result is a dispersed distribution or negative rule.

This model is particularly applicable to traditional societies that do not consider landscape as a cosmology that can be cut into pieces and sold as parcels. Land is seen in terms of social relationships (Bohannan1971; Agorsah 1982, 1985, 1986; Gould 1968, 1969; Kuper 1972; Fletcher 1977; Klepper 1988). Although these relationships may change over time in any given situation, the structural and other cultural features such as houses, storage facilities, burial grounds, and other fixed structures become marks that remain in the archaeological record. On the ground one may recognise the formation of distinctive areas (clustered or dispersed) of features within the settlement. Mathematical (graph theoretical) rules governing social relations between individuals or groups have also been used by Cartwright and Harary (1977) to discover that some non-obvious spatial features that result from a group's social relationships possess a certain spatial organisation. Their approach emphasises the fact that when social relations are balanced (on the basis of the theoretical rules) a group can be characterised as either a single homogeneous unit or two opposing units. This is equivalent to the positive and negative rules of the LR model. Cartwright and Harary's model implies that we should be able to take a sociogram and put all groups who "like one another," as seen by their relationship, into one group (positive local rule) and place all those who do not share common social resources into another (negative local rule).

As has been explained elsewhere (Agorsah 1988) the LR model places emphasis on social resources defined as the opportunities offered to individuals or groups and not the relationship per se. Lorraine and White (1977) describe such a situation as a system of binary relations in which social groups are viewed in a network of mutual role relations and sets of reciprocal expectations. Because such roles impose constraints on the behaviour of individuals or groups, there is a tendency for rules of spatial behaviour to be generated as a result. These considerations should be clearly expectable among societies (prehistoric ones included) which, as part of the natural environment, are intimately linked with the land. In such societies, to belong to a territory or place is a social concept which requires first and foremost belonging to a social unit. The northern Volta basin of Ghana provides useful data for further discussion of relationships between social and spatial factors discussed above.

Test of the Model

The data base

The northern Volta basin of Ghana in West Africa is inhabited by several ethnic groups, the major ones being Gonja, Krachi, Nawuri, and Nchumuru. Some of these groups have been in the Volta basin since prehistoric times (Agorsah 1983, 1985a). They are identified today by the linguistic terms that refer to their individual sub-languages (Dakubu 1976; Hall 1983), but all these groups are considered to belong to one major linguistic group called the Guan (Fig. 1). Occupying the southeastern section is the Krachi group, which, oral tradition says, originated from present Akwapim areas of southern Ghana (Kumah 1964) and share the tradition of the great god and oracle *Lente*, now known by the corrupted name *Dente*, with the Nchumuru presently located to the north and west of the Krachi. The Nchumuru, located in three administrative districts, are also said to have migrated from southern Ghana to their present locations along the banks of the Volta and the Daka rivers (Brukum 1979). The Gonja occupy areas to the north and the west of the Nchumuru. Oral tradition (Braimah and Goody 1967) supported by Arabic documents (Johnson 1965) indicates that they have a long-standing cultural connection with the Mande-speaking country of the Sahel regions of West Africa. The Nawuri, the smallest of the four groups, occupy the area to the northwest of the Nchumuru and also probably migrated from Mande country (Daaku 1969; Kumah 1964).

Archaeological and ethnological evidence indicate that the northern Volta basin constituted a significant catchment area for the ancestors of these four and other (West African) ethnic groups which inhabit the basin and adjoining areas today.

Geographically, the northern Volta basin, the area of this test, consists of shallow-water sediments that were deposited in the subsiding area of pre-Cambrian rocks (Wills 1962). The area is topographically uniform and the topsoil is generally red-brown, well drained, porous, and friable. Soil nutrients are concentrated in this top organic matter, which has little capacity to retain them. The deeper soil over the Voltaian sandstone is admirably suited to the production of yams (*Dioscorea* sp.), guinea corn (*Sorghum guineense*), millet (*Pennisetum cenerum*) and cassava (*Manihot utilissima*). The distribution of these crops is quite uniform northward until the drier (more northern) country is encountered. The uniform topography is cut through by the dense drainage pattern consisting of the Volta, Sene, Oti, and Daka rivers. Because of the seasonal nature of the rainfall, some of the stream beds of this seemingly dense drainage system are dry in the dry season and flood in the wet season. Also, water loss is quite high and is worsened by surface run-off during thunderstorms or rainstorms, which occur in June–July and reach a maximum in August–September. The two regimes of wet and dry seasons caused by the north-south movement of the Intertropical Convergence Zone (ITCZ) has created a remarkable east-west bonding of climate and vegetation zones, which grade from the coast of Ghana with increasing latitude from thick equatorial and semi-deciduous forests to the savannah zone, where a greater portion of the northern Volta basin lies. Environmental and other studies (Asibey 1969, Wills 1962) indicate an irretrievable decline in wildlife population since prehistoric times. Squire (1962) has recorded 186 species of mammals in the geographic area, 52 of which are known to be

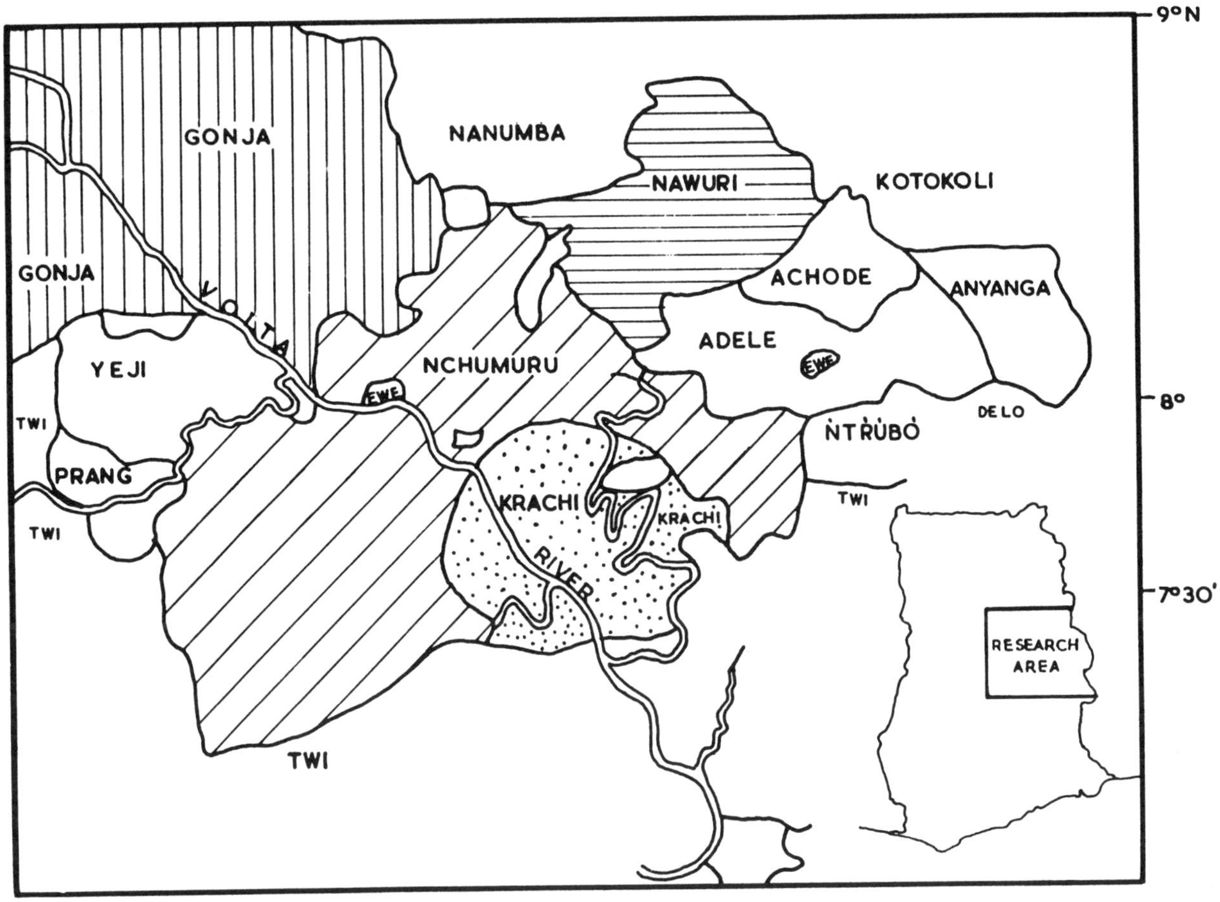

Fig. 1. Distribution of ethnic groups in the northern Volta basin of Ghana.

confined to the area of this study. Adiase (1969) also confirms relatively abundant aquatic resources in the Volta basin, most of them edible. Overall, plant and animal foods are abundant although sustainable yields, both wild and domesticated, are unpredictable.

Spatial pattern development

In his discussions of regional analysis in archaeology, Johnson (1977) clearly stated that a model that systematically analyses the interaction of human groups should consider such variables as the size and the nature of the groups engaged in the interaction, the nature of that interaction, and the physical space over which that interaction occurs. It may be added that in such an analysis one also needs to look at the level of interaction as well as the social resources as defined in this chapter. Obviously, the LR will not be the same at both the regional and the individual settlement levels. Analysis of settlement pattern development in the northern Volta basin of Ghana (Agorsah 1988a) indicates that the rule at the regional level tends to be less positive than at the level of the individual settlement. It means also that one is likely to find different degrees of the rule, be it positive or negative, at different levels. The section which follows will serve to demonstrate the dynamics of the social factor in the spatial pattern development of settlements at:

(a) the regional level,
(b) the individual settlement level, and
(c) the individual structural feature level (e.g., compound).

Regional Spatial Pattern Development

Archaeological and linguistic evidence (Davies 1967, 1971; Andah 1979; Dakubu 1982; Hall 1983; Painter 1966) indicate that settlement in the northern Volta basin could date back several millennia to the Stone Age. The first wave of settlers probably occurred within the confluence of the White and Black Volta. Archaeological survey of the area has revealed several sites with surface material attributed to the Early and Middle Stone Ages. The main artifacts include rolled pebble tools (choppers?), quartz pebbles, and broken Acheulean handaxes (Davies 1967, 1970). Although microlithic and Sangoan cultural material from various sites outside but adjacent to the basin has been recovered, suggesting a date around 50,000 years ago, we cannot generalize and use this as conclusive evidence for the presence of these same early cultural traditions in the basin. However, available evidence indicates that at least 4,000 years ago, and probably earlier, some parts of the Volta basin were inhabited by early food-producing people, although the extent of occupation cannot be definitely determined (Flight 1967; Danes 1970, 1971; Stahl 1985; Agorsah 1976; York and Calvocoressi 1967). The evidence of increase in the number of settlements in the basin is not complemented by adequate chronological data that can be used to demonstrate the actual sequence of the growth of the individual settlements.

The location and distribution of the settlements indicate that many of the early ones in the northern Volta basin developed in valleys, flood plains, fans, confluences, and pediments with soil that receive periodic alluvial deposits (Agorsah 1988a). The streams, springs, and seepage of groundwater probably provided water for permanent settlements in a savannah country with inconsistent rainfall (Wills 1962). The preferred areas were those overlooking valleys (Dombrowski 1976). Evidence has been adduced that points to a second wave of movement of groups into the Volta basin in the early part of the second millennium A.D., which coincides with the familiarity of people with the use of metal, an event which seems to have speeded up the pace of population movements. The two waves of movement of people and settlement in the basin have been discussed in greater detail elsewhere (Agorsah 1988a), which clearly supports the view that early settlement of the basin was environmentally and culturally determined.

Identification of the social factor in the location and the distribution of settlement in prehistoric Volta basin is important but clearly an arduous task. The question is, which social groups settled where in the basin? Linguistic evidence has been a great complementary source to archaeological evidence in African archaeology (Ehret and Posnansky 1982), and this has been useful to some extent in identifying generally the groups which still occupy most of the northern Volta basin. The languages by which we identify the ethnic groups are known to belong to the Niger-Congo linguistic family whose diversification in the area has been dated back some 10–12 millennia (Painter 1966). In the Volta basin specifically, the major languages identified belong to what is known as the Volta-Comoe (Dakubu 1982) which includes Akan, Bia, and Guan, the last one being the most widespread in the Volta basin. The linguistic speculations on the movement and settlement of the Guan group in the Volta basin (Dakubu 1982; Painter 1966; Steward 1960) extend into the Stone Age and indicate gradual increase in the occupation of the basin over time. It is therefore assumed that the present Guan-speakers are the same people who have occupied the basin since prehistoric times, which were the groups that developed the social system that we observe in the area today.

Using their present distribution on the basis of the above (Fig. 1), it appears that the social groupings as they are today generated the spatial distribution that we observe today. One important conclusion of the study of the settlement history of the basin was that cultural and historical variables, land shortages and restrictions, as well as clan attachments may have defined the aggregation of people and thus the production of small scale segmentary societies, and then of larger societies. The social structure in prehistoric times may, also, have been a function of ecology. This does not seem necessarily to apply to later developments, particularly at the single settlement level. Although not directly related to the Volta basin, Mills (1985) has derived a similar generalisation from his study of social structure and function of settlement space in northern Namibia. Mills' study gives important consideration to the "social" as a crucial factor in determining the dynamics of spatial patterning of Ovambo settlements.

Spatial Patterning at the Individual Settlement Level

The first test of the LR model of spatial behaviour was conducted in relation to the archaeological evidence of the origins and the development of traditional settlements in the Volta basin of Ghana. The ethnographic data relates to the Nchumuru ethnic group. Each Nchumuru settlement in the Volta basin belongs to one of its major groupings or phratries: Banda, Chachai, Nchenke, Kpentanai, or Sunwiae. These groupings are traditionally referred to as *nsuro* (*Kasuro*, sing.), each with a male head, its own ancestral shrine, secrets, properties, and relationships with other villages and adjoining areas. Inheritance is by a homogeneous transmission either male or female to the next oldest in the *kabuno* (clan). There are five *mbuno* (Brenaise, Dapoeta, Kpenwiae, Ntrapo, and Tariaso) in the head village of the Banda phratry called Wiae, discussed later below and which is the paramount village of the whole Nchumuru ethnic group. Recognition as an Nchumuru is determined by *kabuno* membership, which consists not only of the living, but also and primarily the ancestors. Consequently, the ancestral shrine of the *kabuno* is the controlling factor within the *kabuno* and traditionally should be located in the *kabuno* head house or compound. In addition, in Nchumuru society as it is with other West African societies such as the Krachi (Agorsah 1986), the Brong (Posnansky 1971, 1976), the Yaluka of Sierra Leone (Decorse 1988), and the Tiv (Bohannan1971), the builder of the environment is the user and at the same time he is the one who maintains it. Social connections, therefore play a vital role in spatial behaviour. One very basic fact about many traditional societies (including prehistoric ones) is that spatial behaviour is not merely a technological problem, but principally one of social relationship, the main goal being the practical adherence to cultural values. This assertion is supported by studies carried out by Mhlanga (1976), Prussin (1969), Mills (1985), Sinclair (1987), and Beattle (1960).

Nchumuru occupation of their present area (the Banda-Wiae area) has been reconstructed into four phases (Agorsah 1983, 1985b, 1988a and b). Each phase is characterised by social and spatial adjustments that have been identified through a study of the location of settlements and changes in house location within settlement. As has been remarked, the development of settlements in the northern Volta basin has been seen as clearly influenced by the social systems of the societies. The case of Wiae settlement succinctly demonstrates this assertion. Archaeological and ethnographic evidence has been used to identify the clan (*kabuno*) areas at Old Wiae (Agorsah 1983; Fig. 2).

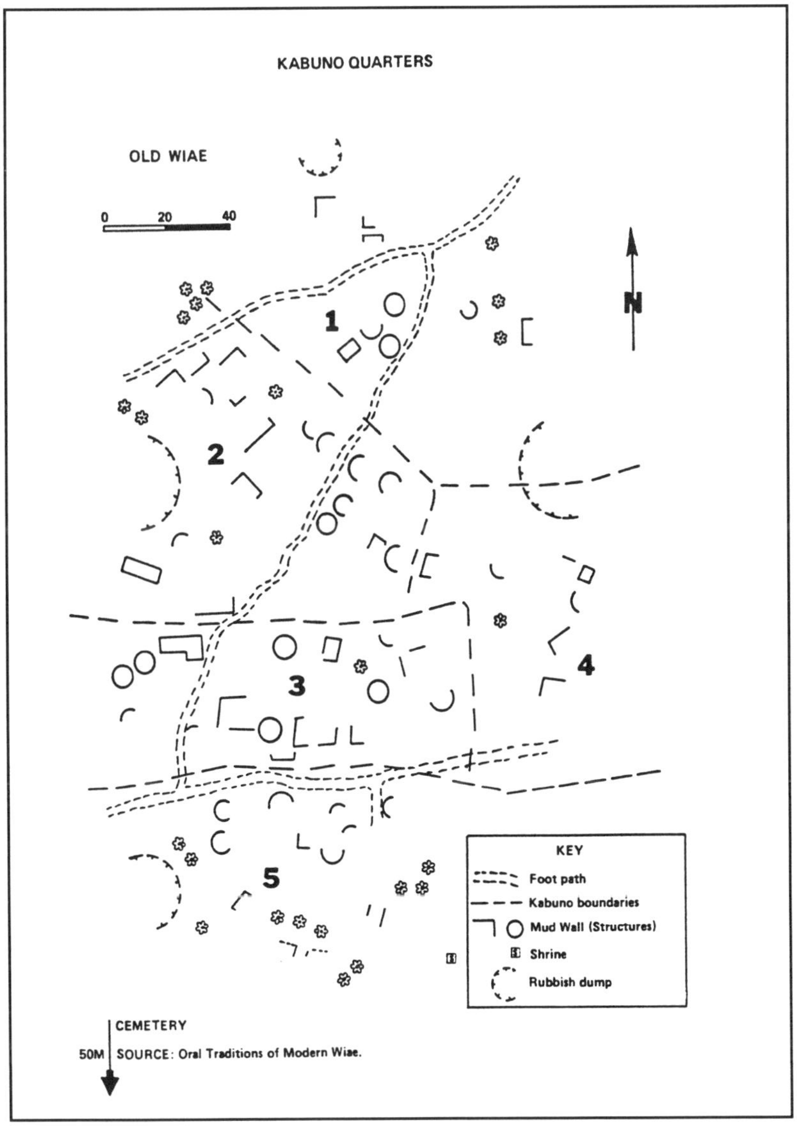

Fig. 2. Boundaries of *kabuno* (clan) quarters at Old Wiae, Ghana. 1=Kpenwiae, 2=Ntrapo, 3=Tarieso, 4=Breniase, 5=Dapoeta.

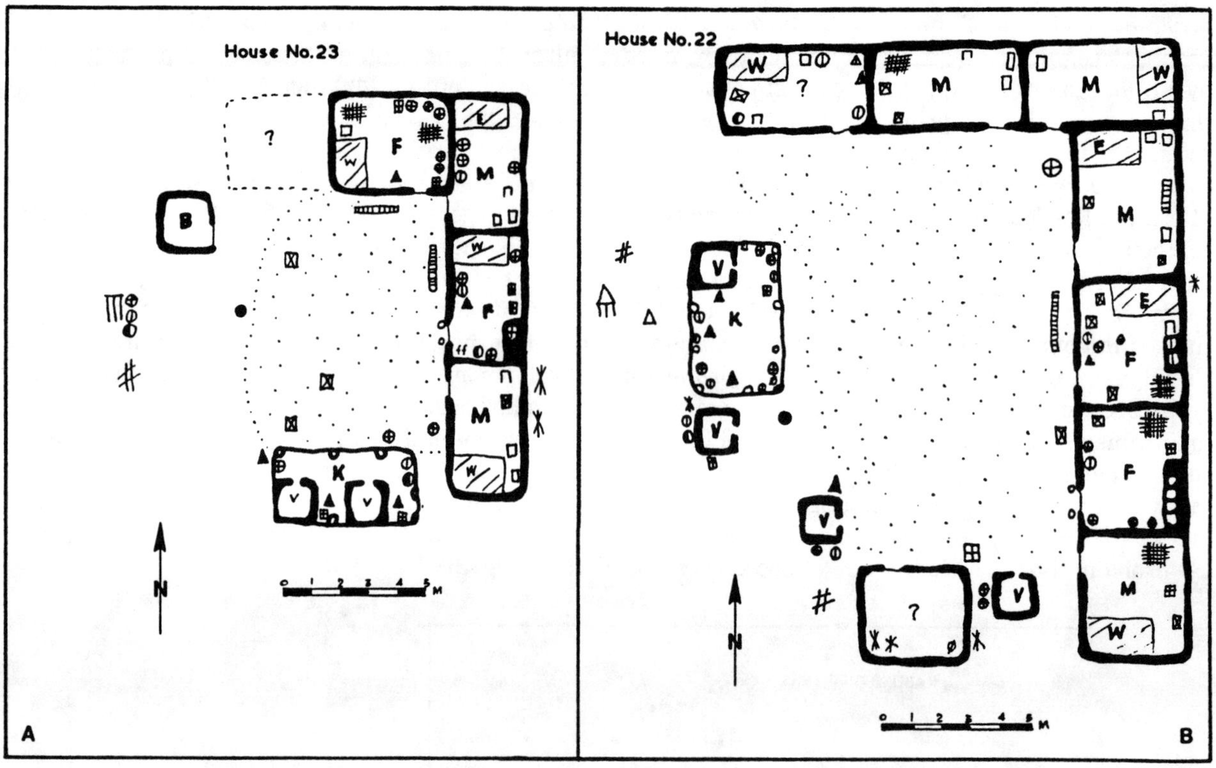

Fig. 3. Location and distribution of structural features and objects in houses with *kabuno* shrines.

The importance of keeping the *kabuno* system intact at Old Wiae is also indicated by the presence of *kabuno* shrines at central locations in the compounds as keepers of the clan spirit (Fig. 3), which has also been noted elsewhere (Kuper 1972). Also we recognize that courtyards of compounds open into each other to maintain *kabuno* connections. These patterns of spatial distribution were carried forward into New Wiae, which in 1972 showed signs of the tendency which ten years later, in 1981, became clearly manifested.

Figures 4 through 6 represent a breakdown of the distribution. Ethnographic evidence from Wiae suggests that a change in social relationships among *kabuno* groups would certainly effect changes in future distribution of *kabuno* compounds. However, over the four hundred years of its existence, the Nchumuru village of Wiae seems to have maintained the spatial features of the settlement in the same conservative fashion that social relationships have been maintained. The Nchumuru example at Wiae also indicates that the effect of the social system on the spatial pattern depends on the strength of the relationship involved, although the nature of the relationship appears to be more crucial. The socio-spatial dynamics among the Nchumuru are also demonstrated when we analyse the development and placement of individual structural features within the settlement.

Settlement Patterning at the Individual Feature Level

The history of the growth of individual houses or compounds in the Nchumuru village of Wiae also provides data that gives strong support to the importance of socio-spatial dynamics in the study of past human behaviour (Agorsah 1985a and b, 1986a and b). The tracing of the growth of individual houses not only provides us with a history of the structural development of the basic units of the settlement, but also the adjustment through which the basic social unit of the society (the family) was going. The examples of houses 1, 51A, and 10 provided below constitute the true pattern of the development of house structures (Figs. 7–9; Agorsah 1983, 1986b).

Fundamentally, the physical development of the house or the compound in Wiae seems to entail more than satisfying purely functional requirements, e.g. the form of the house is consciously conceived (designed) and realized (built) in response to an existing set of conditions accepted by the people as a social group. It is the social factor that provides the continuity between Old and New Wiae house forms, and

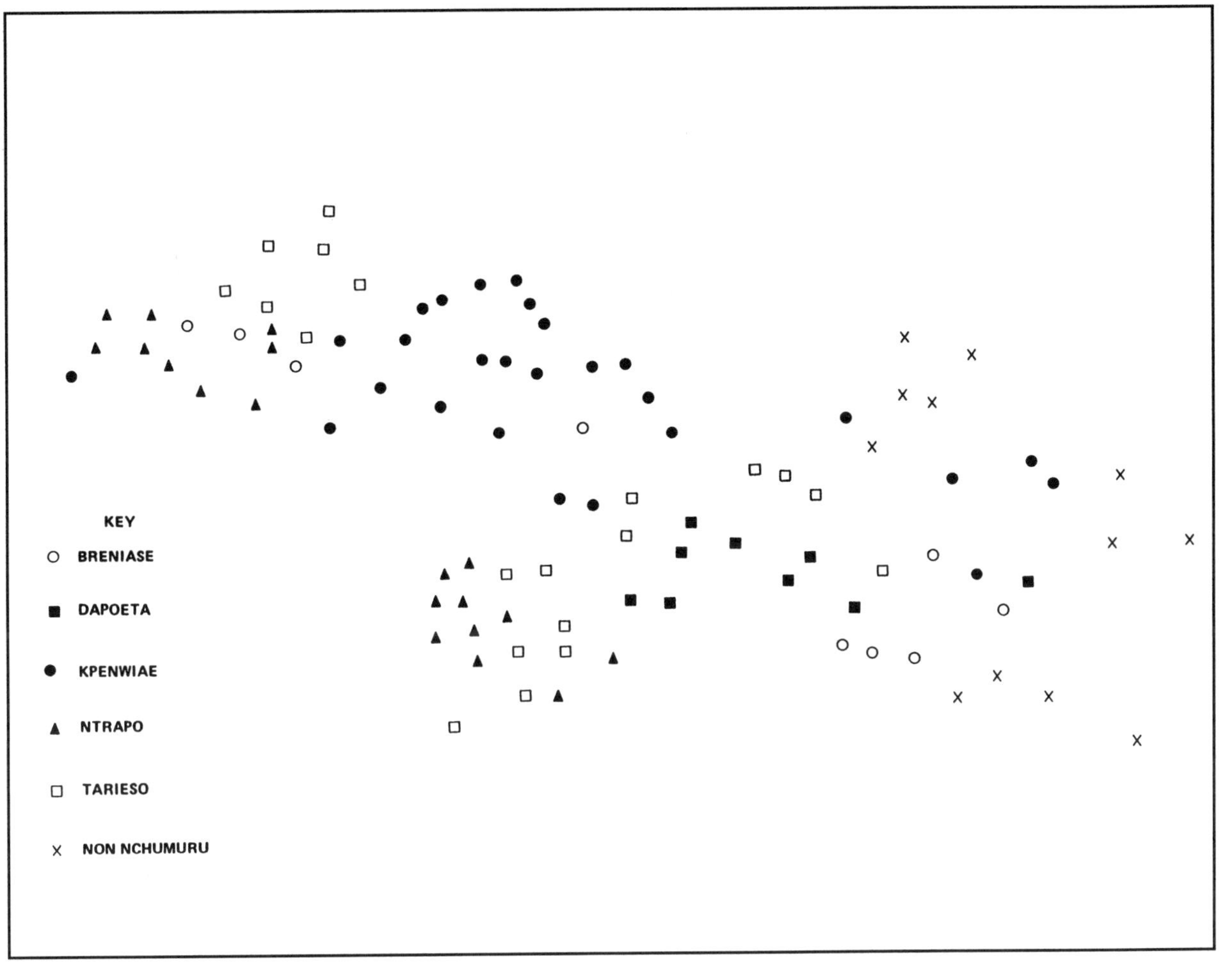

Fig. 4. Summary of the distribution of *kabuno* (clan) houses at New Wiae, Northern Ghana.

their orientation toward *kabuno* kinsfolk as social custom required is a clear illustration of how spatial order was taking form to satisfy social requirements (Figs. 7– 9, Table 1). The socio-spatial relationship shows how the pattern of the building, its maintenance, constraints, and also the patterns of daily life and demography are all fused in the form, thus giving it dual coherence: social and physical (Agorsah 1986b). A closer study of the various parts of the individual house among the Nchumuru (the rooms, courtyard, back yard, kitchen, and similar divisions of the house) also show how all these parts of the individual house and other houses are linked to one another. The connectivity pattern (*connectivity* here meaning the degree of accessibility between houses) is also emphasized by the network of footpaths which accommodate the criss-cross movements among relatives in different compounds and also give access to the main paths leading out of the settlements to the streams, shrines, farms, and other areas.

An interesting aspect of the growth of house form is the data it provides for explaining social transformation, which has been a major concern of scholars in recent years in the context of spatial configurations (Agorsah 1983 b and c, 1988a and b; Webb 1985; Goody 1973, 1975; Tait 1961; Decorse 1988; Holl 1987; Zubrow 1978; Black 1978; Hodder 1977; Clarke 1972;

Table 1. Development of houses: characteristics of households.

House No.	1	51A	10
Location	620M20	900N10	620M20
Kabuno	Kpenwiae	Tarieso	Tarieso
Head	Asofoakye Asabese	Abena Bruku	Kwasi Kyere
No. of Rooms	8	4	8
No. of Inhabitants			
Adult (M/F)	2/2	0/1	3/5
Other (M/F)	1/3	2/4	4/1

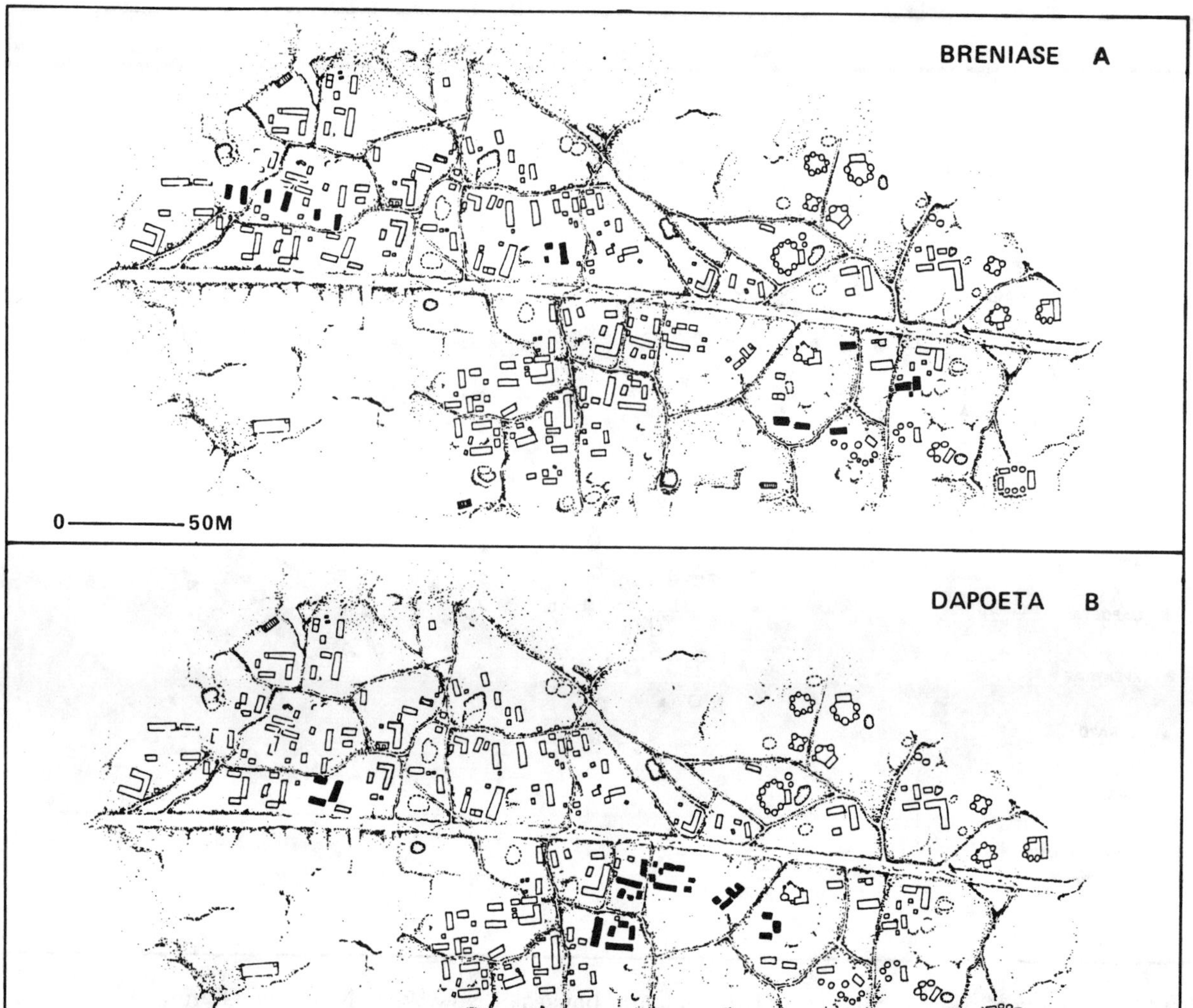

Fig. 5. Distribution of *kabuno* houses at New Wiae.

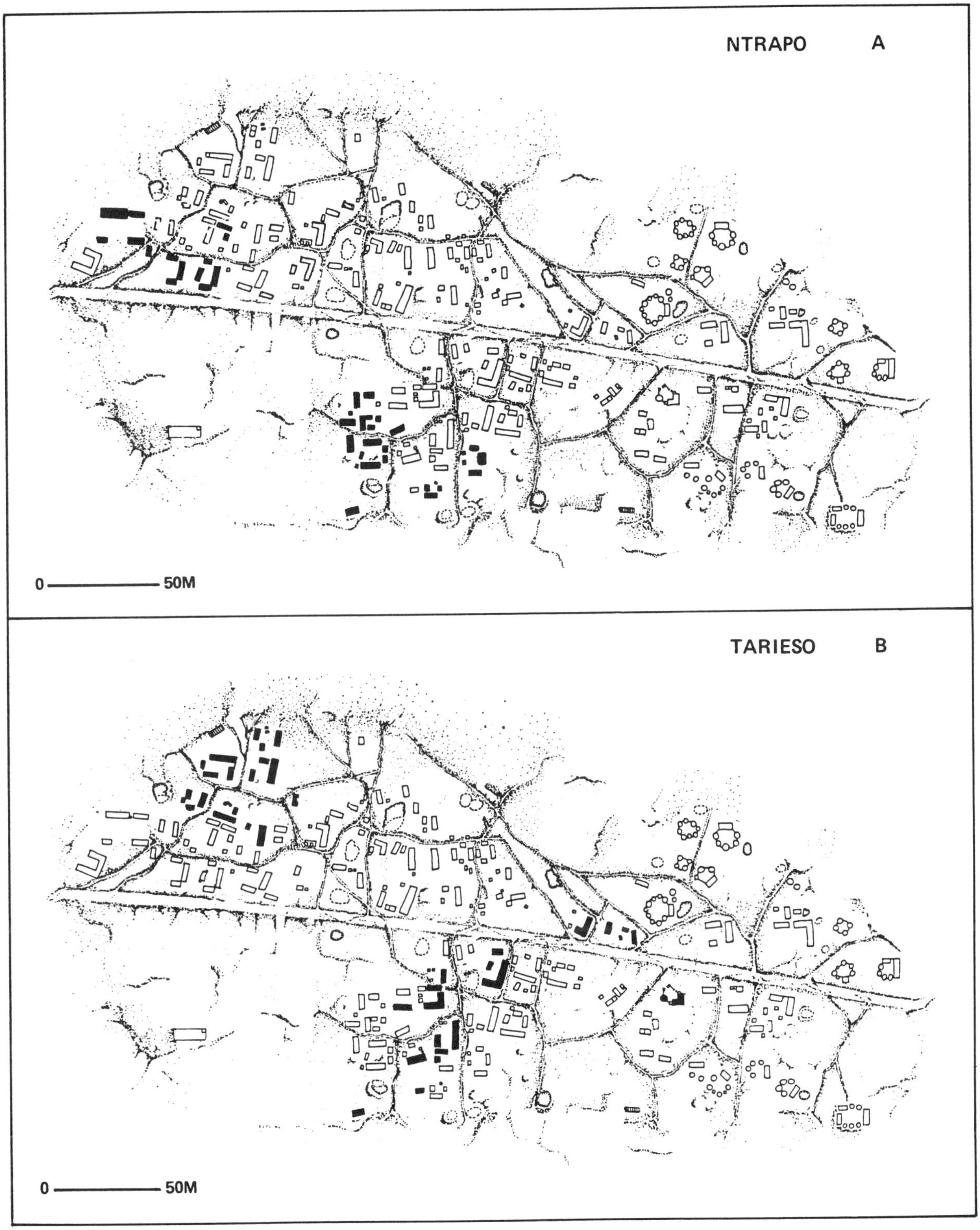

Fig. 6. Distribution of *kabuno* houses at New Wiae.

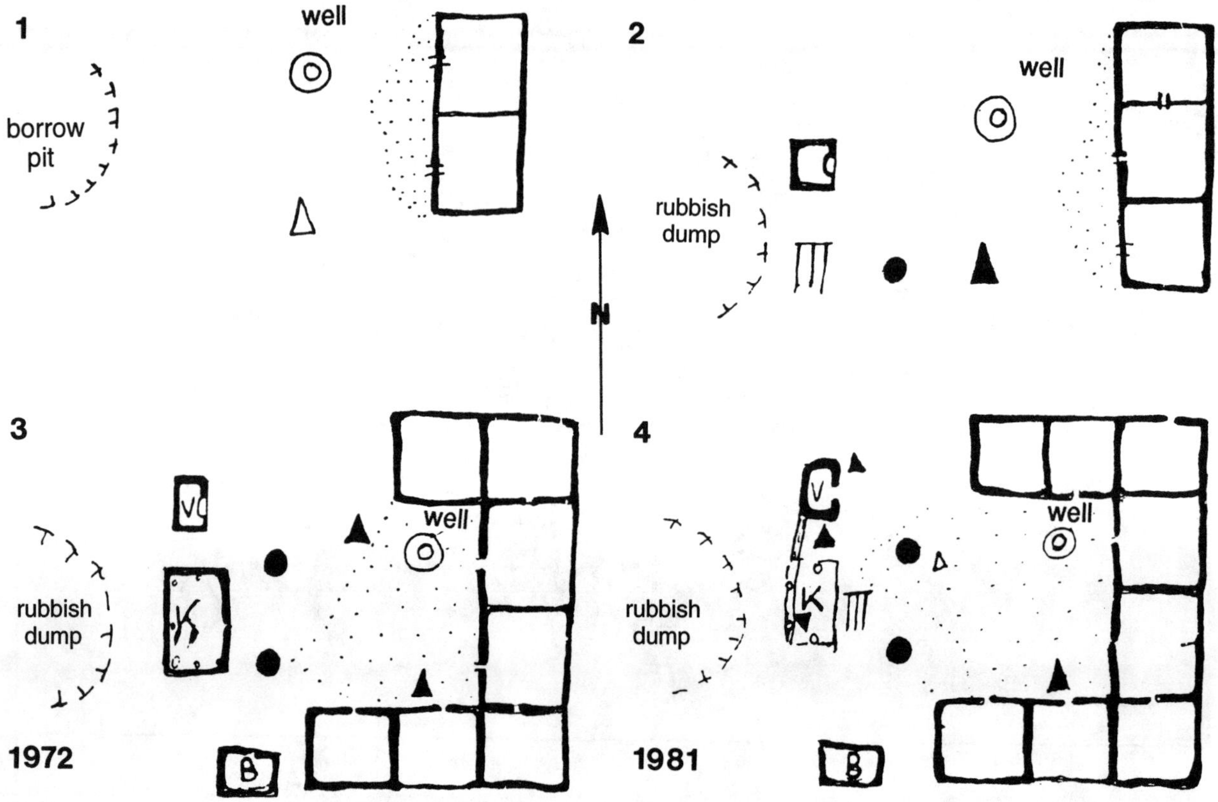

Fig. 7. Development of the house at New Wiae: house 1.

Haggett 1965; Soja 1971; Leach 1978; Hillier et al. 1978). It is not taken for granted that because of the close relationship between the social and spatial factors in human behaviour we should close our eyes to other factors that may at certain points in time exert effective influence on social transformations and which may not be reflected in the data available to the archaeologist. The point being made here is that the social factor cannot be ignored under any circumstance. Studies among the Tiv (Andah 1982), the Mossi of Burkina Faso (Skinner 1960, 1964), the Larteh of Ghana (Brokensha 1966), the Yalunka of Sierra Leone (Decorse 1988), the Akan (Fortes 1970), the Konkomba of northern Ghana (Tait 1961; Fletcher 1972), and among several other societies of West Africa clearly give support to the close interrelationships between the social organisation of these societies not only for purposeful and shared opportunity but also in the placement of structural features within the environments which they occupy at any time. Clan affiliations of these societies need special mention.

Discussion

Most important in the development of the clan (*kabuno)* areas at Old Wiae has been the recurring patterns of aggregation of *kabuno* members in the settlement. Once people became familiar with these patterns of behaviour, they tend to respond to them in terms of the shared opportunities that they offer. The more the shared opportunities gain root, the more positive the rule of cluster. The settlement history and the distribution of features within Old Wiae settlement clearly show that the Local Rule that operated was positive, and this seems to have carried on to New Wiae, even after it was burnt down by fire. The continuity of the pattern at New Wiae gives strong support to the overriding significance of affiliations in the location of family groups and their associated activities and cultural features. Figure 3 represents the distribution of clan compounds or houses at New Wiae in 1972 and 1981. The breakdown of this is represented by Figures 4 and 5, indicating the compounds belonging to specific *kabuno* in the whole settlement. Although the form of settlement is different from that of Old Wiae, the congregation of *kabuno* members provides evidence for continuity. Clearly, the *kabuno* system of the Nchumuru has significant effects on spatial colonisation. It defines locational regularities rather than being constrained by those regularities. At the level of Nchumuru community behaviour, the spatial development of the settlement

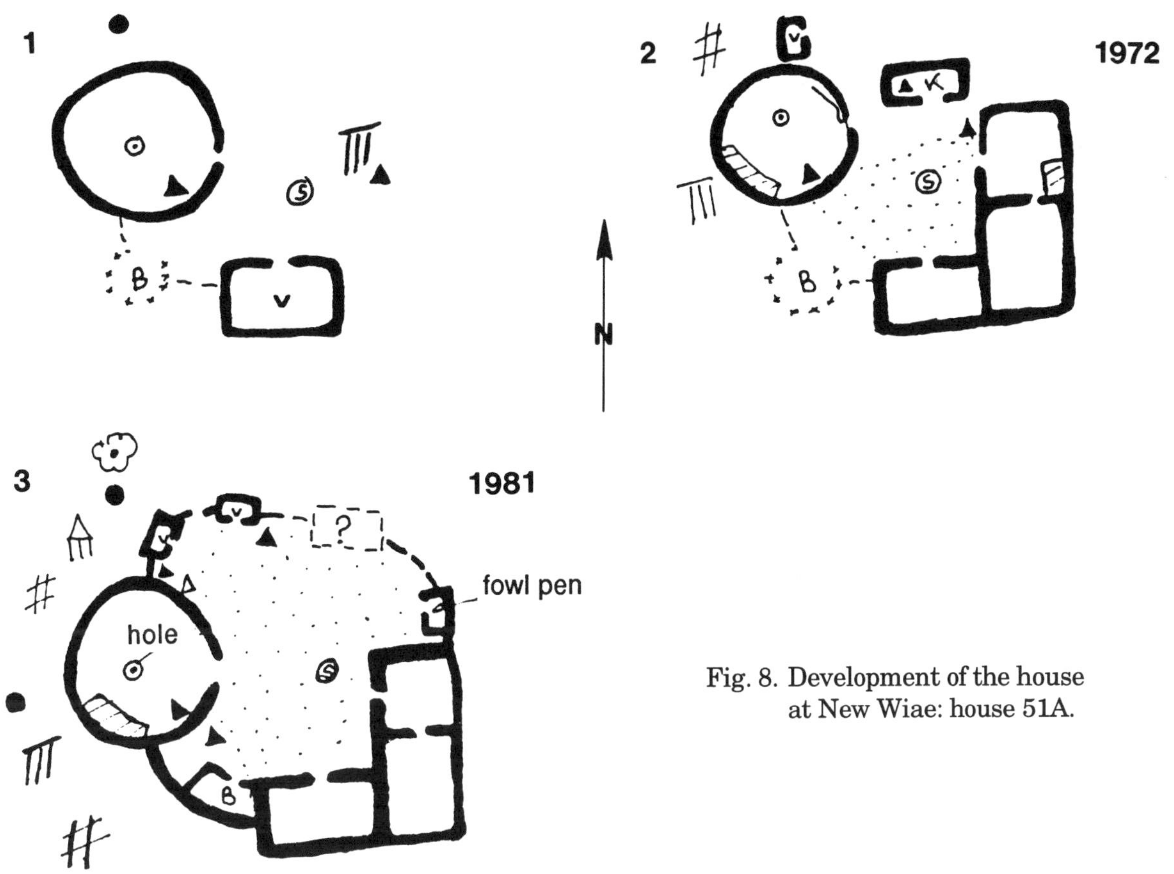

Fig. 8. Development of the house at New Wiae: house 51A.

of Wiae has been considered in relation to the spatial framework in which they had previously lived, perhaps since prehistoric times, as well as in terms of all practical factors that influenced their decisions as to where to locate their family groups in order to maintain the shared opportunities available to them. The speculation made before the test of the model with archaeological evidence was that, since the Nchumuru perception of the location of the *kabuno* houses was repetitious and carried through time, the development of any Nchumuru settlement would, theoretically, assume the pattern observed at New Wiae. The correlation between spatial configuration and social structure may in some cases be obvious, and in others it may be extremely difficult to discover. But this study demonstrates that Nchumuru spatial configurations reflect not only the true, unconscious organization, but a model existing consciously in their traditional mind, although its nature may be illusory and even contradictory in reality. Herein lies the relationship between social and spatial dynamics.

The patterns that often result from such interaction have been explained by Hillier and his colleagues (1978) by their space syntax theory in terms that demonstrate that there is a means of producing an overall differentiation in the man-made landscape without a clear idea of the limits of the settlement that a society occupies. I have explained elsewhere (Agorsah 1985) why it is easy to make strong arguments against the proposition that the cultural process which produced a pattern of settlement can be inferred from spatial form. The case of New Wiae is an obvious indication that this has some support in the realm of human behaviour, the basis of which is the *kabuno* system in this case. But the discussion also indicates that the social process which produced a spatial pattern may not necessarily be spatial in character, because generally different processes may give rise to similar patterns. Even societies that are similar in many respects could generate different patterns of settlement as a result of relatively basic differences between them, making it difficult to recognise differences in patterning. These difficulties are due to the individual as well as the combined dynamic nature of the social and spatial factors in the formation of patterns. The discussion of this chapter clearly, therefore, supports the assertion made by Mills (1985) in his study of the Ovambo concept of

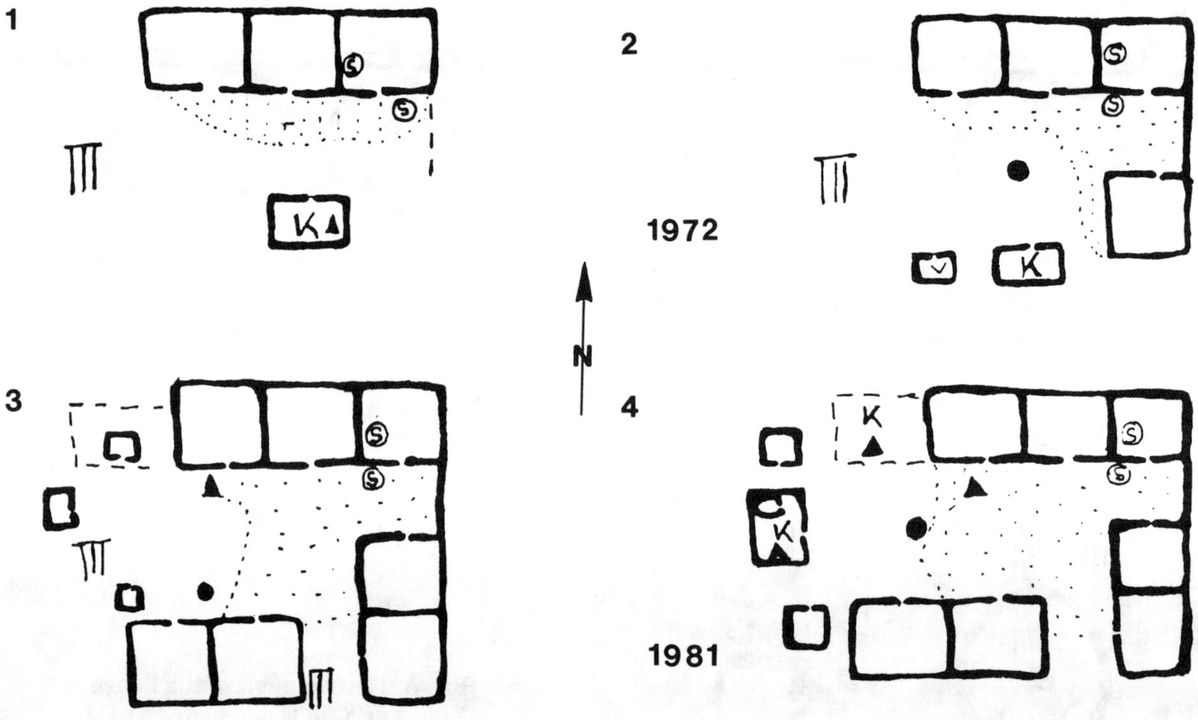

Fig. 9. Development of the house at New Wiae: house 10.

space that "in order to understand settlements, it is necessary to analyse their forms in relation to the social patterns that generate them, not only at the level of their appearance or what they look like, but more importantly in what they are as physical organization of society." The use of such models as the LR model of spatial behaviour should provide useful means towards the realization of this goal.

Studies that deal with the growth or development of individual features in settlements such as compounds or houses are very few and far between. Unfortunately, this is one of the areas of study where the true relationships between social and spatial dynamics can be observed. The importance of the use of evidence related to socio-spatial relationships has been demonstrated in the study of the development of the Nchumuru compound (Agorsah 1983). By use of ethnographic data, family history, and demography in the village of New Wiae, an attempt has been made to discover regularities, if any, of development of the compounds and to find out how they relate to the Nchumuru social system. The question here is: to what extent is the house form determined by the *kabuno* or family system of the Nchumuru?

Concluding Remarks

Human spatial behaviour is strongly dependent on an individual society's cognition of its environment and experiences over time, which are defined by a convenient set of symbols (in the case of the Nchumuru, the pattern of the placement of structural features in their settlement). As Downs and Stea (1973) have pointed out from their own studies, these elements of definition are influenced by the society's cultural and social environment. Among the Nchumuru the demographic development of the household (Figs. 6 and 7) is linked more to family structure and social values than the size of the compound. For example, some of the houses, despite their bigger sizes, have far fewer inhabitants than smaller ones (Agorsah 1983). It is difficult to explain such a discrepancy if one has to rely on demographic factors only. When Zubrow (1975) proposed a model for population growth and settlement and the procedure for simulating them, his data appeared quite attractive, but so far it could not be a working tool for adequately explaining the dynamic relationships between social and other factors and for the explanation of spatial growth. Such a model cannot deal with a society in which the builder is the one who takes the locational decision and the one who, on the basis of his social relationships, maintains not only his social position but the continuity of his ancestry in his society. Zubrow's model defines four components such as a population resource check, settlement location, and a longevity function (Hodder 1978). These obviously do not take into account the social structure, which more than anything else determines the dynamics of spatial patterning.

References

Adiase, M. K.
1969 Preliminary account of the food and feeding habits of fish in the Volta Lake. In *Man-made Lakes*, L. Obeng (ed.), 238-241. Accra: University Press.

Agorsah, E. K.
1976 *Some Considerations on the Archaeology and Oral Traditions of the Begho area*. M.A. Thesis. Legon: University of Ghana.
1982 Spatial expressions of traditional behaviour: An archaeological study. In *Archaeology at UCLA* 2(6), E. Elster (ed.). Institute of Archaeology, UCLA.
1983a *An ethnoarchaeological study of the settlement and behaviour patterns of a West African traditional society*. Ph.D. dissertation. Los Angeles: University of California.
1983b Patterns of spatial behaviour among the Nchumuru. *Nyame Akuma* 23:6-8.
1983c Social behaviour and spatial context. *African Study Monographs* 4:119-128.
1985a Archaeological implications of traditional house construction among the Nchumuru of northern Ghana. *Current Anthropology* 26(1):103-115.
1985b The internal spatial organisation of traditional houses in the northern Volta basin of Ghana. *Research Review* 2(2): 104-134.
1985c Excavation in the northern Volta basin. *West African Journal of Archaeology* 15:11-40.
1986a House forms in N. Volta basin, Ghana (Evolution, internal organisation and social relationships depicted). *West African Journal of Archaeology* 16:25-51.
1986b *Settlement pattern analysis in the Northern Volta basin*. Volta basin Archaeological Project Report for 1983-85. Legon: Department of archaeology, University of Ghana.
1988a Evaluating spatial behaviour of Prehistoric societies. *Journal of Anthropological Archaeology* 7(3):231-247.
1988b The settlement history of the Northern Volta basin of Ghana. *National Geographic Research* 4(3):371-385.

Andah, B. W.
1978 Excavations at Rim, north-central Upper-Volta. *West African Journal of Archaeology* 8:75-138.
1979 The Later Stone Age and Neolithic of Upper-Volta viewed in West African context. *West African Journal of Archaeology* 9:85-108.
1982 The Bantu "Homeland" Project: Ethnoarchaeological Investigations in parts of the Benue valley region. *West African Journal of Archaeology* 13:23-60.

Anozie, F. R.
1979 Early Iron Technology in Igboland (Lejja and Umunda). *West African Journal of Archaeology* 9:119-134.

Armstrong, D. V.
1986 An Afro-Jamaican slave settlement: Archaeological investigation at Drax Hall. In *The Archaeology of Slavery and Plantation Life*, T. Singleton (ed.), 261-285. New York: Academic Press.

Atherton, J.
1983 Ethnoarchaeology in Africa. *African Archaeological Review* 1:75-105.

Bailey, K. D.
1982 *Methods of Social Research*. London: McMillan.

Beattle, J.
1960 *Bunyoro: An African Kingdom*. New York: Holt, Rinehart and Winston.

Binford, L. R.
1983 *Working at Archaeology*. New York: Academic Press.

Black, S.
1978 Polynesian outliers: a study of a small population. In *Simulation Studies in Archaeology*, I. Hodder (ed.), 63-76. Cambridge: Cambridge University Press.

Boachie-Ansah, J.
1986 Smoking pipes and the dating of the 16th century in Ghana: the evidence from Ahwenekoko. *West African Journal of Archaeology* 16:71-98.

Bohannan, P.
1963 *Social Anthropology*. New York: Holt, Rinehart and Winston.
1968 *Tiv Economy*. London: Longmans.
1971 *Africa and Africans*. New York: Natural History Press.

Boomert, A.
1980 Hertenrits: An Arauquinoid complex in the NW Suriname: Part I. *Archaeology and Anthropology* 3(2) 68-104.

Braimah, A.A. & J. Goody
1967 *Salaga: The Struggle for Power*. London: Longmans.

Brokensha, David W.
1966 *Social Change at Larteh, Ghana*. Oxford: Clarendon Press

Brukum, K.
1979 *A brief History of the Nchumuru People*. B.A. Long Essay, Legon: University of Ghana.

Cartwright, D. & F. Harary
1977 Structural balance: a generalization of Heider's theory. In *Social Networks: a Developing Paradigm*, S. Leinhardt (ed.), 9-27. New York: Academic Press.

Chang, K.C.
1968 Study of Neolithic social groupings: examples from the New World. *American Anthropologist* 60:298-334.

Clarke, D.L. (ed.)
1977 *Spatial Archaeology*. London: Academic Press.

Crossland, L. B.
1973 *A study of Begho Pottery in Light of the Excavation conducted at Begho B-2 Site*. M.A. Thesis. Legon: University of Ghana.

Dakubu, K. E.
1976 *West African Languages Data Sheets*. Vol. 1. Accra: African Linguistic Society.
1982 The peopling of Southern Ghana: a linguistic viewpoint. In *Archaeological and Linguistic Reconstruction of African History*, C. Ehret and M. Posnansky (eds.), 245-255. Berkeley: University of California Press.

Davies, O.
1967 *West Africa before the Europeans*. London: Methuen.
1970 *Ghana field notes, Part 2: Northern Ghana*. M. Posnansky (ed.), Legon: University of Ghana.

Decorse, C.
1980 An archaeological survey of prehistoric defensive sites in Sierra Leone. *Nyame Akuma* 17:48-53.
1981 Additional notes on archaeological fieldwork in northeastern Sierra Leone. *Nyame Akuma* 19:14-15.
1988 Material aspects of Limba, Yalunka and Kuranko ethnicity: Archaeological research in NE Sierra Leone. In *Archaeological Approaches to Cultural Identity*, S. J. Shennan (ed.). London: Allen and Unwin.

Deetz, J.
1977 *In Small Things Forgotten: the Archaeology of Early American Life*. New York: Archer Books.

Doby, J.T.
1967 *An Introduction to Social Research*. New York: Appleton Century-Crofts.

Dombrowski, J.
1976 Mumute and Bonoase - two Kintampo sites. *Sankofa* 2:64-71.

Donnan, C. B. & C. W. Clewlow (eds.)
1974 *Ethnoarchaeology*. Los Angeles: Institute of Archaeology, UCLA.

Downs, R. M. and D. Stea
1973 *Image and Environment: Mapping and Spatial Behaviour*. Chicago: Aldine.

Earle, T.
1976 A nearest neighbour analysis of two formative settlement systems. In *The Early Mesoamerican Village*, K. V. Flannery (ed.), 196-223. New York, Academic Press.

Ehret, C. & M. Posnansky (eds.)
1982 *Archaeological and Linguistic Reconstruction of African History*. Berkeley: University of California Press.

Eidt, R. C.
1984 *Advances in abandoned settlement analysis*. Milwaukee: University of Wisconsin Press.

Fletcher, R.
1972 Settlement studies (Micro and semi-micro). In *Spatial Archaeology*, D. L. Clarke (ed.), 47-162. London, Academic Press.
1978 Issues in the analysis of settlement space. *British Archaeological Reports*, International Series 47 (II):225-240.

Flight, C. R.
1967 Kintampo. *Research Review* 3:72-77.

Fortes, M.
1970 *Kinship and Social Order*. London.

Gould, P.
1969 The structure of space preference in Tanzania. *Area* 1:29-34.

Gould, R.
1968 Living Archaeology: the Ngatatjara of West Australia. *Southwestern Journal of Anthropology* 24:101-122.
1969 Subsistence behaviour among the Western desert aborigines of Australia. *Oceania* 39:251-74.
1980 *Living Archaeology*. Cambridge: Cambridge University Press.

Haggett, P.
1965 *Locational Analysis in Human Geography*. London: E. Arnold.

Hall, L. T.
1983 *Ghanaian Languages*. Accra: Ghana Publishing Co.

Hillier, B., A. Leaman, P. Stansal & M. Bedford
1978 Space syntax, social organisation and settlement. *British Archaeological Reports*, International Series 47(II):343-384.

Hodder, I. and M. Hassal
1971 The non-random spacing of Romano-British walled towns. *Man* 6:391-407.

Hodder, I. and C. Orton
1976 *Spatial Analysis in Archaeology*. Cambridge: Cambridge University Press.

Holl, A.
1987 Mound formation processes and societal transformations: A case study from the Perichadian plain. *Journal of Anthropological Archaeology* 6:122-158.

Johnson, G. A.
1972 A test of the utility of central place theory in archaeology. In *Man, Settlement and Urbanism*, P. J. Ucko, R. Tringham and G. Dimbleby (eds.), 769-785. London: Duckworth.
1977 Aspects of regional analysis in archaeology. *Annual Review in Anthropology* 6:479-508.

Keat, R. and J. Urry
1975 *Social Theory as Science*. London: Routledge and Keagan Paul.

Klepper, E.
1988 Divine kingdoms in Northern Africa: Material manifestations of social institutions. Paper presented at the 21st ICAES, Zagreb, Yugoslavia, July 1988.

Kumak, J. E. K.
1964 *Traditions from Kete-Krachi*. Legon: Institute of African Studies.

Kuper, H.
1972 The language of sites in the politics of space. *American Anthropologist* 74:411-425.

Laux, F.
1971 *Die Bronzezeit in der Lüneburger Heide*. Hildesheim.

Leach, E. R.
1978 Does space syntax really constitute the social? *British Archaeological Reports*, International Series 47(II):385-401.

Lösch, A.
1954 *The Economics of Location*. New Haven: Yale University Press.

Mills, A.
1985 An inquiry into the structure and function of settlement space in northern Namibia: parts I and II. *Architecture S.A.* Feb. 1985:33-35 and April 1985: 46-58.

Mlanga, L.
1976 The impact of technology on the African environment. *African Environment* 76-77.

Muehrcke, P. C.
1980 *Map use (reading, analysis and interpretation)*. Madison: J.P. Publications.

Okpoko, A.
1979 Settlement archaeology in the Anambra River Valley: A short note. *West African Journal of Archaeology* 9:167-171.

Painter, C.
1966 The Guan and West African historical reconstruction. *Ghana Notes and Queries*. Legon: University of Ghana.

Parsons, J. R.
1972 Archaeological settlement patterns. *Annual Review in Anthropology* 1:127-150.

Posnansky, M.
1971 Opportunities for American students to excavate in Africa. *Archaeology* 24:363.
1976 Archaeology and the origins of the Akan society in Ghana. In *Problems in Economic and Social Archaeology*, G. de Sieveking, I. H. Longworth and K. E. Wilson (eds.), 49-59. London: Duckworth.

Prussin, L.
1969 *Architecture in Northern Ghana*. Berkeley: University of California Press.

Roberts, B. K.
1978 Rural settlement in County Durham: forms pattern and system. *British Archaeological Reports*, International Series 47(II) 291-322.

Schiffer, M. B.
1977 Behavioral chain analysis: Activities, organization and use of space. *Fieldiana Anthropology* 65:103-119.

Shinnie, P.
1985 Comments. *Current Anthropology* 26:111-112.

Sinclair, P.
1987 *Space, Time and Social Formation*. Upsala: Societies Archaeological Upsallensis.

Skinner, E. P.
1960 Labour migration and its relationship to socio-cultural change in Mossi society. *Africa* 30:375-99.
1964 West African Economic systems. In *Economic Transition in Africa*, M. Herskovitz and W. Hartwitz (eds.). London.

Soja, S. W.
1971 The political organization of space. In *As-*

sociation of American Geographers on College Geography. Los Angeles

Soper, R.
1971 Early Iron Age pottery types from East Africa: comparative analysis. *Azania* 6:39-52.

South, S.
1977 *Method and Theory in Historical Archaeology*. New York: Academic Press.

Squire, C.
1962 Mammalian fauna. In *Agriculture and Land-use in Ghana*, J.B. Wills (ed.), 126-140. London:Oxford University Press.

Stea, D. & E. Soja
1975 Environmental and spatial cognition in African society. *Journal of Social Science Council* 37(3):37-40.

Steward, J. M.
1960 *Comparative African word list N° 1*. Legon: Institute of African Studies.

Tait, D.
1961 *The Konkomba of Northern Ghana*. Oxford: Oxford University Press.

Thomas, D. H.
1972 A computer simulation model of Great Shoshonean subsistence and settlement patterns. In *Models in Archaeology*. D. L. Clarke (ed.), 671-704, London: Methuen.

Ucko, P. J., R. Tringham & G. Dimbleby (eds.)
1972 *Man, Settlement and Urbanism*. London: Duckworth.

Whallon, R. Jr.
1973 Spatial analysis of occupation floors I: Application of dimensional analysis of variance. *American Antiquity* 38(3):266-278.

White, J. P.
1967 Ethnoarchaeology in New Guinea: Two examples. *Mankind* 6:409-414.

Wills, J. B. (ed.)
1962 *Agriculture and Land use in Ghana*. London: Oxford University Press.

Willey, G. R.
1956 *Prehistoric Settlement in New World*. New York: Viking Fund Publication in Anthropology N° 23.

York, R. & D. Calvocoressi
1967 *Archaeology in the Volta basin 1963-66*. Legon: University of Ghana.

Zubrow, E.
1975 *Prehistoric Carrying Capacity: A Model*. Menlo Park: Cummings.

3. Agrarian Settlement and the Spatial Disposition of Labor

Glenn Davis Stone

Introduction

Many approaches that archaeologists have used to explain settlement patterns, including central place theory and the "social physics" models of the 1970's (Crumley 1979), are based on the fact that distances between settlements are functionally linked to the nature and intensity of interaction between settlements. Capitalizing on the fact that exotic artifacts and raw materials can be sourced and can serve to index interaction between sites, many 1970's archaeological models stressed trade as a key factor in the understanding of settlement patterns (Renfrew 1975; Earle and Ericson 1977). At the same time, archaeologists were exploring political authority as a pivotal element in settlement (Johnson 1972, 1975), a line of inquiry that has continued and diversified (Steponaitis 1981; Evans and Gould 1982; D'Altroy 1992).

That settlement patterns may be shaped by economic and political interaction was discussed as early as Christaller's (1966, orig. 1933) seminal work. Although mainly concerned with the spatial entailments of economic interaction (as was Lösch [1954, orig. 1940]), Christaller discusses the *sociopolitical separation* principle, which allows for central places to develop for defensive, administrative, or other reasons beyond the marketing of goods.

These archaeological and geographical approaches to interaction in space concerned settlements large enough to take on non-agricultural functions, and it is doubtful that their theoretical underpinnings are appropriate to essentially agrarian settlement systems. Christaller was clear in differentiating between towns and agricultural settlements (1966:1). In understanding landscapes common in the archaeological record where "settlements" are not cities, towns, or even villages, but dispersed farmsteads or hamlets, we need to consider a different kind of interaction, and to "turn ourselves to a locational analysis of cultural systems rather than the economic analysis of regions" (Crumley 1979:156; Marquart and Crumley 1987:3).

My ethnoarchaeological research on Kofyar farmers in the Benue Valley of Nigeria has highlighted relationships between settlement patterns and the daily activity of the Kofyar. This chapter is a case study of the patterning of farm "settlements"—in this case, dispersed residential compounds—and the nature of the interaction among these settlements. I wish to illustrate that agrarian settlement patterns are no more independent of intersettlement relations than are urban settlement patterns, but that the form of interaction is of a qualitatively different kind.

Archaeological models of agriculture have been influenced heavily by ecology and evolutionary biology. These approaches have provided a framework for understanding the evolution of agricultural systems, but they have done no better than regional science models at achieving a locational analysis of culture. My interest here is in how settlement location is affected by daily activities of a rural farming population. The following analysis suggests that an essential component in shaping settlement patterns is the interaction among farms in the conduct of agriculture, and specifically that settlement spacing is closely linked to spatial disposition of agricultural labor.[1] I wish to underscore the importance of viewing farming as a *social* process, contrasting both the social physics approach to settlement patterning and the biological approach to agricultural systems.

Kofyar Background

The Kofyar are a group of farmers originally studied by Robert Netting in the 1960's (Netting 1968). At that time there were roughly 50,000 Kofyar living in and around the rugged hills at the southeastern corner of the Jos Plateau, near the geographical center of Nigeria (Fig. 1). Originally confined to the hills for defensive reasons, their population had reached densities over 300/km^2 in places (Stone et al. 1984). The settlement pattern consisted of contiguous farmsteads, often no larger than an acre in size, with a household living in a compound of mud huts. Agriculture was highly intensive, with annual cropping of grains (principally millet and sorghum), vegetable and tuber crops in heavily composted fields. Much of the hill landscape was terraced. After the British colonial government removed the military threat in the early 20th Century, Kofyar began tentatively to expand to the south and east by establishing sea-

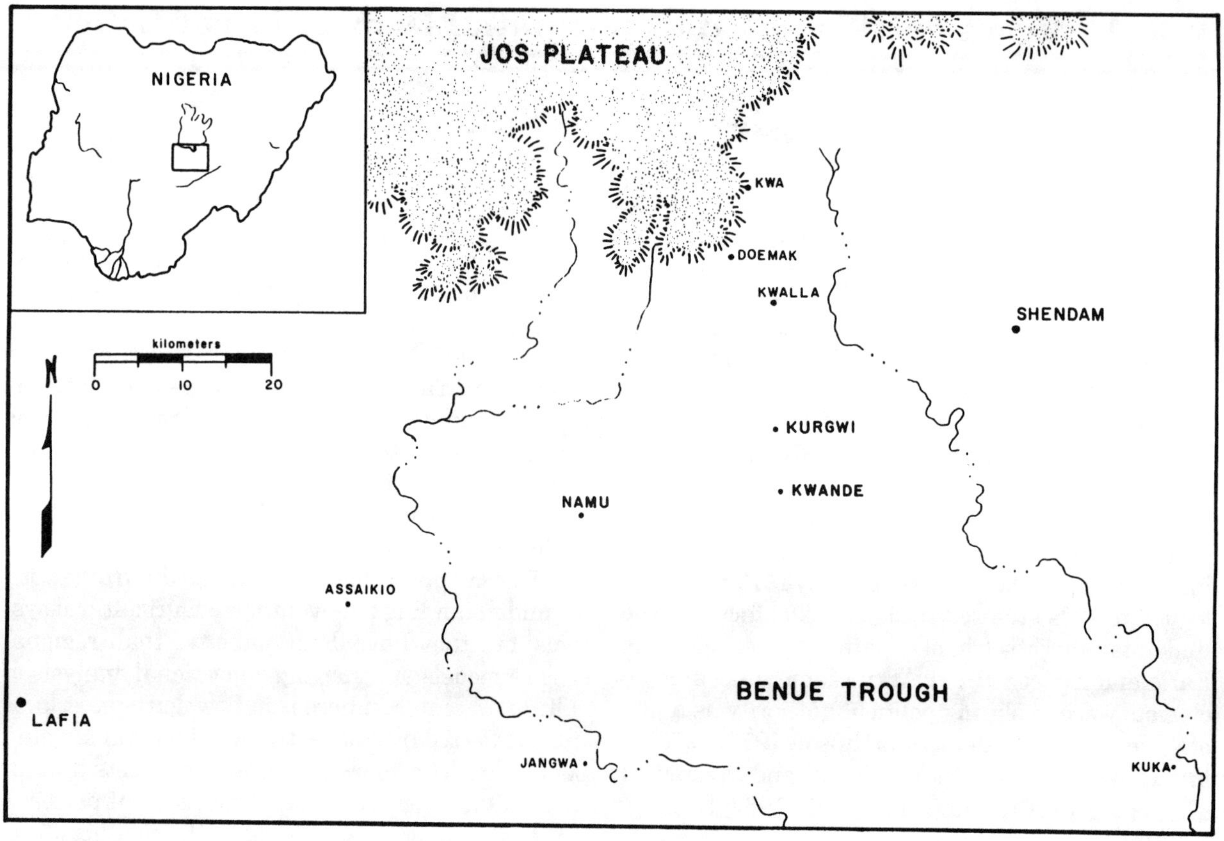

Fig. 1. Jos Plateau and northern Benue valley, Nigeria.

sonal "bush farms". By the early 1950's bush farms were being established on the fertile, virtually empty plains south of Namu. This marked the real beginning of the migration that has since led to depopulation of the homeland communities. The Kofyar were drawn to this frontier area first by two factors. The abundant and fertile land allowed the adoption of extensive agricultural techniques, with their higher marginal returns to labor. Once on the frontier, the Kofyar promptly abandoned the painstaking methods that characterized homeland farming in favor of relatively easy swidden agriculture. Yields per unit land were undoubtedly lower, but farms were as such as ten times larger than home farms, and an impressive surplus could be produced within a few years. The second major inducement came from the marketplace: rising urban populations needed the yams and rice that thrive in the Benue Valley, and while the Kofyar had not grown these crops traditionally, they took them up with immediate success (Netting et al. 1989).

Frontier settlement expanded south and west from the neighborhood (*ungwa*) now known as Ungwa Long (Fig. 2). Aerial photos show that by 1963 compounds had been erected in Ungwa Long, Goewan, Duwe North, Hanyar Kwari, Wunze, Ungwa Kofyar, Bubuak, Dunglong, Kopdogo and Koedoegoer Zang, and parts of Koprume. Population influx has continued in these areas, with virtually no farms being abandoned (Stone 1988b), producing population densities in the range of 100/km^2 by 1984 (Stone 1988a:168). The following discussion concerns this "core area".[2]

Migration and Frontier Agriculture

During the first decade of settlement, many of the new migrants moved in with other farmers, producing a degree of clustering that contrasted the settlement patterns in the homeland and on the later frontier. Of 99 bush farmers censused by Netting in 1962 (9 years after the colony had begun), 49 had first lived in other compounds, for periods ranging from a few months to three years. Of these, 22 had lived in the larger compounds that formed a cluster at the northern end of Ungwa Long, a grouping that might be called a macro-compound. Across the river, in what is now the northern end of the Ungwa Goewan, a single, planned macro-compound was erected around 1955, housing a dozen household heads and parts of

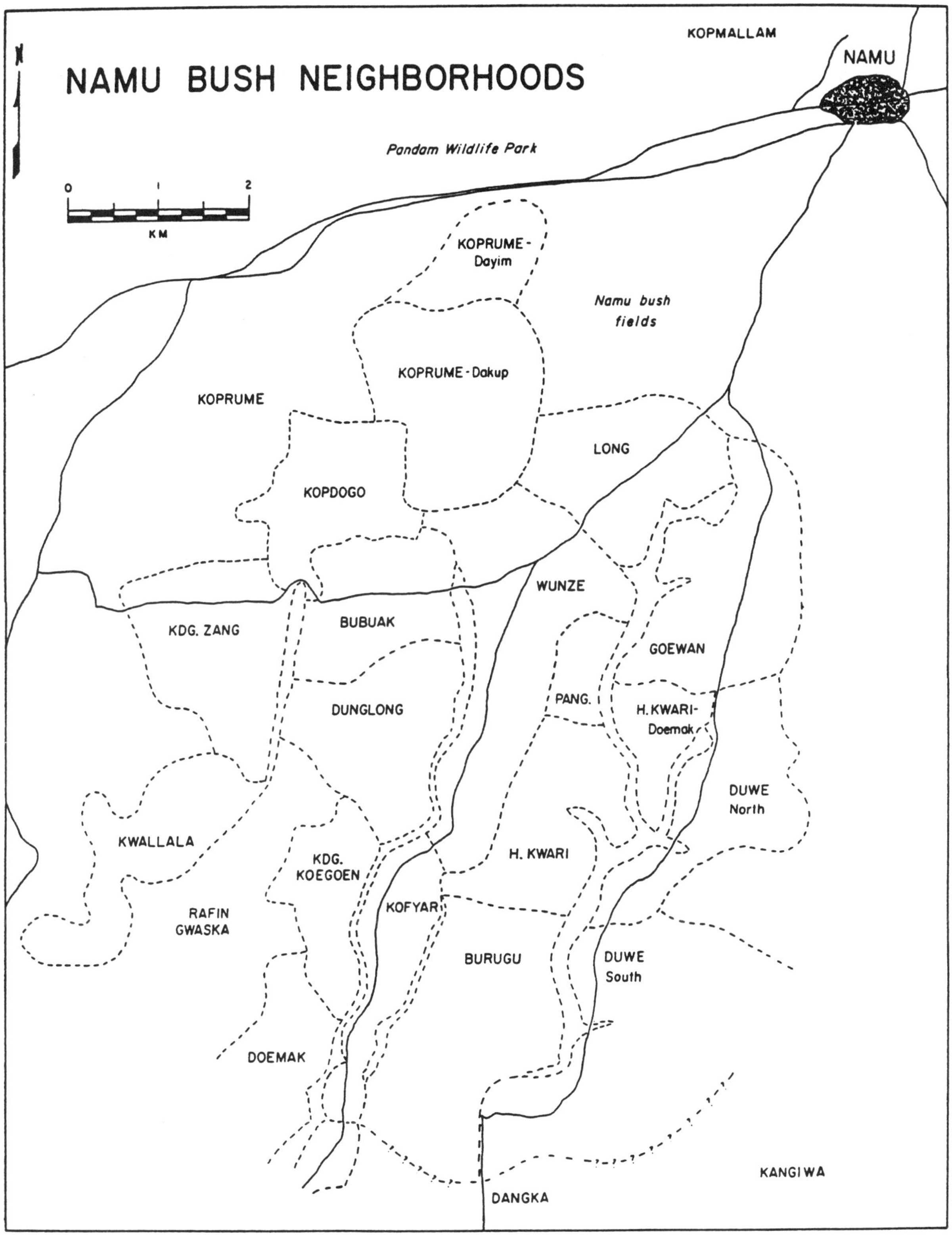

Fig. 2. Kofyar frontier core area.

their families. These arrangements kept the pioneer, already facing the work involved in launching a bush farm, from also having to begin his own residential compound (see also Wilk 1988:138). The large number of residents were better able to protect supplies from wild animals. These pioneers hiked to fields that were sometimes well over a kilometer away, where many built field houses.

While many early settlers lived in macro-compounds, others moved onto their land at the outset, often in rudimentary accommodations. By the early 1960's, most Kofyar pioneers had moved onto their own farms. Figure 3 shows that these farmsteads occurred in ragged lines, generally along footpaths. They were almost never more than 500 m from a stream, and tended to be located between 100 and 250 meters from their nearest neighbors. The present-day settlement pattern is shown in Figure 4.

What underlay this settlement dispersal? One may be tempted to say that the Kofyar gravitated towards the same sort of dispersed settlement pattern they had in their homeland. Yet colonists often amend their traditional pattern of settlement as they move into new ecological situations (Eidt 1977; Ostergren 1979; Brunger 1982). Many pioneers in the American colonies abandoned European village settlements for dispersed farmsteads, largely because of the socioecology of food-production on the frontier (Jordan 1966). Colonists from very disparate Old World traditions settled in similar *Waldhufen*—like strips in the Argentinian frontier studied by Eidt (1977). Indeed, the Kofyar embraced widespread adjustments to the frontier, changing their household size and structure (Stone et al. 1984; Netting 1965), choice of crops and agricultural tactics (Netting et al. n.d.), market orientation (Netting et al. 1989), and patterns of farm abandonment (Stone 1988b). Kofyar pioneers may have brought to the

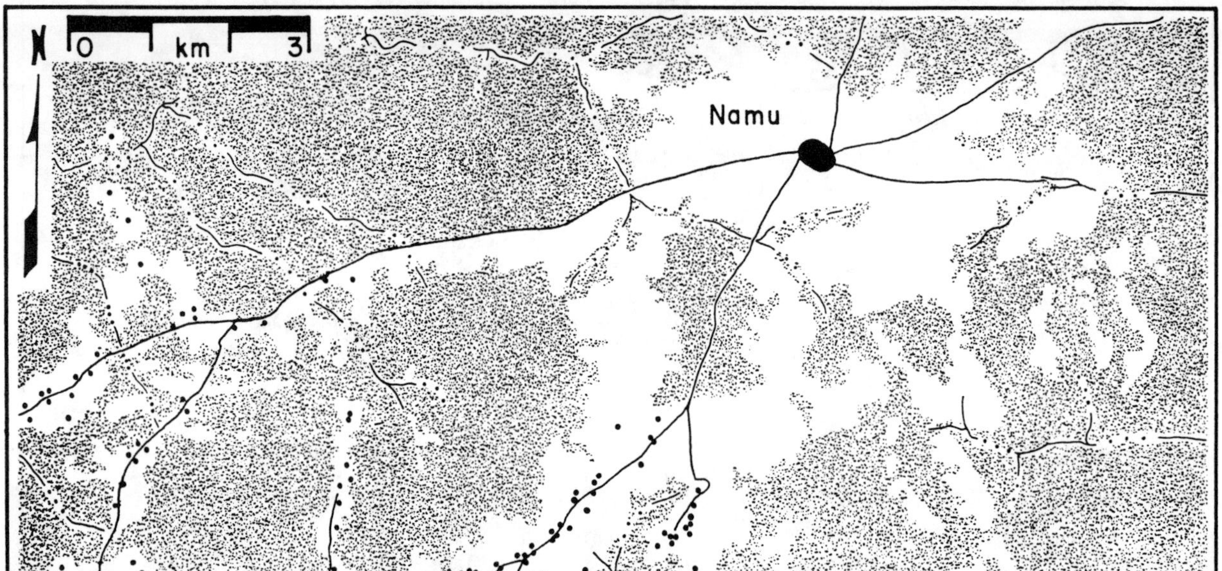

Fig. 3. Detail of core area settlement in 1963, based on air photos.

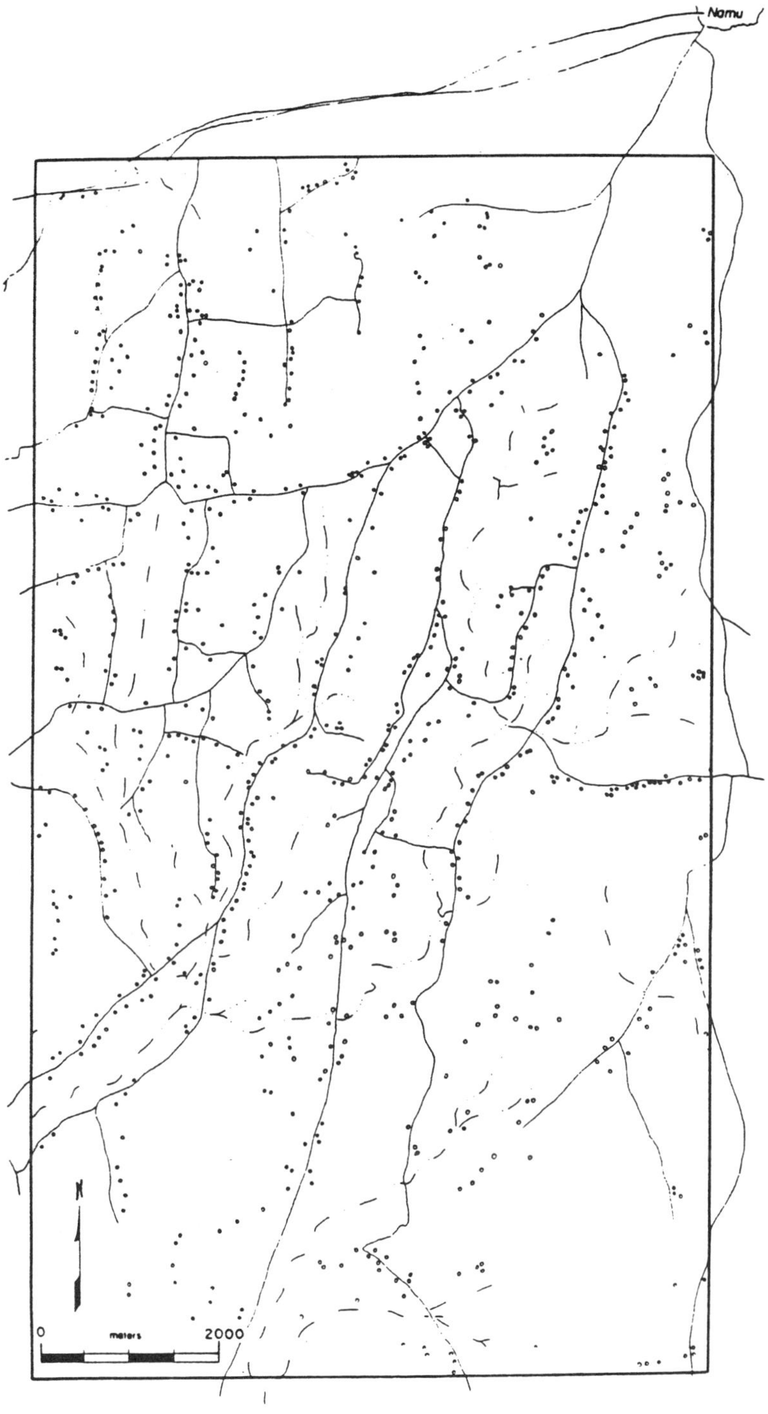

Fig. 4. Settlement pattern, 1977, based on air photos. Each circle is a residential compound or settlement.

frontier the homeland settlement template of contiguous farmsteads, but the pattern that has evolved cannot be explained simply as tradition. It is more profitably seen as a case of the adaptation of settlement pattern to the socioecology of agricultural production.

Intensification and Settlement

In most situations, agricultural plots suffer declining yields after several years of cultivation. Shifting cultivation—i.e., switching the locus of farming to a new plot—has been a basic response to this situation on ancient and contemporary landscapes alike. This is *extensive* cultivation, and its logic is nicely summarized by Thomas Jefferson's comment on agriculture in colonial Virginia: "we can buy an acre of new land cheaper than manure an old one" (in Margolis 1977). Depending on the natural reclamation of the farm plots, settlements themselves may be relocated (i.e., shifting settlement), especially in the tropics (Stone 1988a:92-97). However, in some situations, farmers elect not to relocate but to stay put and amend their farming methods to increase (or to check the decline of) yields per unit of land, and this is *intensification*.

Although conventionally treated as a single fundamental process with more than one manifestation (Boserup 1965), from the perspective of settlement pattern it is important to distinguish among different forms of intensification. The goal of intensification is to mitigate the main impediments to production, which vary with the local ecology. Where production is limited mainly by water, and where the landscape is amenable to canalization, intensification often means irrigation. Elsewhere, it requires increased efforts in field preparation, fertilizing, and weeding.[3] Irrigation intensification generally requires concerted efforts at constructing and maintaining canals between the water source and the individual plot; other forms of intensification demand more sustained inputs on the plot itself. Let us consider the nature of Kofyar intensive agriculture, and its effects on settlement:

1) The amount of time devoted to weeding has risen considerably (Stone et al. 1990). Such an emphasis on weeding is unheard of in extensive systems, and certainly did not occur in the early days on the frontier.

2) Crops have come to be cultivated more densely, both in space and in time. Spatial density is increased by intercropping, and it is now common for millet, sorghum and groundnuts to be growing in a field simultaneously. Temporal density is increased, lengthening the agricultural calendar, leaving almost no dry season break. At the same time, various cropping strategies are used to absorb labor during slack times, which evens the profile of labor inputs across the season (Stone et al. n.d..

3) Although it is not (yet) particularly common, some of the core area farmers have returned to the composting method used in the homeland to raise soil fertility levels. Basketfuls of animal dung are dumped on the land closest to the compound where cropping tends to be perennial and which often supports a kitchen garden as well as crops. Use of chemical fertilizers is also on the rise. By 1984, Kofyar in the core area were putting in an average of 1,205 hours of work into their own fields, which is extensive by cross-cultural standards and much higher than most farmers in tropical Africa (Stone et al. 1990; Cleave 1974).[4]

The relationship between agricultural intensification and settlement pattern has sometimes been misunderstood. On one hand, aggregation, which may result from many factors (Glassow 1977), raises local population density and can force agricultural intensification (Nichols 1987:596). However, intensification such as that experienced by the Kofyar promotes dispersal rather than aggregation, by increasing the amount of time spent on one's field. Rather than the relatively infrequent field visits that characterize extensive cultivators, Kofyar in the core area are on their fields virtually every day from March through October. As intensification amplifies the time and energy spent in commuting to the field, the premium grows in locating the residence near the center of the farm (Netting 1968; Brookfield 1972:32; Stone 1988a; Drennan 1988). Intensification's pull to the field may of course be overridden; a familiar cause of this in the archaeological record is defense (Rowlands 1972), but other causes of nucleation include land fragmentation and attraction to central places. But in intensive systems, if pull to the plot is overridden, secondary residences (field houses) are commonly constructed near the plot.

The underlying logic of the pull of the farmer towards the land as intensification increases also underlies central place theory and von Thünen's theory of land use. It is the principle that the attraction of residence to any landscape feature increases with the rate at which that feature is accessed. In farming systems, intensification's pull toward the land is usually coincident with development of more enduring rights to land (Boserup 1965; Netting 1982; Kohler 1992), which further encourage physical presence of the farmer.

On the Kofyar frontier, the pattern that has emerged is one in which most household compounds are located near the center of more or less rectangular farmstead boundaries (Fig. 5). The mean farm size is 5.5 ha; the mean size of the coresident group is 6.6.[5]

Geographers have shown that concentric land-use zonation is most characteristic of settlements with populations in the range of a few thousand (Morgan 1969:316) in regions with moderate population densities (Grove 1961:125). But as Chisholm points out, the pattern should occur on the level of the individual farm as well, and it does occur on most Kofyar farmsteads. The land surrounding the typical Kofyar compound is used for the rotation of yams with millet and sorghum (and sometimes groundnuts) which is the most intensive use to which land

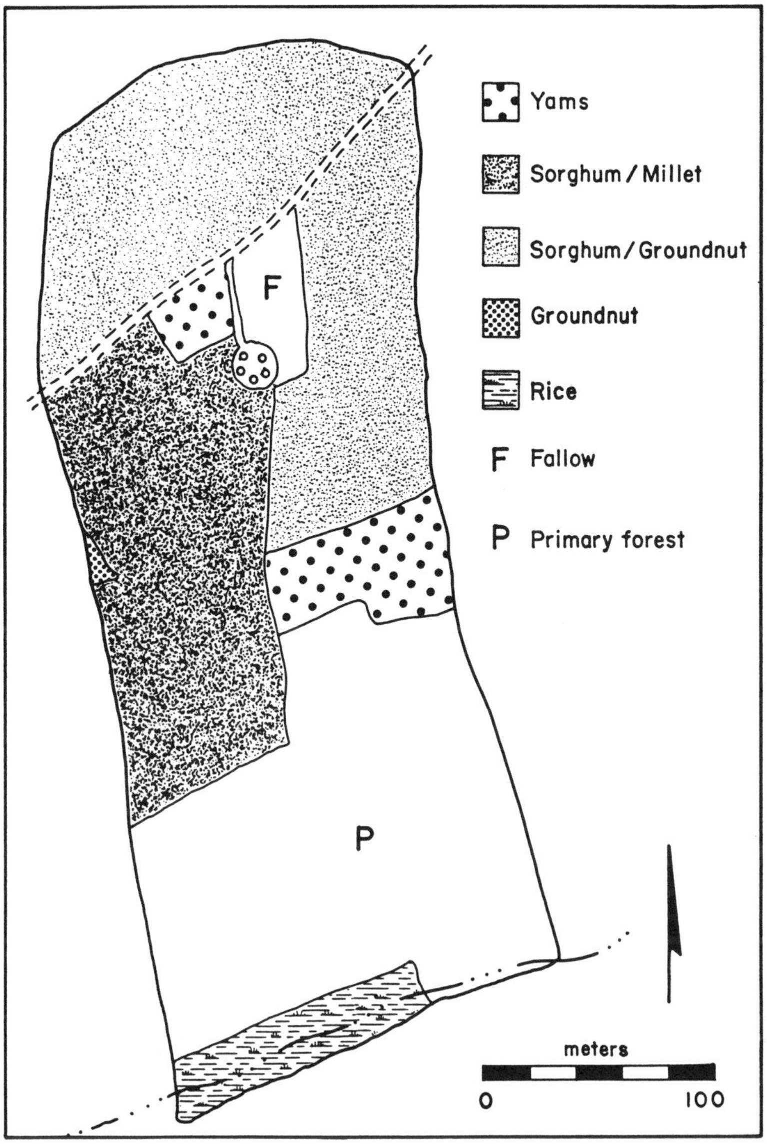

Fig. 5. A core area farm.

is commonly put. Immediately adjacent to the compound, sauce crops or tobacco may be grown amid the staple crops, and this "kitchen garden" (Killion 1992) constitutes an innermost ring of high land-use intensity. Fallow or virgin land is most likely to be near the farm boundaries (Fig. 5).

Thus the Kofyar frontier is a case of intensive cultivation by farmers living in dispersed residential compounds, which are located near the center of farmstead plots. This pattern is explained by the same general principles underlying familiar theories of land-use and central places.

Interaction and Proximity

To say that intensification disperses Kofyar settlement by pulling residences to the land is not to say that it pushes farmers away from each other. While ecological and economic factors militate for settlement dispersal, social factors on the Kofyar landscape encourage proximity among residences (cf. Earle 1976). Inasmuch as archaeological settlement models have assumed settlements to be pulled towards each other, often without a clear explanation of why this "attraction" should occur (Keegan and Machlachlan 1989:614; Hamond 1981; Plog and Hill 1971), it is helpful to know why it occurs in this case.

The most important factor pulling Kofyar farms towards each other is the social organization of labor. The agricultural changes outlined above have had interesting ramifications for the mobilization of labor. Debates on intensification may focus on numbers of hours invested and calories returned—in short, economic problems. But nonmechanized agriculturalists responding to population pressure (or inducements to produce a surplus) face a set of *social* problems: work groups of particular sizes, durations, and abilities must be marshalled to meet the labor demands of production. The demands of production have been shown in varying contexts to play a major role in shaping the size and the composition of residential groups (Sahlins 1957; Netting 1965, 1974; Pasternak et al. 1976). An important component in meeting the labor demands is mobilization of supra-household labor.

In their homeland, Kofyar farmers invested the majority of their productive labor into their own household farms, but also participated in group labor parties on their neighbors' fields. These festive labor parties were called *mar muos* ("beer farming"), referring to the quantities of millet beer which the host prepared to compensate the workers.[6] The main use of the *mar muos* (Fig.6) was to cultivate outfield plots which would take too long if done only by the household (Netting 1968:132-134).

On the frontier, group labor parties have come to play a critical role in the intensive system of agriculture. Here their function is not to expedite cultivation of outlying plots, but to help the farmer cope with a schedule which has become crowded and filled with conflicts as intensification has proceeded. It is significant that Kofyar farmers in the core area spend over 20% of their productive time on their neighbors' farms, and almost all of this agricultural collaboration occurs in groups. Reliance on group labor may not be inevitable, but the *mar muos* system does offer important advantages over entirely household labor.

Mar muos are suited to tasks in which several operations must be carried out at once—what Wilk and Netting (1984) call *simultaneous labor demands*. With the Kofyar, the best example of simultaneous labor demands is the job of storing millet, *lang maar* (Fig. 6). The *lang maar* follows the millet harvest, in which the grain heads are cut and headloaded in bundles back to a drying rack in the compound courtyard. This is a relatively easy chore, generally completed with household labor. The labor demands of the *lang maar* differ sharply because of the many sub-operations, many of which must be conducted simultaneously:

> Grasses are gathered for ropes and thatching; ropes are braided to tie bundles of seed heads while thatch mats are woven; workers throw the bundles up to a high wooden rack, where others arrange them in a conical heap, around which the thatching mat is wrapped.

Fig. 6. A large *mar muos* work group performing the millet storage operation (*lang maar*).

Mar muos are particularly adapted to this task, and account for over 72% of the work (Stone et al. 1990:14).

The need to complete the millet storage during the mid-season break in the rains makes it a bottleneck as well. *Mar muos* are instrumental in handling labor bottlenecks that agricultural intensification has brought. This is shown best in the making of earthen heaps for yam planting, called *bunga*. For several reasons, many farmers make *bunga* for the next year's yams in September.[7] It is advantageous for these farmers to mobilize as much labor as possible for this task, and the work can only be done after the August *lang maar* and before the end of the rains in October. It is difficult for a large yam field to be prepared by household labor, but the *mar muos* system allows these farmers to "bank" their labor, investing in millet production from March to August and then using millet beer to underwrite a large labor party. *Mar muos* for making *bunga* in September and October are among the largest labor groups, with an average size of 57 workers.

Mar muos have further advantages, including the festive atmosphere of the work and party afterwards. But management of labor bottlenecks and simultaneous tasks are most important, as reflected in figures on what is and is not done by group labor: *lang maar* and the September-October *bunga* are easily the most group-oriented agricultural tasks.

Group labor requires regular travel among farms, and the adults in our sample made an average of 59 trips to other farms for group labor. With such frequent travel, distance becomes an important consideration. Figure 7 shows the distribution of distances walked per person for group labor parties in 1984, which is characterized by a sharp drop-off beyond 750 meters (the drop-off actually begins at 700 meters; see Stone 1990). Above, I discussed the frequency-proximity principle that undergirds land-use theory and central place theory, and showed how an effect of this principle is for intensive farmers to be drawn to their land. It should now be clear that even while these farmers are pulled towards their own land, they are pulled toward *their neighbors' land*, because of the social solutions to agricultural labor demands.

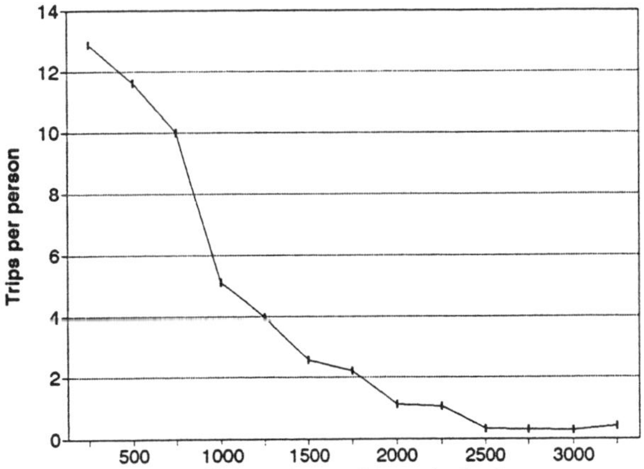

Fig. 7. Travel between farms.

One important effect of this is that Kofyar farms never exist in isolation, and in fact usually abut one another. The frequent access to others' farms also contributes to the elongated rectangular shape that typifies farms. Compounds are normally located near the farm's center, within 100 meters or so of the road. This pattern, resembling what German settlement geographers term *Waldhufen* (Mayhew 1973; Carlstein 1982:205), allows farmers to have relatively large plots while maintaining a low inter-residence distance.

The simultaneous pull of the farmer to his own land and to his neighbors' land is reflected in the variability in nearest neighbor distances, shown in Figure 8. Over 80% of contemporary compounds are located 100–200 meters from their nearest neighbor. As Figure 8 also shows, the nearest neighbor distances have dropped somewhat since 1963; the increase in low nearest neighbor distances has resulted partly from the rise in farm fragmentation.

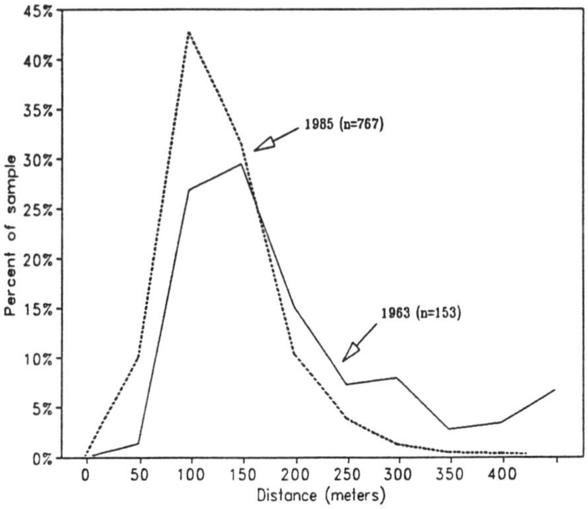

Fig. 8. Distribution of nearest neighbor distances.

Discussion

Kofyar residences are pulled towards their farmland by frequent access to that land, and this is a major factor shaping the pattern of dispersed settlement in the core area. At the same time, reliance on supra-household labor in meeting the demands of agricultural production puts a premium on low intersettlement distances. I have argued that intensification's pull of the residence towards the land is a case of a general principle in the spatial organization of human affairs. It is clearly not the case that intensification always produces dispersed farmsteads (Stone 1988a); farmers may find residence in a nucleated town advantageous if their farmland is fragmented (Bentley 1987), or nucleation may be necessary for defensive reasons (Udo 1965; Rowlands 1972). But the pull remains nonetheless, and there are numerous cases of this phenomenon overriding artificial attempts at nucleation (e.g., Gade and Escobar 1982). When there are compelling reasons for nucleated settlement, cultivation of distant plots generally leads to the construction of secondary residences (field houses), or at least the probability of this increases with distance to plot.

The relationships among agriculture, settlement, and labor mobilization are reflected in cases described elsewhere, especially by geographers. Eidt's (1977) study of agricultural colonization in Argentina provides a striking case of *Waldhufen*-like settlement, to which the settlers gravitated despite government insistence on rectangular grid settlements. Strip settlement allowed greater contact among the farmers, notably in mobilizing group labor. Extensive farmers may also be dispersed, but both the underlying causes and the actual pattern may be different from intensive cases. Jordan and Kaups (1989:100), for instance, describe a pattern that features dispersed transitory farmsteads and an economy based on extensive cultivation mixed with hunting and gathering. The first wave of pioneers in parts of the American eastern woodlands, extracted from the European periphery, practiced this. Their pioneer cabins were located centrally in the plot, from where they could better protect their crops from animals.

Part of this adaptation was to minimize reliance on group labor in agriculture. It is interesting that Jordan and Kaups' American pioneers scrupulously avoided clearing stumps from fields, the one job that Eidt's Argentinian pioneers found worked best with formal labor groups. Nevertheless, some jobs demanded simultaneous labor, especially field clearing (Jordan and Kaups 1989:97-98). Although they present no data, Jordan and Kaups reckon that most of these frontier farms kept within a few miles or less of each other. Wilhelm's detailed study of the Virginia Blue Ridge concludes that loose clusters of two or three cabins were created at the beginning; as in the Kofyar case, isolated farmsteads were rare (Wilhelm 1978; see also Price and Price 1981).

Farmstead settlements, then, are closely related to the nature of interaction between "sites" as are larger settlements that are involved in trade, purveyance of central functions, and exercise of political control. Our ability to interpret patterning in ancient agrarian sites is strengthened by our understanding of how the inhabitants of such sites have interacted.

Notes

1. O'Brien (1984:8-9) discusses the integration of spatial and cultural-ecologic analyses. The role of labor mobilization in shaping settlement has been discussed in a few archaeological studies, including Crown (1987). For examples of settlement models inspired by biological ecology, see Green 1977, O'Brien 1984, Lewis 1984, Pruecel 1987.

2. "Core area" here refers to a more restricted area than in Stone (1988a).

3. Landscapes may be modified to meet various agroecological constraints: growing seasons can be extended by cold air drainage features (Riley and Freimuth 1979; Adams 1979), steep slopes can be terraced (Donkin 1979), and swamps can be drained or transformed into fertile ridges (Denevan and Turner 1974).

4. Labor input figures are based on a sample of households monitored in the core area. A group of young Kofyar farmers were hired and trained as enumerators; each monitored his own and at least one neighboring household, making up a total sample of 39 workers in 11 households. Using their own observations as well as interviews, they recorded each adult's daily activities, noting the task, the crop, the approximate amount of time spent and the farmstead on which each task was performed. Time spent on each activity was rounded to the nearest hour, and activities less than ca. 45 minutes in duration were omitted. The daily returns were carefully checked on a weekly or biweekly basis. Further details of the labor study are reported in Stone et al. (1990). Figures in Stone et al. (1990) are slightly higher because they include crop processing time.

5. The coresident group is in most cases the same as what may be called a household. I have avoided that term here because of the ambiguity caused by two-farm households.

6. There are other conventions for mobilizing group labor as well (Stone et al. 1990), including small reciprocal labor groups composed mostly of close neighbors. In this chapter, however, I will treat supra-household labor as a single category.

7. Late rainy season *bunga* are made in the sorghum field, where the millet plants had recently been

removed. Heap-making effectively weeds the sorghum at the same time it prepares the field for the next season's crop. The heaps also buttress the sorghum stalks against winds which whip through the thinned field; they may be used for a last-minute sesame crop as well (Stone et al. 1990).

Acknowledgements

I am grateful to Terry D'Altroy, Bob Netting, Priscilla Stone and Carole Crumley for discussion relating to this paper. The Kofyar Research Project was supported by the National Science Foundation (grants BNS-8318569 and BNS-8308323) and the Wenner-Gren Foundation. Further support was provided by a Weatherhead Fellowship at the School of American Research, Santa Fe, and by a grant from the Councils for Research in Humanities and Social Science at Columbia University. Finally, thanks to John Speth.

References

Adams, E. C.
1979 Cold air drainage and length of growing season in the Hopi Mesas area. *The Kiva* 44:285-297.

Bentley, J. W.
1987 Economic and ecological approaches to land fragmentation: in defense of a much-maligned phenomenon. *Annual Review of Anthropology* 16:31-67.

Boserup, E.
1965 *The Conditions of Agricultural Growth*. New York: Aldine.

Brookfield, H. C.
1972 Intensification and disintensification in Pacific agriculture. *Pacific Viewpoint* 13:30-48.

Brunger, A. G.
1982 Geographical propinquity among pre-famine Catholic Irish settlers in Upper Canada. *Journal of Historical Geography* 8:265-282.

Carlstein, T.
1982 *Time Resources, Society and Ecology*, Vol. 1. London: Allen and Unwin.

Christaller, W.
1966 *Central places in Southern Germany*. Translated by C. W. Baskin. Englewood Cliffs: Prentice-Hall. [Orig. 1933]

Cleave, J. H.
1974 *African Farmers: Labor Use in the Development of Smallholder Agriculture*. New York: Praeger.

Crown, P. L.
1987 Classic period Hohokam settlement and land-use in the Casa Grande ruins area, Arizona. *Journal of Field Archaeology* 14:147-162.

Crumley, C. L.
1979 Three locational models: an epistemological assessment fcr anthropology and archaeology. In *Advances in Archaeological Method and Theory*, Vol. 3. M. B. Schiffer (ed.), 141-173. New York: Academic Press.

D'Altroy, T. N.
1992 *Provincial Power in the Inka Empire*. Washington DC: Smithsonian Institution Press.

Denevan, W. M. & B. L. Turner II
1974 Forms, functions and associations of raised fields in the Old World tropics. *Journal of Tropical Geography* 39:1-24.

Donkin, R. A.
1979 *Agricultural terracing in the aboriginal New World*. Viking Fund Publications in Anthropology 56.

Drennan, R. D.
1988 Household location and compact versus dispersed settlement in prehispanic Mesoamerica. In *Household and Community in the Mesoamerican Past*. R. R. Wilk and W. Ashmore (eds.), 273-293. Albuquerque: University of New Mexico Press.

Earle,T. K.
1976 A nearest-neighbor analysis of two formative settlement systems. In *The Early Mesoamerican Village*. K. V. Flannery (ed.), 196-223. New York: Academic Press.

Earle, T. K. & J. E. Ericson (eds.)
1977 *Exchange Systems in Prehistory*. New York: Academic Press.

Eidt, R. C.
1977 *Pioneer Settlement in Northeast Argentina*. Madison: University of Wisconsin Press.

Evans, S. & P. Gould
1982 Settlement models in archaeology. *Journal of Anthropological Archaeology* 1:275-304.

Flannery, K. V.
1986 A visit to the master. In *Guilá Naquitz: Archaic Foraging and Early Agriculture in Oaxaca, Mexico*. K. V. Flannery (ed.), 511-519. Orlando: Academic Press.

Gade, D. & M. Escobar
1982 Village settlement and the colonial legacy

in southern Peru. *Geographical Review* 72:430-449.

Gall, P. L. & A. A. Saxe
1977 The ecological evolution of culture: the state as predator in succession theory. In *Exchange Systems in Prehistory*. T. K. Earle and J. E. Ericson (eds.), 255-268. New York: Academic Press.

Glassow, M. A.
1977 Population aggregation and systemic change: examples from the American Southwest. In *Explanation of Culture Change*. J. N. Hill (ed.), 185-214. Albuquerque: University of New Mexico Press.

Green, S. W.
1979 The agricultural colonization of temperate forest habitats: an ecological model. In *The Frontier: Comparative Studies*, Vol. 2. W. W. Savage and S. I. Thompson (eds.), 69-103. Norman: University of Oklahoma Press.

Grove, A. T.
1961 Population densities and agriculture in northern Nigeria. In *Essays on African Population*, K. M. Barbour and R. M. Prothero (eds.), 115-136. London: Routledge and Kegan Paul.

Hamond, F.
1981 The colonization of Europe: the analysis of settlement process. In *Patterns of the Past: Studies in Honor of David Clarke*. I. Hodder, G. Isaac, and N. Hamond (eds.), 211-248. Cambridge: Cambridge University Press.

Hess, D. W.
1979 Pioneering as ecological process: a model and test case of frontier adaption. In *The Frontier: Comparative Studies*, Vol. 2. W. W. Savage and S. I. Thompson (eds.), 123-151. Norman: University of Oklahoma Press.

Johnson, G. A.
1972 A test of the utility of Central Place in Archaeology. In *Man, Settlement and Urbanism*. P. J. Ucko, R. Tringham and G. W. Dimbleby (eds.), 769-785. Cambridge, MA.:Schenkman.
1975 Locational analysis and the investigation of Uruk local exchange systems. In *Ancient Civilization and Trade*. J. Sabloff and C. C. Lamberg-Karlovsky (eds.), 285-339. Albuquerque: University of New Mexico Press.

Jordan, T. G.
1976 Abandonment of farm-village tradition in new-land settlement: the example from Anglo-America. In *Geographic Dimensions of Rural Settlement*. R. L. Singh, K. N. Singh and R. P. B. Singh (eds.), 84-88. Varanasi: National Geographic Society.

Jordan T. G. & M. Kaups
1989 *The American Backwoods Frontier: An Ethnic and Ecological Interpretation*. Baltimore: The John Hopkins University Press.

Keegan, W. F. & M. D. Machlachlan
1989 Evolution of avunculocal chiefdoms: a reconstruction of Taino kinship and politics. *American Anthropologist* 91:613-630.

Killion, T. W. (ed.)
1992 *Gardens of Prehistory: The Archaeology of Settlement Agriculture in Greater Mesoamerica*. Tuscaloosa: University of Alabama Press.

Kohler, T. A.
1992 Field houses, villages and the tragedy of the commons in the early northern Anasazi Southwest. *American Antiquity* 57:617-635.

Lewis, K. E.
1984 *The American Frontier: An Archaeolgical Study of Settlement Pattern and Process*. New York: Academic Press.

Lösch, A.
1954 *The Economics of Location*. Translated by W. H. Woglom and W. F. Stolper. New Haven: Yale University Press. [Orig. 1940]

Margolis, M.
1977 Historical perspectives on frontier agriculture as an adaptive strategy. *American Ethnologist* 4:42-64.

Marquardt, W. H. & C. L. Crumley
1987 Theoretical issues in the analysis of spatial patterning. In *Regional Dynamics: Burgundian Landscapes in Historical Perspective*. C. L. Crumley and W. H. Marquardt (eds.),1-18. San Diego: Academic Press.

Mayhew, A.
1973 *Rural Settlement and Farming in Germany*. New York: Barnes & Noble.

Morgan W. B.
1969 The zoning of land-use around rural settlements in tropical Africa. In *Environment and Land-Use in Africa*. M. F. Thomas and G. W. Whittington (eds.), 301-319. London: Methuen.

Netting, R. McC.
1965 Household organization and intensive agriculture: the Kofyar case. *Africa* 35:422-429
1968 *Hill Farmers of Nigeria: Cultural Ecology of the Kofyar of the Jos Plateau.* Seattle: University of Washington Press.
1974 Agrarian ecology. *Annual Review of Anthropology* 3:21-56.
1982 Territory, property and tenure. In *Behavioral and Social Science Research: A National Treasure*, 446-502. Washington: National Academy Press.
Netting, R. McC., G. D. Stone & M. P. Stone
n.d. Agricultural expansion, intensification, and market participation among the Kofyar, Jos Plateau, Nigeria. In *Population Growth and Agricultural Intensification in Africa.* B. L. Turner II, G. Hyden & R. Kates (eds.). Gainesville: University of Florida Press.
Netting, R. McC., M. P. Stone & G. D. Stone
1989 Kofyar cash cropping: choice and change in indigenous agricultural development. *Human Ecology* 17:299-319.
Nichols, D. L.
1987 Risk and agricultural intensification during the formative period in the northern basin of Mexico. *American Anthropologist* 89:596-616.
O'Brien, M. J.
1984 *Grassland, Forest and Historical Settlement.* Lincoln: University of Nebraska Press.
1987 Sedentism, population growth and resource selection in the Woodland Midwest: A review of coevolutionary developments. *Current Anthropology* 28:177-197.
Ostergren, R.
1979 A community transplanted: the formative experience of a Swedish immigrant community in the Upper Middle West. *Journal of Historical Geography* 5:189-212.
Pasternak, B., C. R. Ember & M. Ember
1976 On the conditions favoring extended family households. *Journal of Anthropological Research* 32:109-123.
Plog, F. & J. N. Hill
1971 Explaining variability in the distribution of sites. In *The Distribution of Prehistoric Population Aggregates.* G. J. Gumerman (ed.), Prescott College Anthropological Reports 1.
Preucel, R.
1987 Settlement succession on the Pajarito plateau. *The Kiva* 53:3-33.
Price, C. R. & J. E. Price
1981 Investigations of settlement and subsistence systems in the Ozark border region of southwest Missouri during the first half of the 19th century: The Widow Harris cabin project. *Ethnohistory* 28:237-258.
Renfrew, C. A.
1975 Trade as action at a distance. In *Ancient Civilization and Trade.* J. Sabloff and C. C. Lambert-Karlovsky (eds.), 3-59. Albuquerque: University of New Mexico Press.
Riley, T. J. & G. Freimuth
1979 Field systems and frost drainage in the prehistoric agriculture of the Upper Great Lakes. *American Antiquity* 44:271-285.
Rowlands, M. J.
1972 Defence: A factor in the organization of settlements. In *Man, Settlement and Urbanism.* P. J. Ucko, R. Tringham and G. W. Dimbleby (eds.), 447-462. Cambridge, MA.: Schenkman.
Sahlins, M. D.
1957 Land use and the extended family in Moala, Fiji. *American Anthropologist* 59:449-462.
Steponaitis, V. P.
1981 Settlement hierarchies and political complexity in nonmarket societies: the formative period in the valley of Mexico. *American Anthropologist* 83:320-363.
Stone, G. D.
1988a *Agrarian ecology and settlement patterns: An ethnoarchaeological case study.* PhD dissertation. Ann Arbor: University Microfilms.
1988b Agricultural intensification and residential mobility: An archaeological perspective on Boserup. Paper presented at the annual meeting of the Society for American Archaeology, Phoenix.
1990 Agricultural territories in a dispersed settlement system. *Current Anthropology* 32:343-352.
Stone, G. D., M. P. Johnson-Stone & R. McC. Netting
1984 Household variability and inequality in Kofyar subsistence and cash-cropping economies. *Journal of Anthropological Research* 40:90-108.
Stone, G. D., R. McC. Netting & M. P. Stone
1990 Seasonality, labor scheduling and agricul-

tural intensification in the Nigerian savanna. *American Anthropologist* 92:7-23.

Stone, M. P., G. D. Stone & R. McC. Netting
n.d. The sexual division of labor in Kofyar agriculture. *American Ethnologist*, in press.

Thompson, S. I.
1977 The cultural ecology of pioneer agriculture in contemporary South America. In *The Frontier: Comparative Studies*, Vol. 1. D. H. Miller and J. O. Steffen (eds.), 297-316. Norman: University of Oklahoma Press.

Udo, R. K.
1965 Disintegration of nucleated settlement in eastern Nigeria. *Geographical Review* 55:53-65.

Wilhelm, E. J.
1978 Folk settlements in the Blue Ridge Mountains. *Appalachian Journal* 5:204-245.

Wilk, R. R.
1988 Maya household organization: Evidence and analogies. In *Household and Community in the Mesoamerican Past*. R. R. Wilk and W. Ashmore (eds.), 135-151. Albuquerque: University of New Mexico Press.

Wilk, R. R. & R. McC. Netting
1984 Households: changing forms and functions. In *Households: Comparative and Historical Studies of the Domestic Group*. R. McC. Netting, R. R. Wilk & E. J. Arnould (eds.), 1-28. Berkeley: University of California Press.

4. Community Interaction and Settlement Patterning in Northern Cameroon

Augustin Holl

Introduction

Pastoral nomadic communities of northernmost Cameroon distinguish themselves or are distinct from other communities not only by their mode of subsistence, animal husbandry, but also by a wide range of material variables. These include: the choice of the species of animals to be reared (cattle), their house-building techniques, the raw material used, and the specific spatial patterning of their camps. My general hypothesis is that the maintenance of specific pastoral traits which may be observed in the internal patterning of domestic space—the structure of domestic space relative to public or communal space, is a general strategy with twofold consequences: that of maintaining the cultural homogeneity and integrity of pastoral groups and, at the same time, of enhancing systemic complementarity with neighboring sedentary agriculturalists belonging to more complex sociopolitical systems. As far as this differentiation appears at the first glance to parallel ethnic identities, I intend to examine different categories of data including settlement patterns and artifact assemblages, which are left within seasonally abandoned pastoral camps. This is done in order to assess the potential of an archaeological approach for the study of sociological and ideological features transferable in the material record with an attempt to understand the processes implied in the maintenance of ethnic identities.

This research is an integral part of a current archaeological project initiated in the northernmost part of Cameroon to understand and explicate the nature of sociocultural dynamics of late prehistoric communities in that part of Africa (Connah 1981, 1985; Lebeuf et al. 1980; Holl 1987, 1988). According to general archaeological and historical knowledge, the Chadian plain, in which our study area is located, was a crossroad of peoples, cultures and techno-economic complexes. Many models have been presented to explain the incredible complexity of ethnic and linguistic distributions in that part of Africa; some of them are related to ecological theories (Connah 1981) and many others concern the development of theories of migrations (Lebeuf 1979, 1981; Tijani 1986). Both of these forms of models may be true and we may thus avoid an a priori decision concerning the research potentials of these complementary models of explanation. However, we need a larger and more comprehensive base of factual data in order to test the fitness of each of these models. The research presented in this paper is thus a modest contribution to this exciting research undertaking concerned with the explanation of processes of sociocultural dynamics and transformations.

The Archaeological Background

According to the archaeological and historical record available to date, there have been different forms of animal husbandry developed in the Chadian plain during the past 4,000 years. The earliest form of pastoralism is attested by the presence of bones of domestic bovines and ovicaprines in the archaeological record of the mounds of Daima and Kursakata, Nigeria, excavated by Connah (1969, 1981). Unfortunately, the nature of this mode of pastoralism is still unexplained in terms of its dynamics and structures. We do have some data concerning the taxonomic composition of faunal assemblages as well as some domestic animal figurines:

> Much of the material is unidentifiable but it does appear that the inhabitants of the village [Kursakata] kept both cattle and small stock (sheep and goats). (Connah 1981:98)

Variations in the relative proportions of animal bones of different domestic species show that cattle herding was dominant during the earlier Daima I–II (ca. 600 B.C.–700 A.D.) chronological sequences, and was later complemented by an increasing proportion of small stock of sheep/goats during Daima III (ca. 700–1200 A.D.) (Connah 1981:192-3). The late prehistoric peoples of Bornu province of northeastern Nigeria were thus practising a mixed economy in which hunting, fishing, plant collecting, stock herding, and grain farming were combined in various ways as complementary food procurement strategies. These archaeological findings suggest that the socioeconomic specialization and ethnic diversity presently observed in the Chadian plain (Adamu and Kirk-Greene 1986), and which consists of ethnic and cultural variability between pastoralists and sedentary agriculturalists, emerged from a more generalized economic basis. This is a very exciting archaeological challenge; our task is therefore to uncover the processes which led to these new social, cultural and economic patterns in the Chadian plain. In short, what were the driving forces which generated the emergence of specialized pastoralism in this region and how did this new socioeconomic system interact with sedentary agriculturalists?

Another interesting category of information can be gathered from the historical and ethnographic record (Tijani 1986; Zeltner 1979; Hagenburger-Sacripanti 1977a, 1977b; Conte and Hagenburger-Sacripanti 1977). In this regard, according to Tijani (1986:62-3), the main pastoral nomad group, the Shuwa-Arabs, first appeared in the history of Kanem-Bornu kingdom as early as the late fourteenth century A.D., entering that country from Egypt, "possibly as a result of the wars of Islamic expansion in the seventh century A.D."

Since that time the Shuwa-Arabs posed a challenge to the central authority of Bornu, first through wars, and second because of their successful adaptation to the ecology of the Chadian plain environment through pastoralism, "an occupation which keeps them mobile and generally renders them unwilling to adopt most of the homogenizing cultural traits of the predominantly settled populations of Borno" (Tijani 1986:63). It was through these economic activities that they have always managed to keep their pastoral mode of living and identity. According to Tijani (1986), the reason for the failure of Bornu rulers to integrate the Shuwa-Arabs in their sociopolitical system lies primarily in the policy of their central administration, which aimed at incorporating whole community units in order to reap the benefits of mass tutelage at minimum cost. This historical information is very interesting, but it is neither peculiar to the ancient Bornu kingdom nor to Africa; the features presented by Tijani (1986) are a constant in the policy of central monarches in their relations with their pastoral-nomadic neighbors as has been cogently demonstrated by Briant (1982) and others (Charles 1939; Luke 1965) in the Near-East during the 2nd–1st millennium B.C. Concerning our research purposes, the most interesting fact is that new, specialized pastoralists are recorded in the Chadian plain in the 14th century A.D. Since then, they added significant complexity to an already complex set of socioeconomic interactions between different modes of subsistence and ethnic groups. We do not know a great deal about the development of earlier mixed economies attested in the archaeological record from the mound sites of Bornu in which small stock of sheep/goats were increasingly herded at the expense of cattle. Why the shift from a dominantly cattle-based animal husbandry system to a sheep/goat herding system? Finally, what is the impact of the arrival of a new cattle-based socioeconomic system on the Perichadian protohistoric polities? Research focussing on these problems is of crucial importance if we intend to understand the processes involved and the specific nature of pastoral nomadic–sedentary agriculturalist interaction in the Chadian plain.

Research Perspectives

Let us consider that the present ethnic diversity observed in the Perichadian plain is primarily a result of various sociocultural transformations which have occurred during the past 4,000 years. It is obvious that a wide range of evolutionary processes are implied in the patterns of change observed in the archaeological, historical, and ethnographic record. In general, evolutionary processes operative in human cultural systems are very complex, diversified and difficult to identify. They are constituted of changing structures and their continuous mutual interaction and multiple feedback mechanisms. All these features may result in the emergence of specific time/space situations which may be termed techno-complexes, economic systems, cultures, ethnic groups, linguistic entities, and so on. The provisional model considered in this research context focuses primarily on a sample of the cultural dimensions of evolutionary processes as well as a discussion of the nature of ethnicity. As pointed out by Boyd and Richerson (1985:34),

> To understand the evolutionary process of an organism with cultural transmission one must understand the forces that affect the frequency of different culturally transmitted variants in a population.

Thus, in the perspective presented here, the most important aspect to analyze is the inherent structure of social learning which is defined as "any long-term homogeneity of behavior resulting from the transmission of patterns of behavior from individual to individual within a population as a consequence of social interaction" (Galef 1976, in Boyd and Richerson 1985:34). In terms of archaeology we will consider that learned and successfully transmitted patterns of behavior are attested in the archaeological record by the relative frequencies of material items uncovered in each specific time/space sequence and context. In this regard, convergent and/or divergent sequences of change in the material record may signal the reorganization of actual social systems. We assume that in human cultures both trial and error learning as well as rational calculation are potent mechanisms for producing similar patterns of behavior in similar cultural and physical environments, because each individual independently tends to adopt the behaviors appropriate to these environments (Boyd and Richerson 1985). However our model must be simple enough to represent generic processes, to be intelligible, easy to analyze, and useful for prediction.

A Model

Archaeological research on the Chadian plain indicates that its earliest inhabitants were Late Stone Age communities with mixed economies including fishing, hunting, the gathering of plants, and animal husbandry (Connah 1981, 1985; Griaule & Lebeuf 1948, 1950, 1951; Lebeuf 1979, 1981; Lebeuf et al. 1980; David 1980; Rapp 1984; Holl 1986a, b, 1987, 1988, n.d.). However, we do not know yet if they were practising agriculture. Archaeological data relevant for that sequence have been uncovered at Shilma, Bornu 38, Kursakata, Daima, Sou Blame Radjil, and Mdaga and range in time between 2000 years B.C. and 500 years B.C. Dwelling structures were built with wood and grass and it seems that sites were small and nucleated seasonal camps (Holl 1987). The Early Iron Age lasted from 500 B.C. to 500–700 A.D. Iron items belonging to this sequence have been uncovered, many of them belonging to heavy duty tools such as axes and hoe blades uncovered at Mdaga (Lebeuf et al. 1980) which occur along with the appearance of circular mud-walled houses. The number of pottery sherds and items was more important than in the previous sequence. The Late Iron Age (A.D. 700–A.D. 1400) witnessed for the first time the appearance of prestige items in bronze and exotic carnelian beads. Circular mud houses were still in use and the manufacture of large "so pots" began during that sequence. At Daima the heavy reliance on cattle was more and more balanced by small stock of sheep/goats. At Mdaga in Chad cattle bones appear for the first time in the archaeological record. During the last sequence, which I have termed the "Islamic period" (Holl 1987, 1988), there were quadrangular houses with flat roofs at Mdaga with the import of large amounts of carnelian beads, numerous large pots, bronze items, and very few iron artifacts. These categories of data suggest a major change in subsistence-settlement strategies with a decreasing degree of mobility towards more sedentary ways of living. They also suggest technological changes and increasing densities of population in the Chadian plain. One possible evolutionary pathway associated with these changes may be the development of new adaptive strategies connected with the emergence of patterned interaction between specialized pastoralism and sedentary agriculturalists.

A certain number of production activities can be identified from the material evidence recorded at Chadian sites. However, only some of these will be considered in the following model. These include food production and food gathering activities, iron and bronze metallurgy, pottery production, and long distance exchange. In order to perform these activities societies had to devise adequate procedures to have access to information, to acquire desired raw materials, to process and to use the items produced. There are also organizational problems related to time budgeting, the mobilization of the labor force, and the creation of necessary decision-making structures. In this regard, each of the five general activities mentioned above can be considered as a socio-technological system, each with its own dynamics, organizational properties and scheduling mechanism. Their mutual interaction may cause deviation-amplifying or deviation-inhibiting feedback within the global social system.

During the Late Stone Age cattle husbandry and many other food procurement strategies were the major set of activities practised, along with small scale pottery manufacture, and bone and stone tool production. A high degree of mobility may have been the main subsistence-settlement strategy articulated between rainy season and dry season camps. With the advent of iron technology, settlements appear to have been more intensively occupied, and consequently the degree of mobility may have been reduced. Even if we do not yet know the real impact and structure of iron metallurgy among Early Iron Age societies of the Chadian plain, two important sets of activities had to be managed within the same annual time budget. The drift between two socioeconomic components of the same social system may have begun at that time, with domestic stock kept outside the cultivated area located near the main settlement in which iron was used to manufacture agricultural tools, weapons, and other items of equipment. Following this line of thought, craft specialization may have been one of the major driving forces which led to the emergence of specialized pastoralism. Conversely, the relations between the two systems were necessary for the maintenance of both; it is this kind of double bind (Bateson 1984) between two divergent but complementary socioeconomic subsystems which may explain the necessary coexistence of pastoralists and agriculturalists in the same area. During the Late Iron Age, the introduction of bronze metallurgy, the advent of an intensive production of ceramic items, and long distance exchange networks amplified the divergence already set in motion during Early Iron Age. Thus there is no real surprise that at Daima during the Late Iron Age the relative proportion of sheep/goat bones increased at the expense of cattle bones. In this perspective, the finding made by Connah (1981:170) is very interesting:

> ...I find a fragment of "fireplace" wall (spit 4) that was made up of no fewer than six parallel components difficult to explain in domestic terms.

A similar fireplace has been uncovered at Houlouf level III (2.20 m) and both findings are very similar to pastoral nomadic hearths found in the Houlouf region today. This does not automatically mean that the archaeological features recorded at both sites have been built by pastoral nomadic groups, but this stylistic similarity must be explained.

During the following "Islamic period," agriculturalists with small stock and pastoralists with cattle and a nomadic way of life were the main socioeconomic components of the Chadian basin, with some fishing communities located along the major rivers and the lake Chad.

In the model presented here, the maintenance and reproduction of specific cultural traits may be better explained by the concept of double bind. According to this concept, individuals are constrained by cultural forces within their own community to adopt the patterns of behavior expected of them if they intend to be recognized as members. At the same time, depending on the actual economic and political relations between the communities sharing the same territory, the maintenance of community-specific patterns of behavior may be amplified or inhibited. The cultural differentiation thus constructed may enhance interaction which may lead to conflict from time to time, but in the long term it is a strategy of systemic complementarity. The following research has been conducted to test this simple model. In our research perspective, the emergence of specialized pastoralism and its ethnic characteristics may be considered as a result of socioeconomic specialization within the context of competitive social formations. Centralized polities constituted mainly of settled agriculturalists and fishing communities always tried to control and dominate the pastoral nomadic groups which reacted to political pressure by reinforcing their ethnic identity. Even in the modern Cameroonian political and administrative system, these processes of competition are still at work. In this regard, each settlement "may be perceived in terms of social space—physical, ecological, and structural distance—so that there is a relativity of reference points for the groups involved in interaction. Thus, the same site may be differently manipulated according to the specific group interests, but the total spatial arrangements form a general network of communication" (Kuper 1972:421).

Understanding Ethnicity

Anthropologists have proposed different definitions of ethnicity which emphasize various kinds of characteristics (Abruzzi 1982; Barth 1956, 1969; Cohen 1969, 1974a, b; Duncan 1981; Dragadze 1980; Hjort 1981; Knutsson 1969). It appears that ethnic groups are primarily characterized by shared world views, language, and a common territory. According to Dragadze (1980:162), *ethnos* can be defined as a firm aggregate of people, historically established on a given territory, possessing in common relatively stable particularities of language and culture, and also recognizing their unity and difference from other similar formations (self awareness) and expressing this in a self-appointed name (ethnonym).

If we consider ethnicity not only as a sociological category but as a social construct, we should like to know more about the processes leading to the emergence of ethnic groups and the social conditions of their maintenance. It is obvious that ethnicity is a complex phenomenon involving psychological, historical, economic, and political factors. It may be better considered as a variable which in any sociocultural milieu is interdependent with many others. Faced with the complexity of the subject, one way of tackling this problem is to analyze ethnicity in terms of the interconnections of economic and political relationships within a larger social formation. In this regard, "an ethnic group can be operationally defined as a collectivity of people who share some patterns of normative behavior and form a part of a larger population interacting with people from other collectivities within the framework of a social system" (Cohen 1974:ix). The problem of interest for the research perspective presented here is to clarify the relations between ethnicity and political and economic organization in the Houlouf study area and to examine how this set of relations is connected to regional settlement patterns and the spatial organization of pastoral sites. In short, in terms of my research strategy, "what matters sociologically is what people actually do, not what they subjectively think or what they think they think" (Cohen 1974:xi).

The Region of Houlouf: Land and Population

The Houlouf region is situated in the northernmost part of Cameroon along the southern margins of the Sahel (Fig. 1). It is the northern portion of the Canton of El-Birké, a lower-order, present-day, administrative subdivision, and covers an area of about 400 km^2 (20 km E-W and 20 km N-S) limited in the east by the Logone river. The vegetation is characterized by an arbustive savanna with a climatic pattern of two contrasting seasons: six months of a relatively rainy season and an important dry season of equal duration. This region is thus characterized by very sharp seasonal variation in moisture and available water. With the exception of the Logone river, all the remaining streams are temporary, and many of them are presently almost inactive. In terms of micro-environmental features, there are two major sets of characteristics which are critical in regard to settlement patterns: firstly, the overall distribution of seasonally flooded/non-flooded areas and, secondly, the patterning of ecological microzones.

Approximately, three fifths of the 400 square kilometers of the Houlouf region are composed of seasonally flooded lowlands and two fifths are permanently above flood level. In this flat Chadian plain, constituted of montmorillinitic clay as the dominant type of soil, the location of permanent habitation sites is thus severely constrained. Three main ecological microzones have been identified in the study area: 1) the marshy micro-area of the hinterland characterized by grassland and the presence of more or less permanent ponds and marshes, 2) the arbustive savanna micro-area which is the most extensive zone, and 3) the Logone river valley in the east. The distribution of these features appears to have conditioned the pattern of settlement as well as the location of productive economic activities.

Population

Data concerning the various populations inhabiting the Houlouf region have been collected from the administrative census of 1969 (Elingui 1978) and the

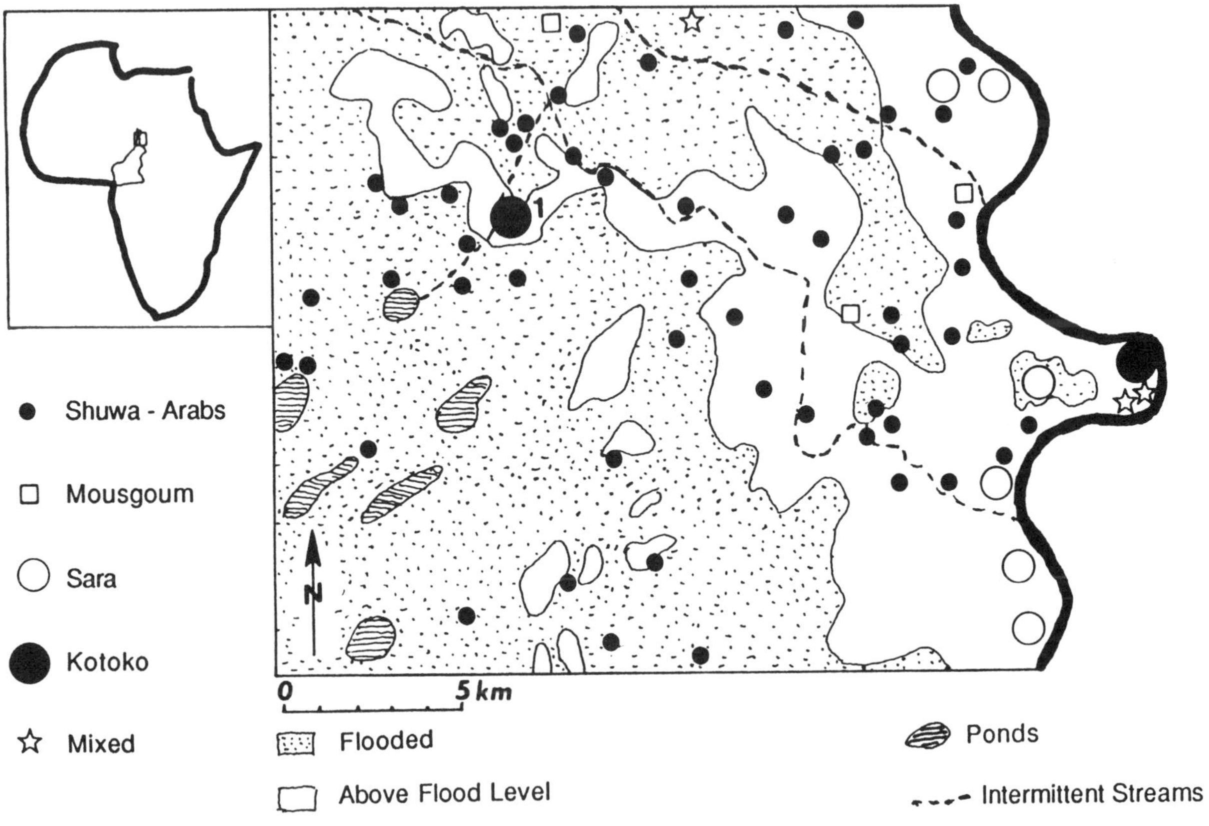

Fig. 1. The Houlouf region: location map and distribution of settlements. 1 = Houlouf.

general census of population and habitation of 1976 (Bureau Central du Recensement 1985; Table 1). It appears that between 1969 and 1976 the total number of inhabitants increased by 2,847 (69.84%), meaning that population densities increased as well (Tables 2 and 3). The ethnic affiliation of these people is quite clear. They are mostly Shuwa-Arabs sometimes in association with the Massa, Mousgoum and Bornouan groups, however, never with the Kotoko.

Concerning the distribution of dominant economic activities, a number of interesting patterns of change emerge from the comparison of these censuses. In 1969, pastoralists and agropastoralists were quantitatively dominant, both in terms of absolute number of inhabitants and number of settlements recorded (Table 2, Fig. 1). In the 1976 census, within the general trend of increasing numbers of inhabitants, pastoralists and agriculturalists/ pastoralists witnessed a decline relative to agriculturalists and agriculturalists/fishers (Table 3, Figs. 2 and 3), even though the number of agricultural settlements was reduced from 9 to 5 and that of agriculturalists/fishers remained the same. Conversely, the number of agriculturalist/pastoralist villages increased very slightly during this period. The total increase in population resulted from a combination of factors: natural population growth and the arrival of a large number of settlers due to critical sociopolitical problems (i.e., the civil war) in the nearby Chad Republic. On the other hand, changes in economic activities can be ascribed to the severe Sahelian drought of 1973–4 as well as technological modifications which resulted from an extensive Cameroonian government campaign to install deep bored wells which had the effect of converting many pastoralists to an agriculture and pastoral economy. As can be seen in Figure 2, almost all agriculturalist and pastoralist/agriculturalist settlements are preferentially located in the zone permanently above the flood level and the Logone river valley. Pastoralist settlements are located in the seasonally flooded zones. In my opinion, this differential use of environmental variability is an ecologically induced phenomena which is superseded from time to time by social and ideological elaboration which further conditions the interaction between the peoples and ethnic groups of the Houlouf region.

Kotoko and Shuwa-Arabs

Unlike the other ethnic groups in the Houlouf region, the Kotoko claim possession of the land through their mythical ancestors, the "Sao" (Griaule and Lebeuf 1948; Lebeuf 1969). In fact, they had, in the recent past, the strongest and the most structured sociopolitical organization in the region. Kotoko societies were organized into competing peer polities fighting against each other for political control of the southern part of the Perichadian plain. In these political, and certainly also economic, conflicts, the Kotoko were always looking for the support of the pastoralists, who were very mobile and preferentially enrolled as soldiers and border guards within the different Kotoko polities. Traditionally, the Kotoko attitude toward the Shuwa-Arab pastoralists has been explicitly characterized by exclusion and paternalism. According to oral information collected in the field, the Shuwa-Arabs are considered to be untrustworthy, thieves, violent, and bad Muslims, an assertion which is in total contradiction to the eagerness of the Kotoko rulers to have them as allies. On the other hand, Shuwa-Arabs consider the Kotoko as witches, chauvinistic, and greedy for power. However, these groups live together on the same land and have to share and use the same space. The range of different kinds of socioeconomic interaction is very interesting. Exchanges take place at weekly markets organized in each cluster of villages. At Houlouf, for example, the vast majority of sellers and service performers at the weekly market are Shuwa-Arabs and most of the Kotoko are selling pots or are merely customers. It is also noteworthy that the Shuwa-Arab language is the lingua franca used among peoples of the entire region and even between the Kotoko from different settlements. But the Shuwa-Arabs do not have access to higher regional political offices. Their respective villages are governed by a chief (*Bilama*) elected among the elders, who is subordinate to a local chief (the lower-order Sultan or *Adjia*) who is always a Kotoko inhabiting Houlouf or any of the Kotoko settlement. Above this chief is the paramount chief (the Sultan) of Logone-Birni. My fieldwork observations show that the exclusive control of higher order sociopolitical offices by the Kotoko is one of the basic reasons for their arrogance toward the Shuwa-Arabs.

In terms of archaeology, our research project was conducted in order to uncover the material manifestation of this situation in spatial patterning of settlements among both sedentary and pastoral peoples, as well as in the material record which remains at abandoned pastoral sites. One of the key question to be investigated is, how do the Shuwa-Arabs manage to maintain and reproduce their cultural identity in this regional setting characterized by social, economic, and political competition and inequality between different ethnic groups?

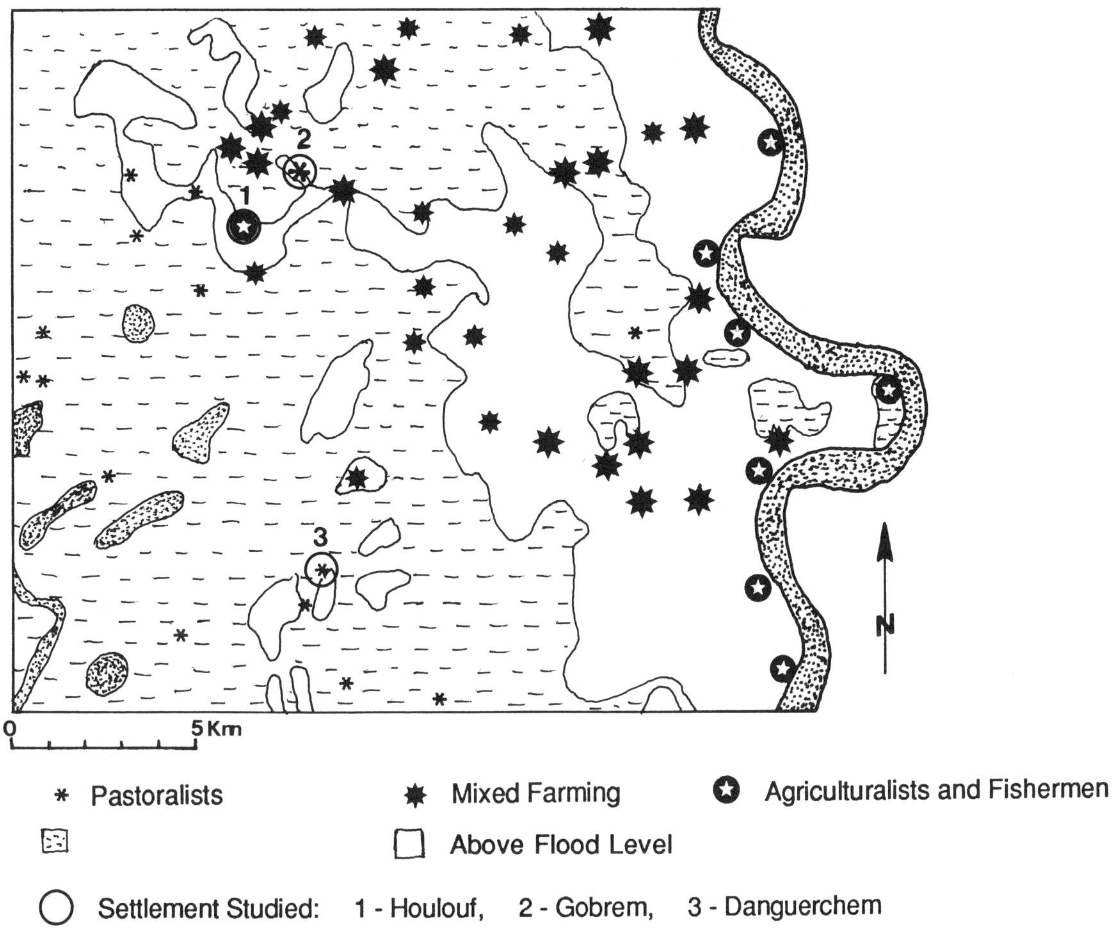

Fig. 2. Nature of land, economic activities and distribution of settlements.

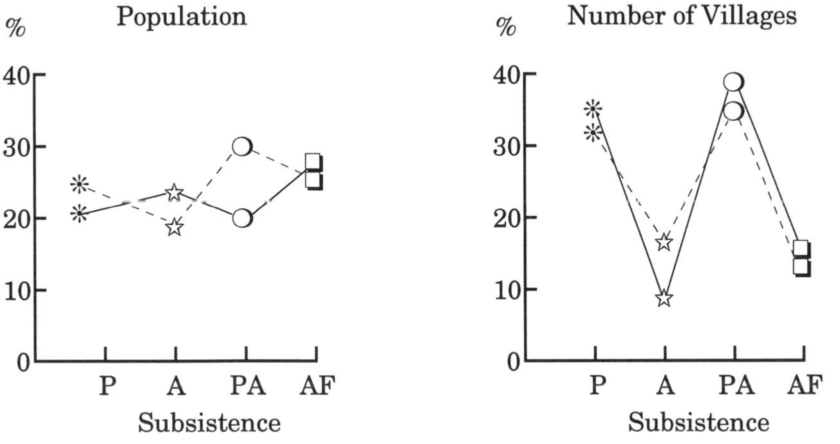

Fig. 3. Subsistence systems and changes in the distribution of population and number of settlements between 1969 and 1985.

Table 1. Localities, ethnic groups, population, and economic activities.
A = Agriculturalists, PA = Pastoralists and agriculturalists, AF = Agriculturalists and fishermen.

N°	Locality	Ethnic groups	Population 1969	Population 1985	Growth No.	Growth %	Economy
1	Houlouf	Kotoko	286	1127	841	294.04	A
2	Riggil	Kotoko/Mousgoum	22	340	318	1445.45	A
3	El Birké I	Arabs	77	138	61	79.22	PA
4	El Birké II	Arabs	23	51	23	121.73	PA
5	Mawak	Arabs	55	194	139	252.72	P
6	Abouzrega	Arabs	21	—	—	—	P
7	Ibou	Arabs	192	253	61	31.77	PA
8	Madana	Sara	174	247	73	41.95	AF
9	Mainani	composite	41	245	204	497.56	AF
10	Gabak	Mousgoum	11	—	—	—	AF
11	Lacka	composite	194	—	—	—	A
12	Massilakanam	Arabs	140	101	- 39	- 27.85	PA
13	Ndou	Arabs/Massa	55	102	47	85.45	PA
14	Kawadji	Mousgoum	102	80	- 22	- 21.56	A
15	Ardebe Gadjar	Sara	134	180	46	34.32	AF
16	Dabaye-Diguine	Arabs	110	—	—	—	P
17	Koumbala	Arabs/Mousgoum	55	145	90	163.63	PA
18	Djagare	Arabs	146	218	72	49.31	PA
19	Wadjetouna	Arabs	46	80	34	73.91	P
20	Ngoudoum	Arabs/Mousgoum	48	89	41	85.41	PA
21	Kellou	Arabs	22	52	30	136.36	P
22	Miguil	Arabs	26	35	9	34.61	P
23	Fachar	Arabs	22	39	16	72.72	P
24	Marle	Mousgoum	8	15	7	87.50	A
25	Kabela	Massa/Mousgoum	183	239	56	30.60	AF
26	Sabakallé I	Sara	49	121	72	146.93	AF
27	Sabakallé II	Arabs	64	62	- 2	- 3.12	P
28	Sabakallé III	Arabs	66	98	32	48.48	P
29	Kabé-Bekoro	Mousgoum/Sara	81	131	50	61.72	AF
30	Kabé-Kilam	K/M/B	377	652	275	72.94	AF
31	Kabé-Malo	Mousgoum/Massa	26	33	7	26.92	AF
32	Wadang	Mousgoum	38	88	50	131.57	A
33	Ngoumati	Arabs	63	52	- 11	- 17.46	P
34	Abendroua	Arabs	29	35	6	20.68	PA
35	Missiskoua	Arabs	54	66	12	22.22	P
36	Magourdé I	Arabs	18	37	19	105.55	PA
37	Magourdé II	Arabs	20	27	7	35.00	PA
38	Magourdé III	Arabs	20	50	30	150.00	PA
39	Djidat I	Arabs	37	63	26	70.27	PA
40	Djidat II	Arabs	79	134	55	69.62	PA
41	Madaf	Arabs	62	130	68	109.67	PA
42	Chouaram	Arabs	63	151	88	139.68	P
43	Mahanna	Arabs	26	40	14	53.84	P
44	Ndom	Arabs	28	49	21	75.00	P
45	Alaya	Arabs	116	53	- 63	- 54.31	P
46	Dambe	Arabs	17	35	18	105.88	P

Continued on next page

Table 1—*Continued*

Nº	Locality	Ethnic groups	Population 1969	Population 1985	Growth No.	Growth %	Economy
47	Gaou Brahim	Arabs	42	77	35	83.33	P
48	Lelewaya	Arabs	36	106	70	194.44	P
49	Massaki	Arabs	146	195	49	106.52	PA
50	Adjaine	Arabs/Bornouans	162	264	102	62.96	PA
51	Atti Ngezoya	Arabs	14	14	0	0	P
52	Ngoch	Mousgoum	12	—	—	—	A
53	Ouzougouboua	Mousgoum	82	—	—	—	A
54	Koulkoulé	Arabs	—	19	19	—	PA
55	Marafaine I	Arabs	46	88	42	91.30	PA
56	Marafaine II	Arabs	10	10	0	0	PA
57	Ngada	Arabs	—	73	73	—	P

Sedentary Settlement Patterning: A Case Study from Houlouf

The Kotoko have centralized sociopolitical institutions characterized by the existence of a paramount chief and lower order local chiefs. Before and even during the colonial period, their different peer polities were organized in a two-tiered settlement hierarchy. The spatial organization of the different Kotoko political centers shares the same basic structure and has been observed by ethnographers at a number of settlements such as Makari, Gulfey, Kusseri, Logone-birni, Houlouf, Kala-kafra, etc. (Griaule and Lebeuf 1948, 1950, 1951; Lebeuf 1969). All the settlements are walled settlements, and their spatial patterning is focused on the Sultan's palace. Habitation units which are organized in individual compounds are composed of various numbers of houses according to the wealth and the number of members of the household. The compounds are mainly quadrangular in shape, with flat roofs, separated from each other by walls built with sun-dried bricks. Aggregates of compounds are organized into distinct quarters or wards separated from each other by narrow streets, and each of them is ruled by a chief elected or appointed among the elders. These elders are members of different councils which manage the community's business under the leadership of the Sultan, who resides in the center of the settlement. The central location of the Sultan's palace is thus a spatial representation of the leading position of his office within the Kotoko social system.

The settlement patterning of Houlouf, which is the sole Kotoko village of our study area shares the same characteristics presented above (Fig. 4): the Sultan's palace (1) is located at the center of the village near a large plaza with a well and numerous trees (2), and the elders meet each other formally and informally under a shelter built next to the palace. The Friday mosque (3) and the residence of one of the most important elders are situated on the southern side of the plaza. Before the installation of deep bored water pumps in 1985, the well was the informal meeting place of the women of the whole village, and different kinds of information were thus exchanged and dispatched. From 1982, which was the year of my first visit to Houlouf, some changes have occurred with the arrival in 1984 of a Moslem scholar called *marabout* (4), who rules a mosque (3) and a Koranic school (5). The primary school (10) excepted, all the compounds located on the northern side of the main east-west street were built between 1984 and 1988 and are inhabited by recent settlers. The traditional authority of the Sultan is being steadily eroded by the modern Cameroonian administrative organization, so that in the modern context, he is mainly a tax collector, unable to initiate a policy of his own. The Moslem local organization is relatively free of the burden of the administration, so that there seems to be a competition for followers between the Kotoko traditional organization, represented by the proximity of the Sultan's palace and the Friday mosque, located at the center of the village, but with decreasing influence of its political system, and the relative Islamic revival shown by the presence of three mosques in such a relatively small settlement, and their organizational necessities. The meeting place in front of the *marabout* compound and the Koranic school has seen during the last years a higher frequency of gathering of the village elders at the expense of the plaza located in front of the Sultan's palace. This competition between Kotoko traditional

Table 2. Population census of 1969.

Economy	Population		Villages		Ethnic Combination				Density	Descriptive Statistics					
	No.	%	No.	%	1	2	3	Comp.	Inh./km^2	Mean	Min.	Max.	R	SD	CV
Pastoralists	1012	24.82	19	34.54	21	—	—	—	2.81	46.49	14	146	132	28.38	1.49
Agriculturalists	755	18.52	9	16.36	7	1	—	1	2.06	83.88	8	246	238	91.57	10.17
Mixedfarming	1226	30.07	19	34.54	75	—	—	—	3.40	71.31	38	192	154	55.75	2.93
Agriculturalists/ Fishermen	1065	26.12	8	14.54	3	3	1	1	2.95	13.31	36	377	341	108.04	13.50
Total	4076		55		38	9	12	1	1.32	74.10	8	377	369	71.95	1.30

Table 3. Population census of 1985.

Economy	Population		Villages		Ethnic Combination				Density	Descriptive Statistics					
	No.	%	No.	%	1	2	3	Comp.	Inh./km^2	Mean	Min	Max	R	SD	CV
Pastoralists	1463	21.13	18	35.29	18	—	—	—	4.06	70.88	14	194	180	42.86	2.38
Agriculturalists	1650	23.83	5	9.80	4	1	—	—	4.58	330.0	15	1127	1112	413.66	82.73
Pastoralists/ Agriculturalists	1943	20.06	20	39.21	16	4	—	—	5.39	107.45	10	264	254	74.96	3.74
Agriculturalists/ Fishermen	1848	26.69	8	15.68	3	3	1	1	5.13	231.0	33	652	619	173.80	21.72
Total	6923	51	41	8	1	1	19.23	135.74	10	1127	1117	176.88	3.46		

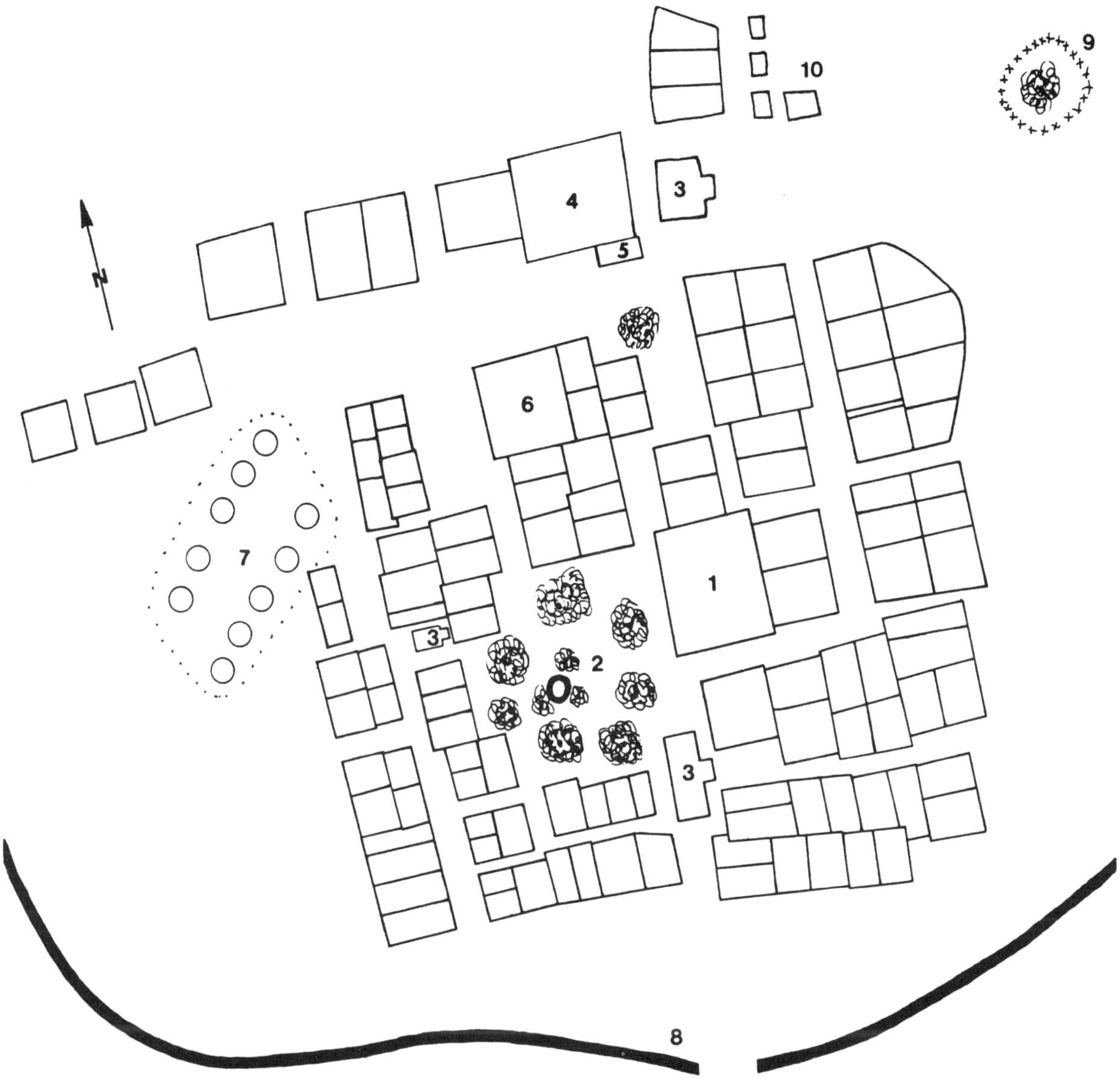

Fig. 4. Schematic map of Houlouf. 1) Sultan's palace , 2) Central plaza, 3) Mosques: the largest is the Friday mosque, 4) "Marabout" compound, 5) Koranic school , 6) "Galadima" compound, 7) Market place, 8) Earthen wall, 9) Sheep/goat enclosure , 10) Elementary school.

system and Islamic organization is not new in this region, however, centers like Logone-Birni have found solutions to lower the degree of competition by building a mosque in close proximity to the Sultan's palace and controlling the appointment of its officials.

This short discussion of the settlement spatial patterning of Houlouf shows that the structure of community space is not a neutral background. Moreover, it shows that the spatial layout of sites is dependent upon the dominant ideological system. The major research problem in this study is thus to understand and explain how the mutual interaction of ethnic groups sharing the same regional space is manifested in the spatial structure of settlement layouts at the polar extremes of the ethnic continuum: the sedentary Kotoko at one extreme and the Shuwa-Arab pastoral nomads at the other.

Spatial Patterning of Pastoral-Nomad Settlement

At this stage of our ethnoarchaeological research project, two Shuwa-Arab pastoral sites have been studied: Gobrem, located three kilometers to the north of Houlouf, and Danguerchem, situated some twenty kilometers to the southeast of Houlouf; both of these

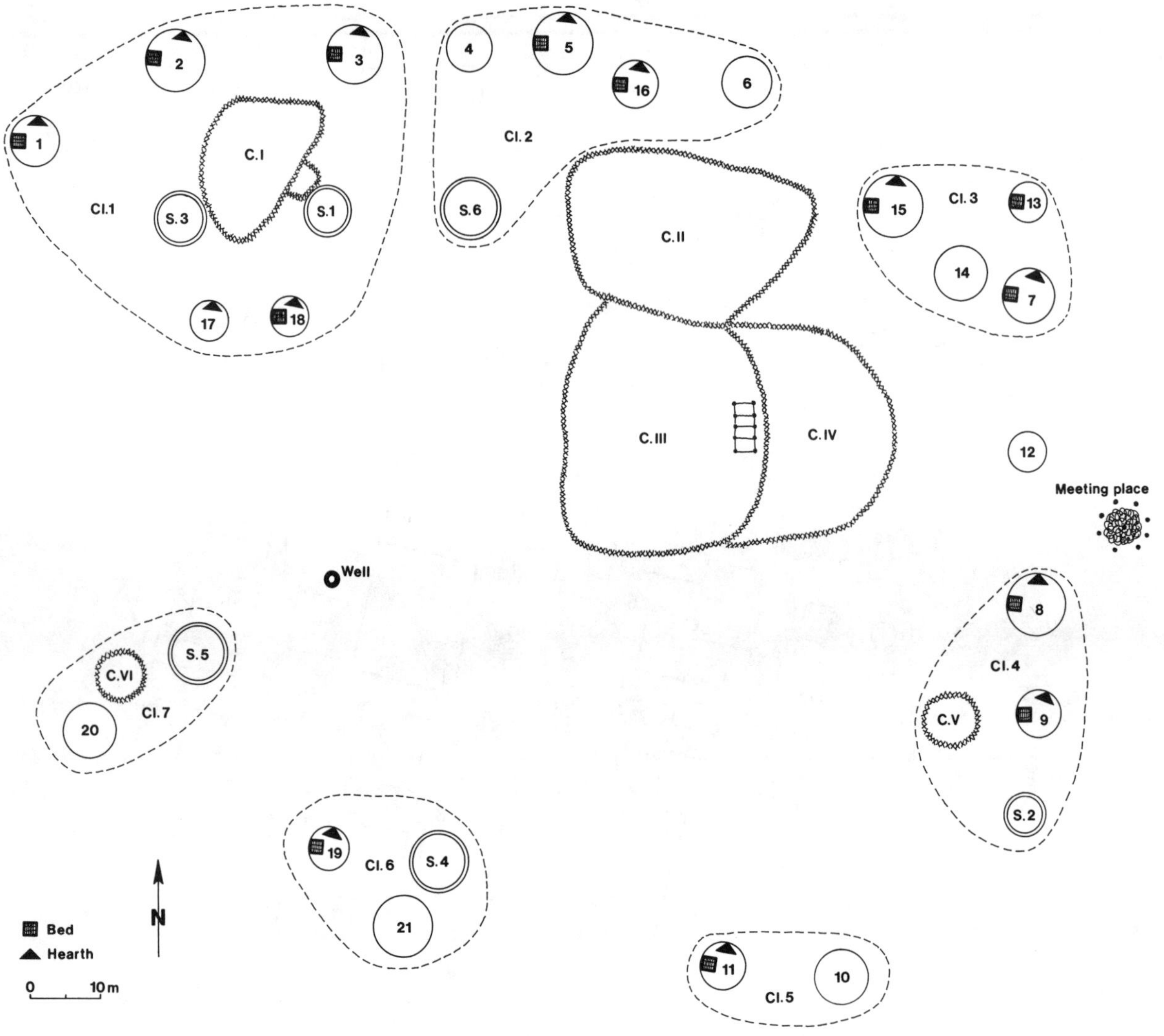

Fig. 5. Spatial organization of a pastoral village: Gobrem.

pastoral sites are located near seasonal river channels. These sites seem to have been abandoned during the severe Sahelian drought of 1973–4 as shown by a series of aerial photographs, census data, and regional maps (Elingui 1976). Thus the abandonment was probably planned and a reoccupation expected.

The site of Gobrem is subcircular in shape, covers a surface of 2.40 ha (with its entrance in the west), in which 34 built features have been mapped comprising 27 circular houses, 6 animal enclosures and one well. A large tree located in the easternmost portion of the site is surrounded by dumps of ash signaling a place of gatherings and probably tea parties (Fig. 5).

Danguerchem is also subcircular in shape, measuring 1.43 ha in surface area and opening to the south. The site layout is composed of 25 built features: 22 circular houses and 3 large livestock enclosures (Fig. 6).

In this chapter, three levels of the spatial patterning of pastoral settlements will be examined. These include: the global community, the familial, and the domestic levels. It will be argued that the organization of houses and settlements is an extremely important aspect of the built environment, embodying not only personal meanings but expressing and maintaining the ideology of prevailing social orders (Duncan 1981:1). In order to understand the meaning of the spatial dimensions which underlie social behaviors, the key role of the social structure of a society, its general institutional and ideational structure must be recognized. All these features form both the supportive and constraining framework in which the behavior of individuals takes place. More

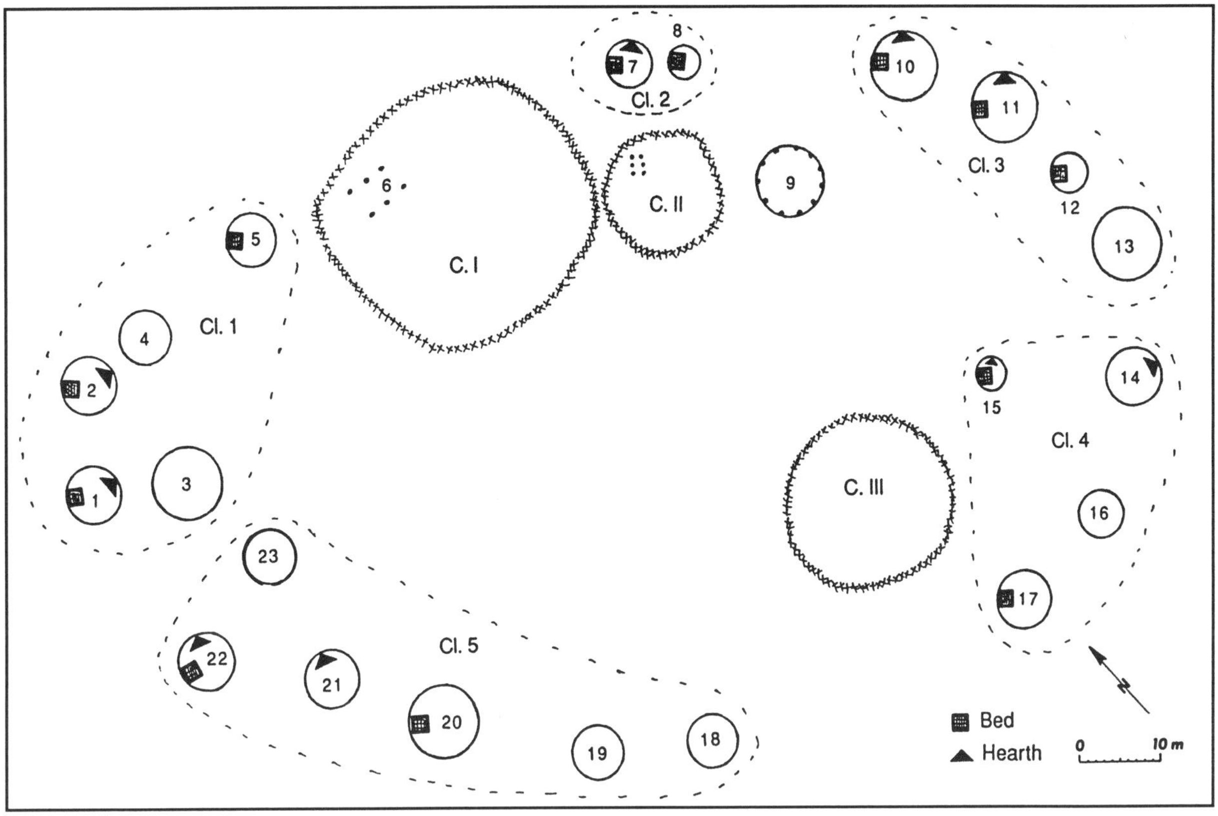

Fig. 6. Spatial organization of a pastoral village: Danguerchem.

attention must be paid to the social worlds of the different groups within and between societies with their shared and contrasting attitudes, interests, values, and experiences (Duncan 1981; Rapaport 1976, 1981; Van Gijn 1986). Regarding the spatial patterning of pastoral sites, it seems that village size and population are heavily constrained by decision-making organization. According to Johnson (1983: 176, 1982), because the links between information processing, decision making, and group organization are clearest in small, face to face task groups, theoretical propositions extending processes of small group dynamics to larger aggregates have been largely implicit. It may be useful to test the accuracy of the three empirical generalizations relevant for the study of pastoral nomad camp size proposed by Johnson with our data on Shuwa-Arab villages.

According to Johnson's model, (1) the development of hierarchical structure (group leadership) from initial non-hierarchical conditions seems to be the most common at group size six; (2) conversely, the maintenance of non-hierarchical structure in groups of size six and greater is associated with declining group decision performance, and (3) in groups of five and fewer individuals, decision performance increases with group size and non-hierarchical groups display superior performance in comparison to those that are hierarchically structured. If families are considered as basic operational organizational units, it is possible to test the empirical fit of the above model.

The Community Level

At the community level, the sites are structured in relation to livestock. Livestock enclosures are located inside the circle of habitation houses which are consequently situated at the periphery, on the frontier between the community and outside. House entrances are all oriented toward the center of the settlement. Gobrem possesses seven livestock enclosures and five barns used to keep calves and sheep/goats. The seven large enclosures were dedicated to cattle as indicated by thick deposits of cattle dung; the surface area of the enclosures vary from 26.87 m^2 for the smallest to 896 m^2 for the largest (Table 4). At this site, the place located under a large tree surrounded by many clumps of ash was probably a place of entertainment: during the day, tea may have been shared under the cool shade and in the night, the light and heat of fires were probably welcomed for

Table 4. Structural features measurements: descriptive statistics.

	Habitation Houses		Livestock Houses		Enclosures		
	Diameter (m)	Surface (m^2)	Diameter (m)	Surface (m^2)	Length (m)	Width (m)	Surface (m^2)
Gobrem							
n	22	22	5	5	7	7	7
Mean	7.02	39.90	7.36	43.91	19.76	14.64	372.36
Minimum	5.00	19.63	5.80	26.42	5.85	5.85	26.87
Maximum	9.30	67.92	8.90	62.21	35.00	28.00	896.00
Range	4.30	48.29	3.10	35.79	29.15	22.15	869.13
Standard deviation	1.22	13.11	1.32	15.33	11.84	7.82	338.62
Coefficient of variation	0.05	0.59	0.26	3.06	1.69	1.11	48.37
Danguerchem							
n	22	22	–	–	3	3	3
Mean	6.79	38.79	–	–	22.06	22.06	425.62
Minimum	3.00	7.06	–	–	14.20	14.20	158.36
Maximum	10.50	86.59	–	–	32.00	32.00	804.24
Range	7.50	79.53	–	–	17.80	17.80	645.88
Standard deviation	1.79	19.93	–	–	7.41	7.41	275.25
Coefficient of variation	0.08	0.90	–	–	2.47	2.47	91.75

many purposes of social interaction between the site's inhabitants. The relative spacing between nearest houses at Gobrem varies between 2.30 m (between A 13 and A 15) and 50 m (between A 17 and A 20) for a mean distance of 19 m (SD = 8.67 m; Fig. 5).

At Danguerchem there are three cattle enclosures ranging from 158.36 m^2 to 804.24 m^2 (Table 4). Small stock seems to have been absent from this site, as no structure related to these animals was found (Fig. 6). The remaining 22 structures are habitation houses, and the relative spacing of nearest neighbor houses varies from a minimum of 1.80 m (between B 2 and B 4) to a maximum of 43.50 m (between B 17 and B 18) with a mean distance of 10.13 m (SD = 9.72 m).

In these two sites the highest distance figures between neighboring house correspond to the village entrance at Gobrem and to the interposition of the largest enclosure at Danguerchem. If these figures are excluded from tabulations, the mean nearest house distances are 11.45 m for Gobrem (SD = 7.23 m) and 7.09 for Danguerchem (SD = 3.64 m), suggesting a more regular linear organization at this settlement.

The Household Level

Following a nearest neighbor approach (Haggett 1973), interesting spatial patterns concerning social arrangements of houses emerge. Families often inhabit groups of houses arranged into more or less coherent clusters. At Gobrem (Fig. 5) seven such clusters can be found; the house clusters identified consist of eight features (5 habitation houses, 2 small stock houses, 1 cattle enclosure) for the largest, five for the second (4 habitation houses, 1 house for calves), four for the third (3 habitation houses, 1 house of unknown function), four for the fourth (3 habitation houses, 1 small stock enclosure), two for the fifth (2 habitation houses), three for the sixth (2 houses, 1 house for small stock), and three for the seventh (1 house, 1 small stock enclosure and 1 house for small stock). The three large central cattle enclosures seem to be features of communal interest.

The same number of central cattle enclosures is attested at Danguerchem, where five house clusters have been identified (Fig. 6). The largest is composed of six houses, the second of five, the third and fourth of four houses each, and the fifth of two. It is interesting to note that the largest house of the village (B 9), which was devoid of walls, was probably a meeting house.

It appears that the most impressive house clusters of these sites are located in the northwestern corner of the settlements; however, if we consider the sample of pastoral settlements studied, this last pattern may only be due to chance; it must thus be tested on a larger sample of sites (Holl et al. n.d.). In the meantime, this spatial patterning fits marvelously with information available on Shuwa-Arab social organization:

> The basic unit of social organization among the Shuwa seems to be the household.... Thus, among the Shuwa when we say the household...we actually mean an extended household, comprising the head of the household and grown-up sons. To this we must add the head's brothers who also have grown-up sons, and so on until in fact, you find a fairly large agnatically linked community working and co-operating together in such essential matters as herding, the seasonal movements and above all, defence and military matters. (Tijani 1986:70-1)

In summary, these two settlements were probably inhabited by seven (Gobrem) and five (Danguerchem) extended families or households: Gobrem was more affluent in livestock and the presence of a well suggests a longer annual occupation if not incentive to sedentary occupation.

Structure of Habitation House

The best clue for the identification of domestic units in the material remains of a site is the presence of cooking hearths, beds, and their associated material artifacts. In the material record of the two sites reported on here, the structural features mentioned above are not attested in each house; however, it appears that clusters of houses are the most significant social unit with respect to the distribution of cooking, storage, and sleeping facilities. In this regard, the distribution of hearths, beds, pottery, and enamel wares is quite balanced among clusters of houses and very variable among individual houses. At Gobrem, all house clusters (with the exception of cluster 7) possess at least one hearth and one bed. The frequency varies from five hearths and four beds in cluster 1, three hearths and beds in cluster 3, two hearths and beds in cluster 4, two hearths and one bed in clusters 2 and 5, to one hearth and one bed in cluster 6.

At Danguerchem, the distribution of the same structural features varies from two hearths and three beds in clusters 1 and 3, two hearths and one bed in cluster 5, two hearths and beds in cluster 4, to one hearth and two beds in cluster 2.

The distribution of these features suggests functional differentiation among houses in terms of domestic activities performed in each house cluster identified in each site, and suggests the presence of main habitation houses whose number varies from one house cluster to another (Figs. 5 and 6). The number of habitation houses is certainly dependent on the number of adult males present in each actual household. The internal spatial patterning of households, which is almost the same in the whole sample studied, is characterized by the presence of sleeping, cooking, storage, and heating facilities (Fig. 7).

The bed, which is used by all the members of the family (father, mother, and young children), is always located at the center of the house (Fig. 7.1), perpendicular to the entrance, and covers approximately half of the house surface. The cooking hearth is usually built of clay with multiple niches and is always located of the right of the entrance near the familial bed (Fig. 7.2). The main storage area in the house is situated along the house wall, on both sides of the cooking hearth and to the right side of the door. It is attested by concentrations of various kinds of containers including pottery as well as enamel wares used for storing, cooking, serving food, and other domestic activities (Fig. 7.3). Finally, a small hearth located near the bed is used for heating the house during the relatively cold nights of the rainy season and keeping mosquitoes away ; it is a featureless structure attested in the material record only by a thin concentration of ash and charcoal (Fig. 7.4).

Material Remains Recovered: the Case of Pottery

The patterning of pastoral villages into structural spatial units at the levels of the community, the household, and the habitation house is also supported by the distribution of other categories of material remains collected, primarily containers made of pottery as well as enamel.

Artifacts abandoned at Gobrem and Danguerchem certainly result from the conditions of abandonment of these two sites. Abandonment seems to have been planned and reoccupation was probably expected but was not realized. In this regard, complete large ceramic vessels were abandoned with an expected reuse in the near future. Conversely, all abandoned enamel vessels were worn out and many of them heavily oxidized; these were probably dis-

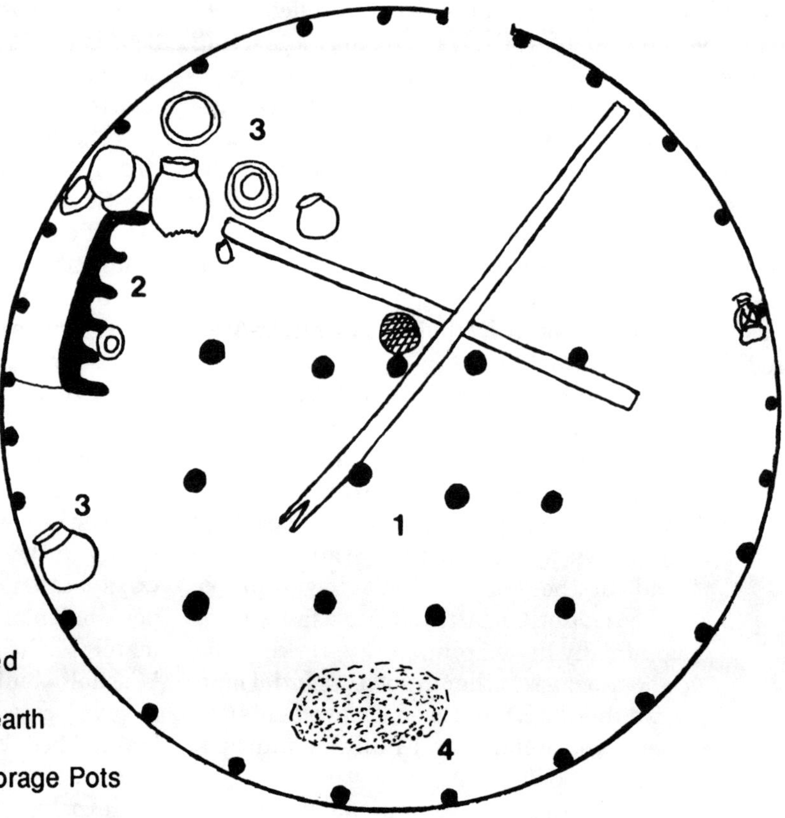

Fig. 7. Spatial structure of a pastoralist habitation house.

1 - Bed
2 - Hearth
3 - Storage Pots
4 - Heating Hearth

carded in the temporally abandoned houses. The total number of vessels, including both pottery and enamel wares, amounts to 39 at Gobrem and 22 at Danguechem. In the first site, 20 ceramic and 19 enamel wares were recorded. In the second, the proportion amounts to 8 ceramic and 14 enamel wares. Thus, the ratio of ceramic to enamel ware varies from 0.57 at Danguerchem to 1.05 at Gobrem, suggesting an interesting variation which is not yet fully understood. The distribution of these categories of material shows that the most significant analytical unit is once again the cluster of houses. At Gobrem, cluster 4 is devoid of any container. Among the others, frequencies vary from five pottery and two enamel wares in cluster 1, four and four in cluster 2, nine (among which three pots filled with fire hardened clay used as "hearth stones") and three in cluster 3, two and one in cluster 1, and one and eight enamel wares in clusters 5 and 7. At Danguerchem, there are three ceramic and two enamel wares in cluster 1, two and one in cluster 2, one and seven in cluster 5, two and one in B 9, the "meeting house," and finally one and two enamel wares in clusters 3 and 4.

The most frequent categories of vessels in terms of shape and function are necked pots and jars for cooking and the storage of liquids such as water and dairy products. Four handled cooking pots have been recorded from both sites, three at Gobrem and one at Danguerchem; in the last settlement, a small footed bowl was uncovered in the "meeting house." The remaining pottery vessels constitute medium to large sized pots and jars. Concerning our research problem, one of the most interesting features to emerge from this class of material evidence is pottery decoration, its design and patterning on the vessels. Fortunately enough, seven out of eight vessels from Danguercherm and the whole sample from Gobrem are decorated (Fig. 8).

In terms of motifs, roulette stamping and grooved lines are combined in a relatively small number of designs. Grooved lines are always situated on the upper tier of the vessel. A striking difference appears between Danguerchem and Gobrem assemblages.

At Danguerchem, with the exception of a footed bowl on which the whole body is decorated with roulette stamped SW-NE lines (the foot and the rim being undecorated), vessels are decorated with bands of stamped roulette and grooved lines always situated at the neck and/or some centimeters under it. Four patterns have been discerned. The first constitutes of a band of five to ten centimeters in width delimited at both top and bottom by a grooved line filled with

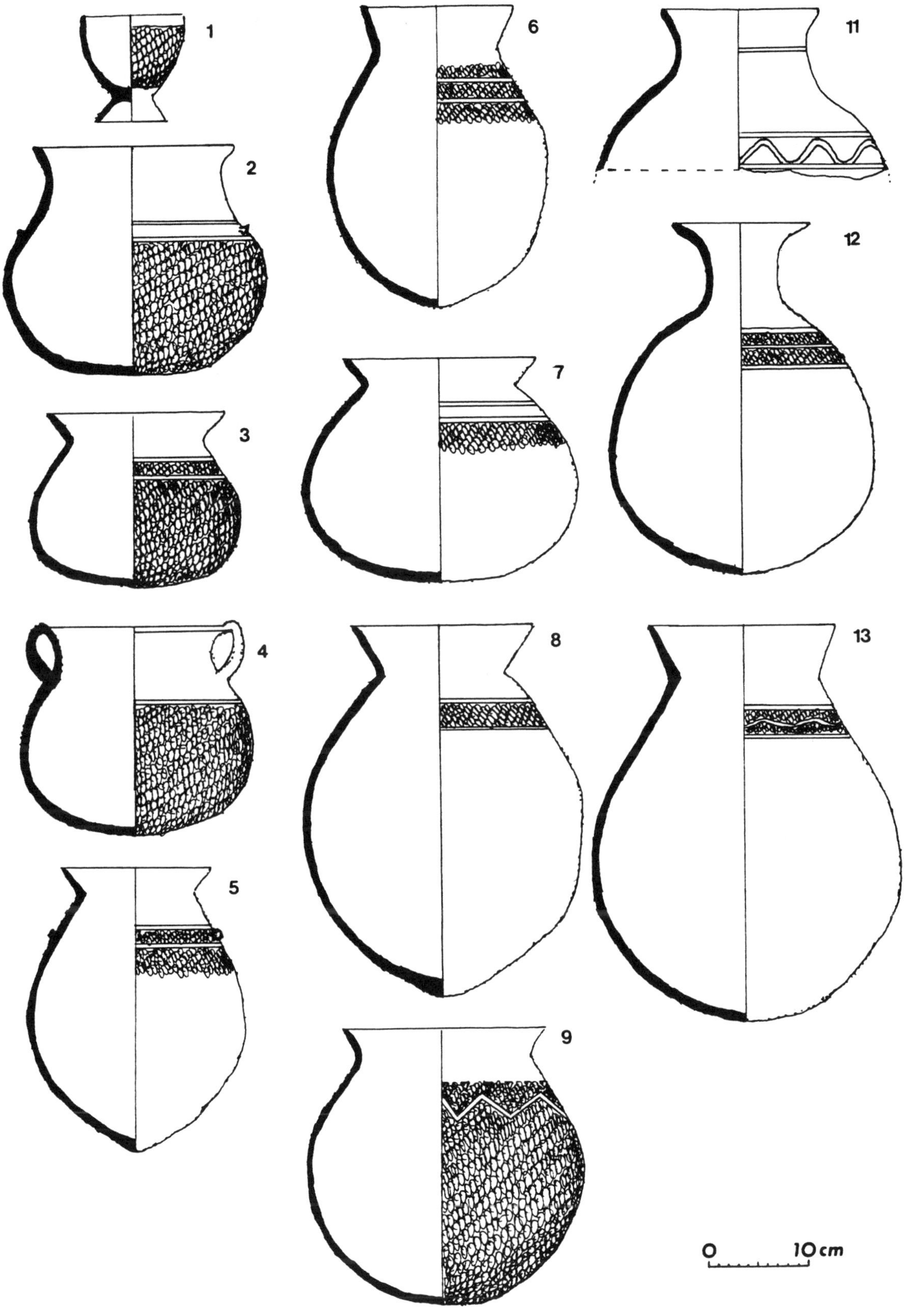

Fig. 8. Patterns of decoration of pots.

stamped roulette and a wavy grooved line (two occurrences). The second (two occurrences) is composed of a band of stamped roulette motifs divided into three micro-bands by two parallel grooved lines. The third pattern (one occurrence) consists of a band of roulette motifs limited at its upper part by a grooved line and divided into two equal micro-bands by another grooved line. Finally, the last pattern (one case) is composed of two parallel grooved lines above a band of roulette motifs.

At Gobrem, the number of combinations is larger, but the basic structure already seen at Danguerchem is the same, i.e., the association between roulette stamped motifs and grooved lines. The major decorative element in the Gobrem assemblage, however, is the existence of roulette stamped motifs covering the entire body of vessels delimited by one (one case) or two grooved lines (eleven cases). In this relatively large class, there are two design patterns: one in which two parallel grooved lines set the upper limit of roulette motif (four cases), and the other characterized by a band of roulette motif created by two parallel grooved lines, one of them setting the upper limit of the decorated surface (seven cases). There is one occurrence of a pot with its whole body surface covered with roulette motif and its upper limit formed by triangular holes and a zigzag patterned grooved line. Another set of design patterns is composed of bands situated near the neck of the vessel; five combinations are attested. The first (two cases) is composed of a band of two parallel grooved lines filled with roulette motif. The second (one case) is a variant of the same pattern with a third grooved line situated inside the band of roulette stamped motif. In the third case (one occurrence), the design is composed of a band of roulette motif divided into two micro-bands by two grooved lines, one of them setting the lower limit. The fourth pattern (one case) is almost the same as the previous one but with one of the grooved lines setting the upper limit. The fifth pattern (one occurrence) is composed of three motifs: a large band of roulette motif delimited by two parallel grooved lines with two parallel zigzag patterned lines inside the band. There are two additional types of design patterns: one is composed of a horizontal line situated at the neck of the vessel plus a band of parallel grooved lines filled with a wavy grooved line located few centimeters above the shoulder; and the other a cordon decorated with short vertical and parallel grooved lines. In total, there are eleven design patterns at Gobrem.

In summary, pottery decoration in both settlements shares the same basic structure, characterized by a combination of roulette stamped motifs and one to three grooved lines which are always situated on the upper part of vessels. How, then, can we explain the variability in design patterning between them? One possibility is that the degree of this variability may be correlated with the intensity of interaction of each settlement with the outside in terms of vessel procurement strategies. In this regard, Gobrem is located between the hinterland and the highest order regional centers of Kousseri and Ndjamena, the capital city of the Chad Republic located on the eastern shore of the Chari river. Consequently, transfer of goods and people is certainly more intensive at Gobrem than at Danguerchem, which is located in the hinterland near the depressions characteristic by the presence of more or less permanent ponds, an area in which mostly pastoral settlements are located. However, this does not mean that people of Danguerchem were living in splendid isolation, it only means that they could have lived with a lower intensity of interaction with the other communities of the study area. One is tempted to say that there seems to be a pastoral way of decorating pottery, which may be one of the possible way to maintain their cultural identity and also to have their craft production identified at market places or in other kinds of exchange. This feature may thus have served a dual purpose, amplifying Shuwa-Arab signs of identity and enhancing interaction with the outside world, which insures that a pastoral nomad remains a pastoral nomad (Khazanov 1984). This explanation is appealing but wrong: the Shuwa-Arabs of the study area do not manufacture pottery; they purchase their pots from the Kotoko potters of Houlouf and at the main market place of Kousseri. Consequently, the similarities observed on pottery shapes and decoration patterns result from an identity of provenience. The greater diversity of the Gobrem sample may thus result from a wider procurement network. As Khazanov (1984:3) points out,

> ...nomads could never exist on their own without the outside world and its non-nomadic societies, with their different economic systems. Indeed, a nomadic society could only function while the outside world not only existed but also allowed for those reactions from it—reactions which were economic, social, political, cultural in a word, a multifaceted response—which ensured that the nomads remained nomads.

Spatial Patterning, Pastoral Ideology and Decision-Making Organization

Following Oswald (1984:297), there is no doubt that site structure is patterned in the archaeological record. Repeated associations of structures and facilities are often found. Refuse is often clustered in dumps or discrete areas rather than being scattered evenly and randomly over an entire site. Thus, spatial patterning of settlements results from the interaction of several categories of factors, among which two major classes will be considered in this study: these include socio-technological factors (activity frequency, periodicity and duration, bulk of associated material and structural features, facility requirements, number of participants, etc.) and socio-ideological factors which depend on the relative hierarchy of performed activities in the maintenance and reproduction of any social system. In this regard, socially bounded space is no more a neutral physical background but is responsive to various categories of social values organized into a more or less coherent symbolic system. The present study is thus a contribution to a larger research field of archaeological interest. According to Oswald (1984:306),

> It remains to be seen whether or not most socio-technological organizations influence site structure and, if so, why and how the influence is. if these patterns do occur under many conditions, what are the implications for archaeological inference? Is it possible to understand the processes relating to components of site structure and successfully use that understanding to interpret the archaeological record?

As already discussed above, the patterning of community space at Gobrem and Danguerchem suggests that sites were structured according to the spatial requirements of livestock (mainly cattle); structural features devoted to them are always located at the center of sites and house entrances were focused on them. Habitation houses were located at the periphery, thus constituting a "closed" social space. The proportion of the site surface devoted to habitation houses at both sites varies from 878.0 m^2 (7.31%) at Gobrem to 853.41 m^2 (11.75%) at Danguerchem (Table 5). That devoted to livestock varies from 2,826.13 m^2 (23.55%) at Gobrem to 1,276.25 m^2 (17.98%) at Danguerchem. Consequently, the area devoted to any kind of structural features varies from 3,704.13 m^2 (30.87%) at Gobrem to 2,130.16 m^2 (30.0%) at Danguerchem. The ratio of site surface to built area at both sites varies from 3.24 at Gobrem to 3.33 at Danguerchem, suggesting a kind of constant in the spatial patterning of a pastoral settlement. This interesting finding must however be tested on a larger sample of pastoral camps to evaluate its accuracy and research potential.

In terms of raw material used and architectural design, pastoral settlements are characterized by circular house shapes built with wood and grass. However, three houses were built with mud brick walls (two at Danguerchem and one at Gobrem). Very large quantities of wood were used for walls and roofs; for instance in house A2 at Gobrem, measuring 9.30 m in diameter, the quantity of wood used to built the superstructure of the house amounts to ca. 34.55 cubic meters composed of twenty one wall posts 0.10 m in diameter and 2.00 m long, four large central poles and four main roof poles all measuring ca. 0.25 m in diameter and 4.00 m in length.

The architectural design, raw material used, settlement spatial patterning, and associated material record strongly emphasized pastoral cultural identity. The site layout reflects a self-sufficient and autonomous social entity in strict conformity with the pastoral-nomadic political system, which is devoid of any super-ordinate sociopolitical decision level, and in which each settlement is a self-contained social and political unit.

Regarding the decision-making organization, the performance of various activities related to such es-

Table 5. Dominant activities and space allocation: intersite comparison.

Site	Site Surface	Habitation Area		Livestock Area		Built Area		Ratio†
	(Ha)	(m^2)	%	(m^2)	%	(m^2)	%	
Gobrem	1.20	878.00	7.31	2826.13	23.55	3704.13	30.87	3.24
Danguerchem	0.71	853.41	11.75	1276.75	17.98	2130.16	30.00	3.33

†Site Surface / Total Built Area

sential pastoral matters as herding, seasonal movement of settlements, and defence are dependent on the pool of information available to the pastoralists. Information pooling and processing may take place in the daily interaction between individuals and specifically in the evening, when adult males from different households meet each other for tea at a communal house (9 at Danguerchem, Fig. 6) or under a tree (at Gobrem, Fig. 5). If households are considered to be the basic operational organizational units, their relative number in each of the sites studied is relevant to assess the performance of decision-making organization in the case at hand. Gobrem was inhabited by seven households and Danguerchem by five. According to Johnson (1983:177), increases in the number of "information sources" within an integrated system increases the probability of either systemic collapse (fission) or of increase in organizational complexity. The maintenance of non-hierarchical structure being associated with declining group decision performance in groups of size six and greater on the one hand, and increasing decision performance in groups of size five and fewer individuals on the other.

The site patterning of Gobrem appears to show declining group decision performance which seems to have shifted from the community to the level of individual household. With seven organizational units, the village patterning shows trends toward nucleation; five of the seven households have built their own livestock facilities, signalling the collapse of the former collective herding system, even if large central enclosures were still visible in the village layout. Although fine-grained chronology of the events is lacking, it seems that these central enclosures were no longer in use at the time of the abandonment of the site, when the systemic collapse (fission) occurred. Interviews with some Shuwa-Arabs of the study area reveal that some of the former inhabitants of the place have founded a new settlement called Alaya II, located four kilometers to the west, and one of my workmen inhabiting this last village was born at the abandoned settlement studied, twenty years ago. With the abandonment of Gobrem, some of the inhabitants joined other pastoral villages, such as the present *Bilama* of Mischiskwa, a settlement located about twenty kilometers to the south of the study area, and another one joined the village of Magourdé, some three kilometers to the east. Faced with scalar stress (Johnson 1982), the Gobrem system collapsed instead of increasing its organizational complexity.

At Danguerchem, none of the five households built a separate livestock facility; the herd of the whole community was kept in the three central enclosures. With five operational organizational units, the Danguerchem system seems to have increased the performance of its decision-making organization. The overall circular arrangement of the houses and the location of central enclosures on the median line of the village attest to the predominance of community co-operation in herding over individual household decisions. This hypothesis is independently strengthened by the location of the communal house near two of the three central enclosures.

In pastoral groups, the socioeconomic system focuses mainly on livestock, and system diversity is therefore minimum. Accordingly, in the context of modern Cameroon, the spatial patterning of their sites is dependent on the decision-making organization concerning matters of herding and the relations with the neighboring societies. Because of their total exclusion from the pan-regional political systems, pastoralist site patterning is inward-oriented in an attitude of self-exclusion; the outside is clearly kept aside. In this regard, one may easily understand the Shuwa-Arabs' attitude toward the sedentary Kotoko which may be characterized as unbalanced reciprocity (Sahlins 1968), a structural incentive to mercantilistic exchange relations. The Shuwa pride and untrustworthiness expressed in popular sayings (Tijani 1986) is thus a metaphorical expression of the symbolic and ideological features resulting from their long-term interactions with their different neighbors, which is attested in their settlement patterning and material record.

Conclusion

More intensive research must be carried out before any satisfactory set of inferences can be constructed concerning the whole range of behavioral information contained in the material record of pastoral nomadic villages of the Houlouf region. Nevertheless, the research already conducted on two abandoned pastoral settlements suggests interesting patterns of variability among structural features within each individual site and between both sites, as well as some degree of intra- and intersite structural consistency. Some of these aspects have been extensively discussed in the paper; many others are yet very poorly understood, for instance the finer-grained aspects of the regional division of labor. In this regard, it is worth noting that presently the largest part of craft activities, such as mat weaving and blacksmithing, in the region of Houlouf are performed by Shuwa-Arab pastoralists and agriculturalists/pastoralists. In general, it appears that Shuwa-Arab ethnicity is always in the making and that they and the Kotoko are ethnic and cultural polar extremes on a continuum of sociopolitical organizations, socioeconomic activities, subsistence-settlement strategies, decision-making organizations, and symbolic and ideological systems. In this perspective, each site considered in this chapter may be defined as a particular piece of social space, a place socially and ideologically demarcated and separated from other places. As such, it becomes a symbol within the total and complex system of communication in the total social universe (Kuper1972).

It is not relevant to ask whether the few variables isolated in this study are valid or not. For any research problem at hand, one can isolate any number of variables from concrete behavior for "it is an axiomatic assumption that all the variables involved in that behavior are, to a lesser or greater extent directly or indirectly interdependent. The question is only whether the variables isolated are significantly interconnected and whether the study of this interconnection is likely to develop systematic hypotheses and to lead to further analysis" (Cohen 1969:222). The Shuwa-Arab socioeconomic system has a lower degree of diversity than the Kotoko one. The former, almost exclusively focused on livestock herding, is nomadic and non-hierarchical, with, on average, lower densities of population. The latter, more diversified, is characterized by social ranking, craft specialization, and sedentarization, with higher densities of population. In the regional sociopolitical context, Shuwa-Arab pastoral nomads are dominated by the sedentary Kotoko. According to Knutsson (1969:99), it is clear that any concept of ethnic group defined on the basis of "cultural content" is not sufficient as a research tool for the analysis of ethnicity in its various interactional contexts. Consequently, it is only when ethnic distinction, stratification, or differentiation are part of the individual's or group's strategies for preserving or increasing control of resources, social status, or other values that a meaningful interpretation becomes feasible. The relevant research perspective is then to concentrate on socioeconomic systems and treat ethnic ascription as one asset among several to get access to needed or attractive resources, be they subsistence niches in a multi-ethnic context, land rights in a predominantly monoethnic area, or some other thing of economic significance (Abruzzi 1982; Hjort 1981). In this regard, Barth (1956:1088) has outlined several propositions relevant for the discussion of environmental factors that may lead to the co-residence of different ethnic groups in the same area:

(1) The distribution of ethnic groups is controlled not by objective and fixed "natural areas" but by the distribution of specific ecologic niches which the group with its particular economy and political organization is able to exploit.

(2) Different ethnic groups will establish themselves in stable co-residence in an area if they exploit different ecologic niches, and especially if they can thus establish symbiotic economic relations.

(3) If different ethnic groups are able to exploit the same niches fully, the militarily more powerful will normally replace the weaker.

(4) If different ethnic groups exploit the same ecologic niches but the weaker of them is better able to utilize marginal environments, the groups may co-reside in one area.

The first and the fourth of this set of propositions seems to be fully applicable to the situation observed in the Houlouf region.

The problem concerning the emergence of specialized pastoralism in the Chadian plain is still poorly understood, and, to date, no serious attempt has been made to clarify its components and transformations. Theoretically, it is possible to consider that the emergence of pastoral nomadism in this part of Africa partly resulted from the failure of past mixed economies to face the increasing complexity generated by conflicting organizational necessities of agriculture, livestock husbandry, craft specialization, and higher concentration of population in the same socioeconomic system. This "system collapse" opened new opportunities to different evolutionary pathways, some of them like pastoral nomadism became more and more specialized in the process of systemic interaction at the regional level. The arrival of the Shuwa-Arab pastoralists in the Kanem kingdom in the 14th century A.D., recorded in the Arabic historical sources, amplified a process already in motion. The major archaeological difficulty is to uncover and identify a pastoral assemblage in the archaeological context, and, as shown here, the artifacts recovered from pastoral villages are not necessarily pastoral-specific. The areal samples of our excavations are too small to allow the exposure of a whole pastoral site's layout; in this regard, the best clue for the identification of a past pastoral settlement is the accumulation of animal dung, which may signal livestock features, along with the other categories of material culture remains. Future research and the collection of a larger sample of pastoral nomad camps should help to clarify the problem of ethnic formation, maintenance, decay, and interaction in the Chadian basin.

References

Abruzzi, W. S.
1982 Ecological theory and ethnic differentiation among human populations. *Current Anthropology* 23:13-35.

Adamu, M. & A. H. M. Kirk-Greene (eds).
1986 *Pastoralists of the West African Savanna.* Manchester: Manchester University Press.

Bateson, G.
1984 *La nature et la pensée.* Paris: Seuil.

Barth, F.
1956 Ecologic relationships of ethnic groups in Swat, North Pakistan.*American Anthropologist* 58:1079-89.

Barth, F. (Ed.)
1969 *Ethnic groups and Boundaries: The Social Organization of Culture Difference.* Oslo: Universitetsforlaget, Bergen.

Boyd, R. & P. J. Richerson
1985 *Culture and the evolutionary process.* Chicago: The University of Chicago Press.

Briant, P.
1982 *État et pasteurs au Moyen-Orient ancien.* London, Paris: Cambridge University Press/Éditions de la Maison des sciences de l'homme.

Bureau Central du Recensement,
1985 *Recensement général de la population et de l'habitat d'avril 1976*, Vol. III. Yaoundé: Ministère du Plan et de l'Aménagement du territoire.

Cohen, A.
1969 Political anthropology: the analysis of the symbolism of the power relations. *Man* (2):215-235.
1974a, Introduction: the lesson of ethnicity, In *Urban Ethnicity*, Abner Cohen (ed.), IX-XXIV. London: Tavistock.
1974b *Two-Dimensional Man.* London: Routledge and Kegan Paul.

Connah, G.
1969 Archaeological work in Bornu 1964-1966 with particular reference to the excavations at Daima mound. In *Actes du Premier Colloque International d'Archéologie Africaine*, J.-P. Lebeuf (ed.), 112-124. Fort-Lamy.
1981 *Three thousand years in Africa.* London, New York: Cambridge University Press,
1985 Agricultural intensification and sedentism in the Firki of NE Nigeria. In *Prehistoric Intensive Agriculture in the Tropics.* Vol. II, I. S. Farrington (ed.), 765-86. Oxford: B.A.R.

Charles, H.
1939 *Tribus moutonnières du Moyen-Euphrate.* Documents d'études Orientales, 8. Damas: Institut français de Damas.

Conte, E. & F. Hagenburger-Sacripanti
1977 Habitation et vie quotidienne chez les Arabes de la rive sud du lac Tchad. *Cahiers ORSTOM Série Sciences Humaines* XIV (3):289-323.

David, N.
1980 History of crops and peoples in North Cameroon to A.D. 1900, In *West African culture dynamics*, B. K. Swartz and R. A. Dumett (eds.), 139-182. The Hague, Paris: Mouton.

Dragadze, T.
1980 The place of "Ethnos" theory in soviet anthropology. In *Soviet and Western Anthropology*, E. Gellner (ed.), 161-170. London: Duckworth.

Duncan, J.
1981 Introduction. In *Housing and Identity: cross-cultural perspectives*, J. S. Duncan (ed.), 1-5. London: Croom Helm.

Elingui, H.
1978 *Dictionnaire des villages du Logone et Chari.* Yaoundé: Office National de la Recherche Scientifique et Technique.

Griaule, M. & J.-P. Lebeuf
1948 Fouilles dans la région du lac Tchad. *Journal de la Société des Africanistes,* 18 (1):1-116.
1950 Fouilles dans la région du lac Tchad. *Journal de la Société des Africanistes* 20(1):1-152.
1951 Fouilles dans la région du lac Tchad. *Journal de la Société des Africanistes* 21 (1):1-95.

Hagenburger-Sacripanti, F.
1977a Les Arabes dits "*Suwa* " du Nord-Cameroun. *Cahiers ORSTOM Série Sciences Humaines* XIV (3):223-249.
1977b Eléments de magie et de sorcellerie chez les Arabes d'Afrique Centrale. *Cahiers ORSTOM Série Sciences Humaines* XIV (3):251-288.

Hjort, A.
1981 Ethnic transformation, dependency and change: the Iligira Samburu of northern Kenya. In *Change and Development in Nomadic and Pastoral societies*, J. G.

Galaty and P. C. Salzman (eds.), 50-67. Leiden: E. J. Brill.

Holl, A,

1986a Systématique archéologique et processus culturels: essai d'archéologie régionale dans le secteur de Houlouf (Nord-Cameroun). Paper presented at the Colloque international d'archéologie camerounaise, Yaoundé, 5-9 January.

1986b Processes of cultural transformations in Sudano-Sahelian belt of West Africa: A case study from the Perichadian plain. Paper presented at the World Archaeological Congress, 1-7 September, Southampton.

1987 Mound formation processes and societal transformations: A case study from the Chadian plain, *Journal of Anthropological Archaeology* 6:122-158.

1988 Transition du Néolithique à l'âge du fer dans la plaine péritchadienne: le cas de Mdaga. In *Le Milieu et les Hommes: Recherches Comparatives et Historiques dans le Bassin du lac Tchad,* D. Barreteau et H. Tourneux (eds), 81-109. Paris: Editions de l'ORSTOM.

1989 Individus et statuts: variabilité mortuaire dans la plaine tchadienne préhistorique. In *Singularités: Les Voies d'émergence individuelle,* 351-367. Paris: Plon.

Holl, A., T. E. Levy, Cl. Lechevalier & A. Bridault

n.d. Of Mound, Cattle and Men: Archaeology and ethnoarchaeology of the Houlouf Region (Northern Cameroon). *West African Journal of Archaeology* 21.

Johnson, G. A.

1982 Organizational structure and scalar stress. In *Theory and Explanation in Archaeology*, C. Renfrew, M. J. Rowlands and B. Abbott Segraves,(eds.), 389-421. London, New York: Academic Press.

1983 Decision-making organization and pastoral-nomad camp size. *Human Ecology*, 11(2):175-199.

Khazanov, M.

1984 *Nomads and the outside world*. London, New York: Academic Press.

Knutsson, K. E.

1969 Dichotomization and integration: Aspects of interethnic relations in southern Ethiopia. In *Ethnic groups and Boundaries: the Social Organization of Culture Difference*, F. Barth (ed.), 86-100. Oslo: Universitetsforlaget, Bergen.

Kuper, H.

1972 The Language of Sites in the Politics of Space. *American Anthropologist* 74:411-425.

Lebeuf, A. M. D.

1969 *Les principautés kotoko: essai sur le caractère sacré de l'autorité.* Paris: Editions du CNRS.

Lebeuf J.-P.

1969 *Carte archéologique des abords du lac Tchad.* Paris: Editions du CNRS.

1981 *Carte archéologique des abords du lac Tchad, supplément*. Paris: Editions du CNRS.

Lebeuf, J.-P., A. M. D. Lebeuf, Fr. Treinen & J. Courtin

1980 *Le Gisement sao de Mdaga (Tchad): Fouilles 1960-1968.* Paris:.Société d'Ethnographie.

Luke, J. T.

1965 *Pastoralism and Politics in the Mari period: A Re-examination of the Character and Political Significance of the Major West Semitic Groups in he Middle Euphrates.* Ann Arbor: University Microfilms.

Oswald, D.

1984 The use of site structure to infer social and technological organization from the archaeological record. In *Frontiers: Southern African Archaeology Today*, M. Hall, G. Avery, D. M. Avery, M. L. Wilson & A. J. B. Humphreys (eds.), 297-309. Oxford: B.A.R.

Rapaport, A.

1976 Sociocultural aspects of Man-Environment studies. In *The Mutual Interaction of people and their built Environment*, A. Rapaport (ed.), 7-35. The Hague, Paris: Mouton.

5. Production, Space, and Social Change in Protohistoric Palestine

Thomas E. Levy

Although village peoples were not the first to practice warfare, they did expand the scale and ferocity of military engagements. Village houses, food-processing equipment, crops in the field, domestic animals, secondary-growth forests, and prime garden lands represent capital investment closely identified with the arduous labor inputs by specific groups of individuals. The defense of this investment laid the basis for the development of stable, exclusive territorial identities. (Marvin Harris 1989:302)

Introduction

Space takes on a new meaning for societies when population increases and more sophisticated methods of production develop. As seen from a neo-evolutionary perspective, the archaeological record of Israel provides an ideal case study for investigating some aspects of this developmental process. By the late 5th–early 4th millennium B.C. the country witnessed its first population explosion. This was accompanied by new means of production associated with agriculture, animal husbandry, and craft production. Compared with the preceding Pottery Neolithic period, more complex forms of social organization also developed. In the northern Negev desert, there is evidence for the emergence of contemporary sub-regional archaeological cultures, which flourished along the major seasonal drainages (wadis) in this area. Although separated by distances of less than 16 kilometers, these tightly knit, wadi-based settlement systems display distinct assemblages of iconographic, domestic, and prestige-related artifacts which may reflect different ethnic affiliations. These wadis include the Nahal (Hebrew for wadi) Beersheva, Patish, Besor, and Gerar (Fig. 1). This chapter explores the relationship between these different archaeological entities by focusing on the problem of differential access to craft production and natural resources in the northern Negev region.

The role of metallurgy in the emergence of Early Bronze Age urban centers in southern Palestine, in particular Tel Arad, has recently been explored by a number of scholars. However, efforts to investigate the social role of metal working in the preceding Chalcolithic period have only recently gained interest among researchers. To date, interpretations of Chalcolithic metal working vary from dismissing it as of little importance to social organization, to viewing it as a key factor in the social integration of some late 5th–early 4th millennium Levantine societies. To reconstruct the role of metallurgy in Chalcolithic societies, a model is presented in which risk management, competition over natural resource space, and the notion of debt are explored in the Beersheva valley, where extensive evidence for early metal production has been found. The production of metal objects, especially items which have been interpreted as having had a prestige/cultic function, are viewed as central to the building and maintenance of bonds between members of the Beersheva valley culture. The discussion focuses on the southern portion of Israel-Transjordan due to the large number of surveys, excavations, and analytical studies of archaeological materials available from the late 5th–4th millennium B.C. for this area.

What is Production?

Production is a social process in which human labor is utilized to manufacture and produce both subsistence goods, commodities and items of social value. A number of schools of thought have developed which focus their analysis of social change on how the control of means of production (land, capital, and technology) and social relations of production are combined to organize the flow of goods to support existing social arrangements (Tosi 1984; Harris 1979; Steward 1955; Rappaport 1971; Sahlins 1974). This materialist approach, which sees the control of economic resources as central to maintaining a society is utilized here (cf. Johnson and Earle 1987:9). In recent studies of the rise of urbanism in Canaan, Amiran (1986), Kempinski (1989), and Ilan and Sabanne (1989) have followed this approach in suggesting that control of copper production during the

Early Bronze II period was a key factor in the rise of stratified societies in southern Canaan. These studies provide clear insights into one of the processes which seem to have stimulated the growth of walled towns during this period. However, in most studies dealing with the rise of complex societies in this region, the role of metallurgy in the preceding Chalcolithic period is left unexamined or interpreted as of little significance. For example, in Gilead's (1988:422-423) recent summary of the Chalcolithic period, the role of copper in "determining the character of the Levantine Chalcolithic society..." is minimized, and, with quotes by Heskel and Lamberg-Karlovsky (1980), Rosen (1987), and Heskel (1983), it is suggested that:

> There is no architectural or other evidence to support a claim that there was any social differentiation or that there existed a social elite that centralized the copper production and monopolized its use. As in Iran, there is no observable social change that can be linked to copper production. The part-time specialization not only is reflected in the copper industry, but also is an attribute of the lithic and pottery industries.

I have argued the opposite and suggest that Chalcolithic settlement in the Beersheva valley represents a chiefdom-style ranked society which emerged as a result of population growth and concomitant new developments in agro-technology, craft specialization, and social organization (Levy 1986, Levy and Holl 1988). In a recent study of early metallurgy in the southern Levant (Levy and Shalev 1989), we touched on the role of copper metallurgy in the emergence of new and more hierarchically organized societies in the Beersheva valley. New data from the recent excavations at Shiqmim provide important information for elaborating on this theme. The shifting socioeconomic role of copper production from the Chalcolithic to Early Bronze Age can be used as an indicator of the greater organizational changes which occurred among the protohistoric cultures of southern Palestine. In this paper, three interrelated themes are explored in order to place Chalcolithic metal working in social perspective: risk management, competition over natural resource space, and the notion of gift giving versus commercially based exchange systems.

Subsistence and Political Economies

If we are to understand the growth of social complexity in the Beersheva valley and southern Canaan, the role of production and debt provide useful concepts for monitoring change. These social processes occur within two interrelated aspects of the primitive economy, one of which is focused on the subsistence economy and the other based on the political economy. The subsistence economy, called the "Domestic Mode of Production" by Sahlins (1974), is organized at the household level to meet individual family needs, including food, clothing, housing, and subsistence technology. According to Johnson and Earle (1987:12), the primary goal of the subsistence economy is to fulfill population needs at the lowest possible cost that affords security. Political economy refers to the structures and rules in an economy that evolve out of the need for societies to adapt to local ecological and cultural environments. At the heart of the political economy is what Hardin (1968) calls "the tragedy of the commons." The archetypal case revolves around the problems which arise when "strangers" seek to exploit the same natural resource space. For example, in societies where pastoralism plays a significant role in the subsistence economy, if one herder aims at keeping the pasture a viable resource by controlling his herd's grazing, the next herder may exploit the situation for extra grazing time for his own herd. Thus, the restraint on the part of the first herder works to his disadvantage, and greed on the part of the second herder only works to his temporary advantage. In the long run, the pasture is damaged by overgrazing and all herders lose. As Johnson and Earle (1987:10) point out, the only solution to this tragedy is for a group's members to practice a code of behavior which regulates all of them and protects the common resource. This is the political economy.

Risk Management

One of the key factors in promoting social evolution is risk management. In general terms, risk management can be related to local subsistence production and regional resource competition. In considering risk management in relation to protohistoric food production, in societies which rely on a small number of domesticates for their basic subsistence, the solutions to crop and pasture failure are limited. As population increases and diets are restricted to a narrow range of products such as grain, meat and the secondary products of herds animals (as opposed to broad spectrum diets of hunters and gatherers, cf. Binford 1968), there are fewer natural food buffers against environmental fluctuations in lean years. In these conditions of environmental risk, more centralized systems of management and food storage can be expected to develop. The second aspect of risk management focuses on the cultural en-

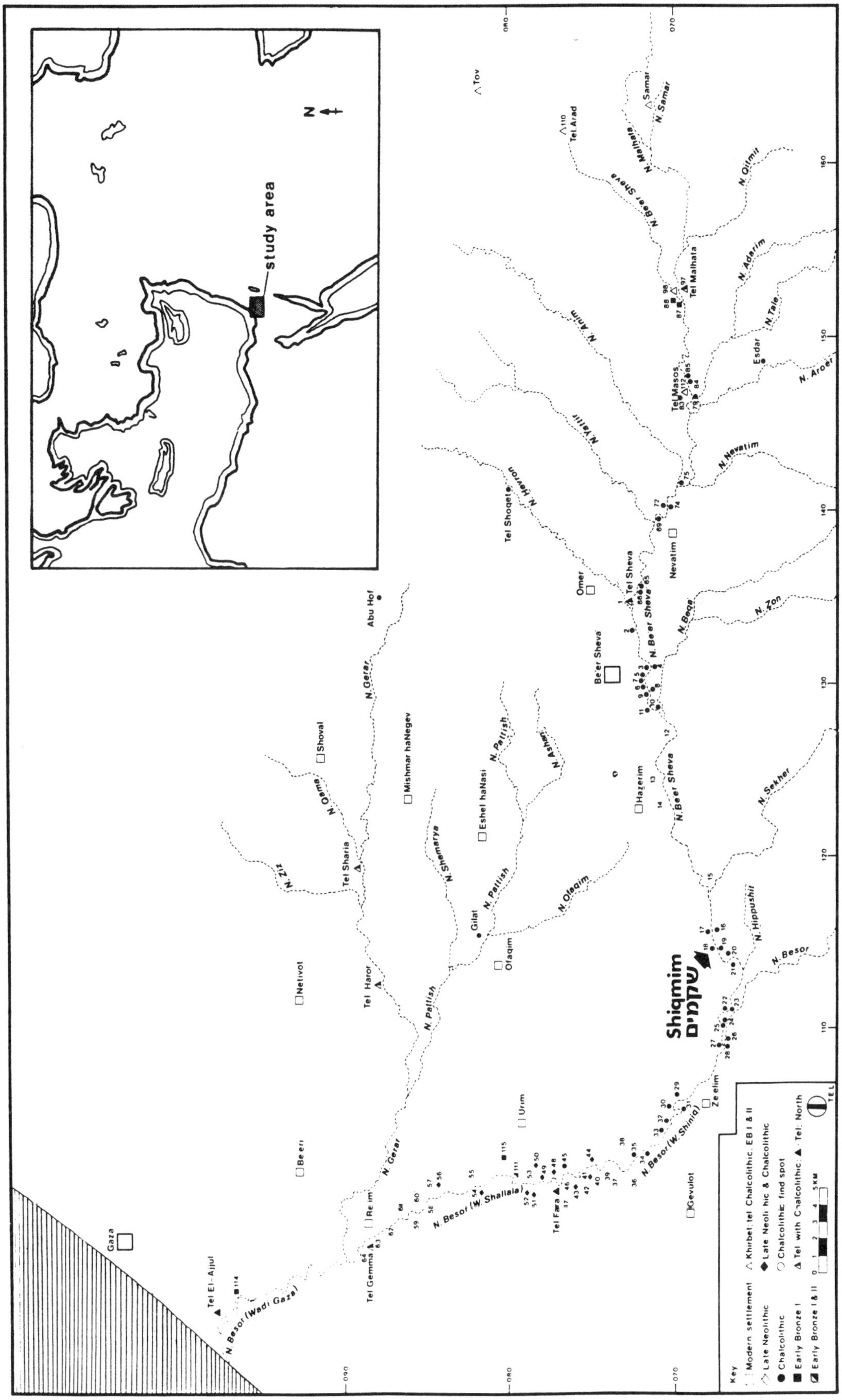

Fig. 1. Map of major sites and wadi drainages in northern Negev.

vironment and resource competition. As pointed out by Johnson and Earle (1987:17), with population growth and intensified land use, locally rich resources such as fertile bottom lands and prime pasture land become even more precious. With intensified land use, the benefits of warfare and the violent seizure of natural resource space in a region rise. Small social groups will form alliances with other small groups for more effective defence or seizure of resources. These factors work together to promote leadership and the potential for social control.

Risk Management and the Archaeological Record

Does the archaeological record of prehistoric Palestine reflect the processes of risk management and warfare? In southern Palestine, clear shifts in regional settlement patterns have been documented from the Late Neolithic through Early Bronze Age (Levy and Alon 1987; Gophna 1979). A marked increase in human population occurred in the Chalcolithic period, when most of the major wadis in the northern Negev were intensely settled for the first time by communities which practised cereal farming and the herding of sheep/goat, cattle and in some micro-environments, pig raising (Gilead 1986; Grigson 1987; Levy 1983). Whereas Late Neolithic settlements were autonomous, of small size, clustered around fresh water sources on the Negev coastal plain, and numbered less than 15 sites, during the Chalcolithic period population increased dramatically as is reflected in the major wadi valleys that were now filled with agricultural producers. For example, in the Nahal Beersheva, 29 village sites were established, 28 hamlets, and 20 find spots (pastoral camps?) during the peak period of occupation (Fig. 1) (Levy and Alon 1987).

From the perspective of social evolution, the emergence of a clear two-tier settlement hierarchy is of great importance, reflecting a chiefdom level of Chalcolithic political organization in the Beersheva valley (Levy 1986; Carneiro 1981). Similar settlement patterns have been recorded for this period along the Nahal Patish and Nahal Gerar (Alon 1961); however, no systematic attempt has been made to define the type of regional political organization which existed along these drainages. By the late Early Bronze Age Ib and Early Bronze II periods, large urban centers of population developed at sites such as Tel Arad and Tel Ereni (Amiran 1979; Amiran and Gophna 1979; Brandl 1989). With the increase in human population observed in the northern Negev during the Chalcolithic period, it can be assumed that there was a concomitant increase in competition over natural resources such as farm land and pasture land.

Settlement history, Risk Management and Competition: the Case of Shiqmim

The recent long term excavations at the Chalcolithic village of Shiqmim, which took place from 1979 to 1989, provide an ideal test case for investigating the processes of growth and decline in the Beersheva valley, one of the main wadi systems in the northern Negev. In this context, the stratigraphic excavations at Shiqmim can be used to test numerous hypotheses concerning the sequence of protohistoric settlement in the Beersheva valley. For example, whereas Perrot (1955, 1984; Commenge-Pellerin 1990) suggests four general phases of Chalcolithic settlement in the valley, based on his excavations at Abu Matar and Bir es Safadi, Gilead (1987) has proposed that the Beersheva sites represent a single phase occupation sequence. While not following Perrot's stratigraphic reconstruction sequence by sequence, the recent excavations at Shiqmim do lend strong support to Perrot's stratigraphic reconstruction, which characterized the pioneer phase of settlement in the Beersheva valley as one made up of underground houses and related subterranean features (Levy et al. 1991). Based on the limited radiocarbon and cultural material studies from the northern Negev (Alon and Levy 1989; Gilead 1988; Levy 1986), we assume that the other wadi systems such as the Nahal Besor, Nahal Patish, and Nahal Gerar were also occupied at this time. Whereas Perrot (1984) has suggested that the Beersheva underground houses were constructed as an adaptive response to micro-environmental conditions in the Beersheva valley, we have interpreted these pioneer settlement structures as a means of defense associated with a settlement process in a relatively virgin area bordered by other cultural groups in the late 5th millennium. There are numerous ethnographic accounts from Africa which associate underground houses with defense (Denyer 1978:67-70). The widespread occurrence of underground rooms and tunnels from the Roman period at sites dating to the Bar Kochba revolt, ca. 128–135 C.E. provide archaeo-historic evidence for this model of settlement defense (Alon, pers. comm.).

At Shiqmim, three major building phases or strata, and possibly a fourth have been distinguished, with the initial pioneer phase characterized by networks of subterranean rooms and the later two phases by a well-planned village laid out on a uniform northwest/southeast axis (Fig. 2).

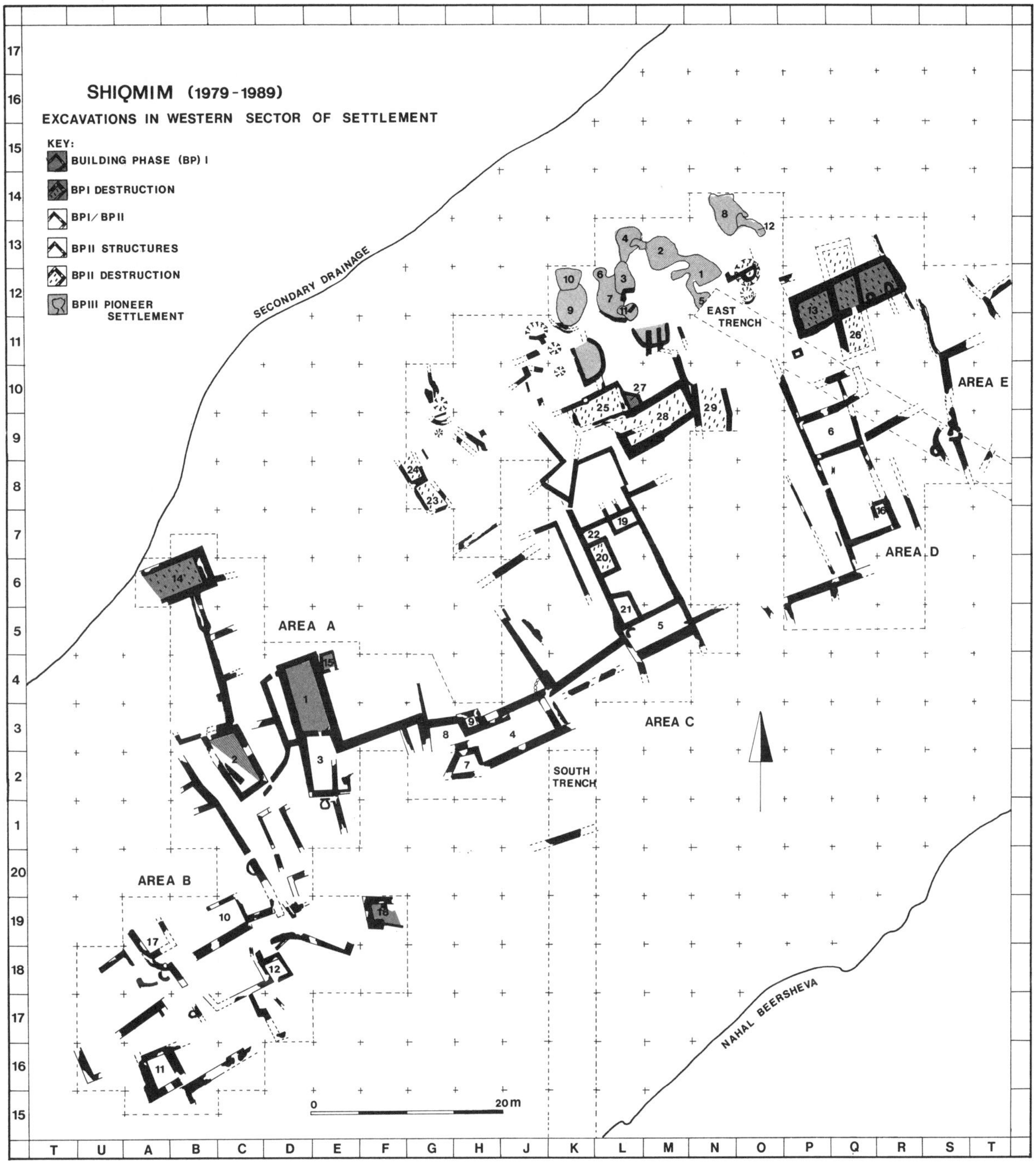

Fig. 2. Map of Shiqmim with destruction levels.

The later village was composed of large and small rectilinear buildings, courtyards, alleys, subterranean storage facilities, and other features. Of interest here is the geomorphological data from the Shiqmim area described by Goldberg (1987; Levy et al. 1990) in conjunction with the growth of the planned village. During the pioneer settlement phase (average calibrated radiocarbon dates, 4450–4350 B.C.), the wadi was a more active agent which deposited thick lenses of gravel, sand, and silt. At this time, the pioneer settlers carved out a terrace from the hillocks of redeposited loessic soil along the north bank of the wadi, erected a large open-air altar (ca. 5.20 x 2.45 x 2.20 m high) along the foot of this terrace, and dug a series of underground room systems laid out in a crescent shape. Thus, during the pioneer phase, settlement was located away from the active wadi channel. Over a period of several hundred years after the initial settlement of the valley, an extensive flood plain was formed throughout the valley bottom. The buildup of gravels, sand, and silt provided an extensive flat plain for both constructing the planned settlement of Building Phases (strata) II and I, as well as an ideal area for farming activities on the floodplain (Levy 1983). Population growth in the village is indicated by the dense packing of buildings in Phases II and I compared with the loosely packed pattern of crescent-shaped underground systems. Of interest here is the clustering of subterranean storage facilities associated with the Building Phase II village in areas where several large non-domestic buildings were found (Fig. 3).

One of these is a silo with a circular stone entrance which led to an underground cavity with a storage capacity of ca. 3 cubic meters (Fig. 4). The planned Phase II village and cluster of storage facilities associated with non-domestic buildings may reflect a moderate redistributive economy which goes beyond the "Domestic Mode of Production" and evidence for risk management in the later phases of occupation when environmental conditions were drier than the pioneer phase of settlement. Large scale storage would be essential for times of drought.

Archaeological Evidence for Resource Competition

Y. Aharoni (1982:47) characterized the Chalcolithic period as a time of peace primarily because of the un-walled nature of the settlements at this time. However, as we have seen in "the tragedy of the commons," problems arise when "strangers" seek to exploit the same natural resources. If we assume that the extensive evidence for Chalcolithic village settlement along the main northern Negev wadis reflects contemporary occupation in the region, then, according to the resource competition model, problems would arise when herders from these different communities chose to move their animals to the same grazing lands or if one group wanted to take over prime agricultural land from another. In earlier settlement pattern studies of the Beersheva valley, site catchment analysis showed that while the carrying-capacity of the valley bottom land was not reached during the peak period of settlement, there was little latitude for additional farming settlements in the valley (Levy 1983). The Chalcolithic period marks the first time in the Levantine archaeological record that cemeteries were established in areas separate from settlement sites. Prior to this, burials were placed within habitation sites (Bar Yosef 1980). This new phenomenon is highlighted by the numerous Chalcolithic cemeteries found along the Sharon coastal plain (Sukenik 1937; Perrot and Ladiray 1980), the lower Jordan valley (Stekelis 1935), most recently in the Samarian hills and in the southern Negev (Avner 1989). In the northern Negev study area, Shiqmim has provided evidence of the only cemetery (over 8 ha in area) in the Beersheva valley. The establishment of separate cemetery sites may reflect a new concern with territory on a scale not previously conceptualized by prehistoric societies in the Levant.

Conflict over grazing and agricultural land in the Negev is reflected in the Bible as early as Gen. 13:5-12 in which Abraham argues with Lot over grazing land. In more recent ethnohistorical data collected by Bailey (1980, 1985) extensive evidence is presented for Bedouin tribal wars, over grazing lands in most cases, in the Sinai and Negev deserts from approximately the 7th through the 20th centuries. Thus, it can be assumed that in the northern Negev, the potential for conflict among various Chalcolithic cultural groups existed in regard to resource competition over agricultural and pasture land. These sources breathe life into the "tragedy of the commons" in the Negev.

The need to organize the protection and exploitation of subsistence resources may have been a key factor in the rise of centralized leadership in the Beersheva valley, and possibly other drainage systems such as the Nahal Patish where the sanctuary center of Gilat evolved (Alon and Levy 1989). The large ceramic statuettes found in the sanctuary, a woman with a churn on her head and a ram with cornets embedded in its back, emphasize a concern with herd animals and their secondary products. In general Ancient Near Eastern terms, these objects point to what Jacobsen (1976) refers to as a metaphor of the "Gods as providers"— a common theme in ancient Mesopotamian religion of the 4th millennium. Seen from the materialist perspective, the location of Gilat at the "gateway" of prime Negev grazing land, away from the moist valley bottom land of the Nahal Beersheva and along the interface of the Negev coastal plain and the northern Negev foothill zone, may indicate the sanctuary's function as a center for mediating use of this resource zone. The positions of Saints' tombs in the Sinai desert along Bedouin tribal boundaries seem to have served a similar socio-political function in historic times (Marx 1977).

What then is the archaeological evidence for warfare in the Chalcolithic? The most obvious technological development is the introduction of finely made mace heads in the Chalcolithic ground stone and metal industries. Yadin (1963:40) was the first scholar to systematically highlight the importance of

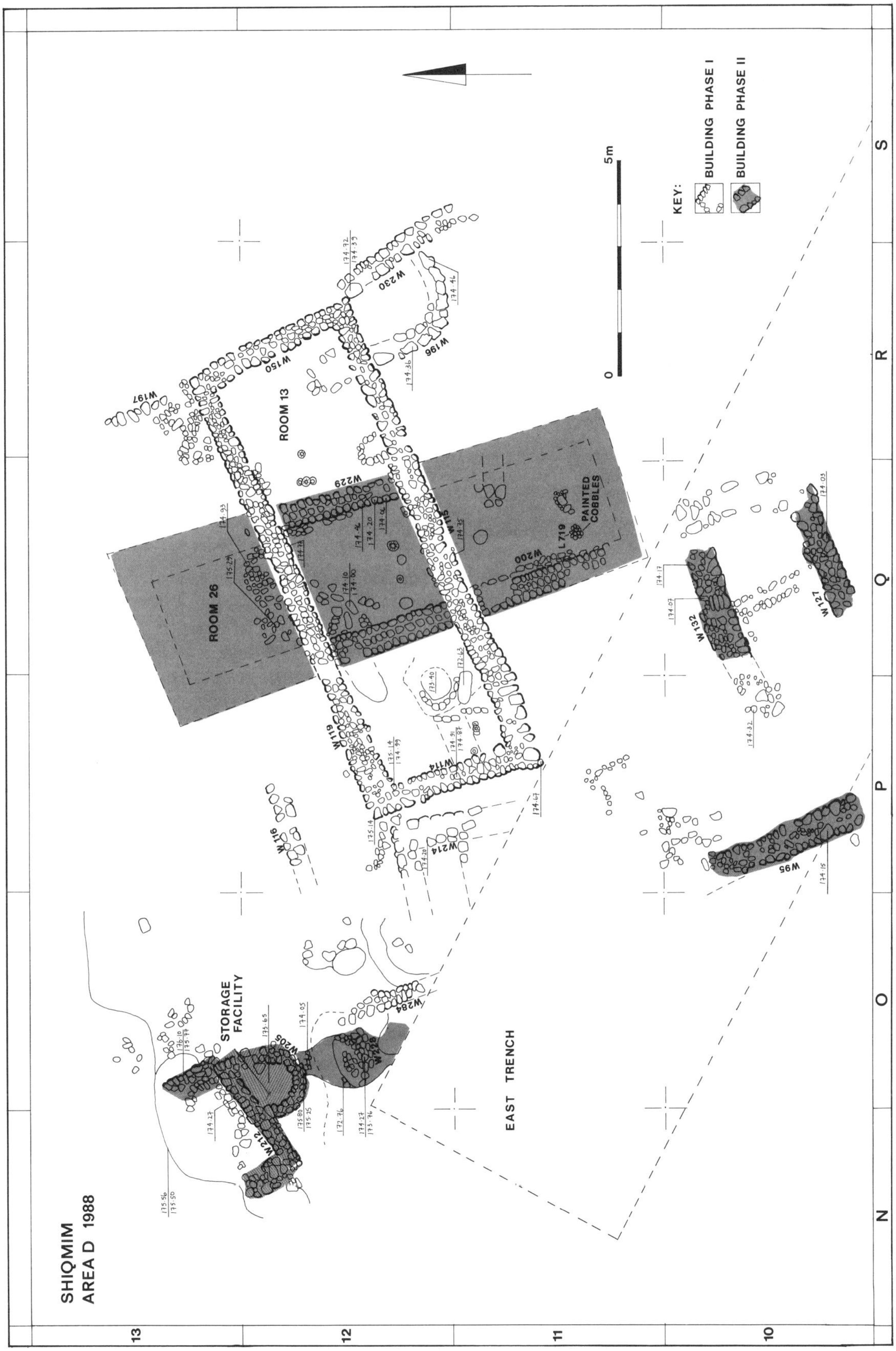

Fig. 3. Area D complex with plan of storage facility 714.

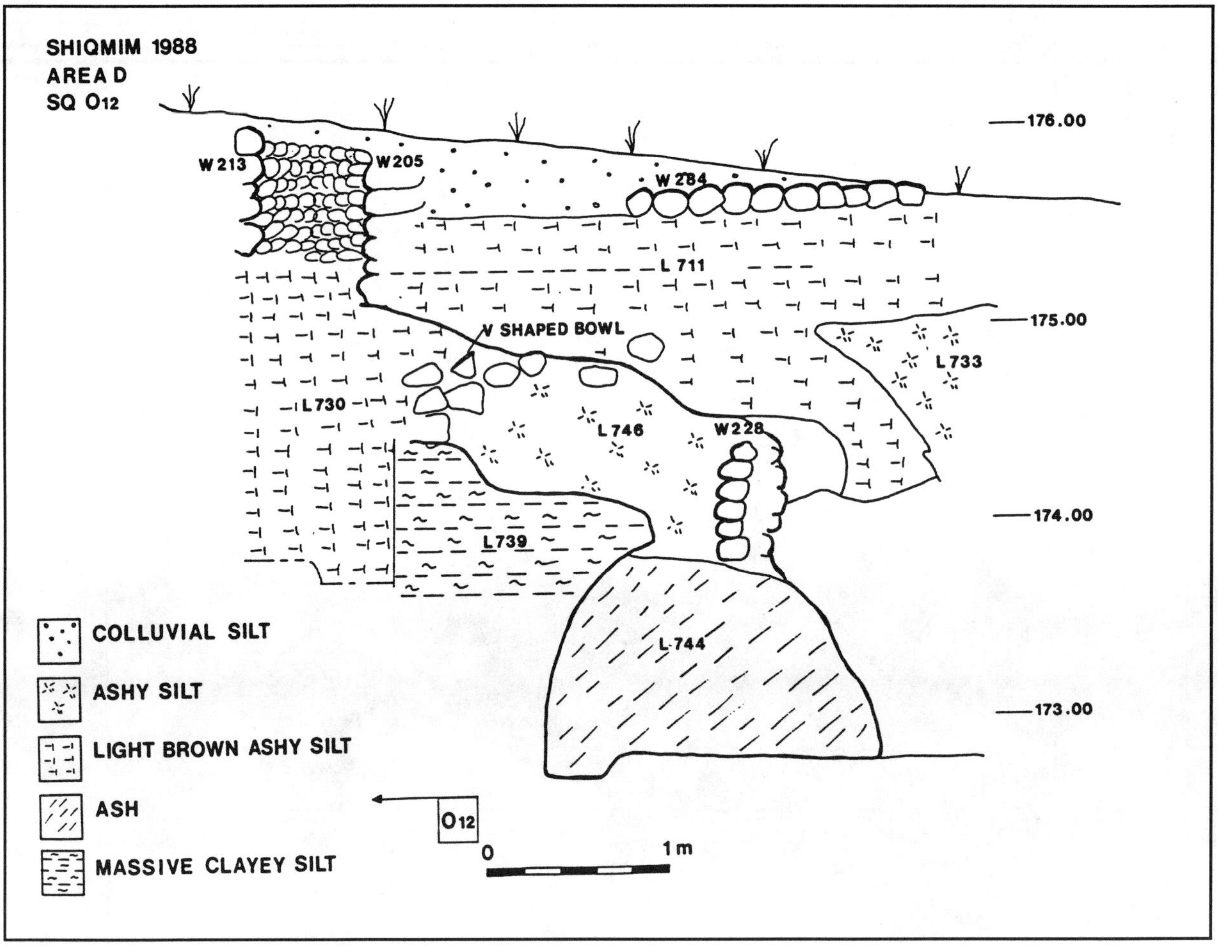

Fig. 4. Section of storage facility 714.

mace heads in short-range hand-to-hand fighting in Chalcolithic Palestine as well as in Egypt and Mesopotamia. While warfare and conflict has no doubt occurred since the Paleolithic periods (Roper 1969, 1975), and almost any stone tool, wooden club, rock, or fist could be used as a weapon, the production of mace heads may represent the first effort to manufacture a weapon specifically for use in inter-group warfare in the Levant. Stager (n.d.) points out that mace heads appear for the first time in Palestine during the Wadi Rabah phase of the Pottery Neolithic and are known from many Halafian sites in northern Mesopotamia and Syria, occurring in Amuq C with imported and locally made Halaf painted pottery. However, in a technological and social study of the mace heads from protohistoric Palestine, Sabanne (n.d.) has shown that mace heads appear in large quantities for the first time during the Chalcolithic period and continue in use throughout the Early Bronze II period.

Mace heads may also have been symbols of rank and authority. The ceremonial mace heads and palettes found in the "Main Deposit," a collection of Protodynastic "antiques" found buried in an Old or Middle Kingdom temple in Hierakonpolis, Egypt, provide invaluable information on the role of these objects in the social milieu of the Protodynastic kings of Nehken, Narmer, and Scorpion (Hoffman 1979:129; Moorey 1988; Quibell 1900, 1901). In this deposit, both inscribed and uninscribed mace heads were found. The Narmer palette illustrates Narmer holding a mace head, clubbing what has been interpreted as an Asiatic (Yadin 1955). That mace heads were also symbols of rank in Protodynastic Egypt is highlighted by the beautifully inscribed mace heads found in the "Main Deposit," which presumably would not have been used in actual fighting, as well as the two examples with gold plated handles discovered in the Late Gerzean "Chiefly" grave in Lower Nubia by Firth (1927:206). The large number of uninscribed stone (primarily limestone), pear-shaped mace heads found in the Main Deposit may also reflect the military campaigns of Narmer. J. Crowfoot Payne has speculated that the kings of Hierakonpolis called in all the mace heads from newly conquered regions to deprive local chiefs of one important emblem of their authority, thus explaining the large quantity of mace heads found in the Main Deposit (Hoffman 1979:302). Based on Egyptian iconography, Hoffman (1979:303) has interpreted the pear-shaped mace heads as symbolic artifacts associated with the king's role as bold warrior—not unlike the American Plains Indian custom of counting coup by touching an enemy with a tomahawk. These observations suggest that the discovery of a mace head associated with an adult male buried in a grave circle at Shiqmim may reflect a warrior's grave (Fig. 5).

To date, a total of 9 mace heads (2 copper, 6 hematite, 1 limestone, and 1 ceramic) have been found in the Shiqmim village. Sabanne (n.d.) has made an inventory of all the known mace heads from Palestine. The fine craftsmanship exhibited in stone mace heads from the Chalcolithic and Early Bronze Age in Palestine may indicate a technological innovation associated with the invention of what Hoffman (1979:303) suggests was an efficient stone-weighted drill for grinding stone in a controlled and rapid fashion. The production of metal mace heads, discussed below and in detail by Shalev et al. (n.d.), represents an even higher level of craft specialization.

Additional evidence for warfare may also be inferred from the cluster of burnt buildings discovered in Building Phase II at Shiqmim. In the central area of the western sector of the site, unlike the majority of the structures, the large buildings and storage facilities all show evidence of destruction by fire, with extensive deposits of ash from the main Building Phase (BP) II occupation. Out of a total of 23 BP II buildings excavated, 7 (30%) were burned, and all cluster together. A similar pattern exists for the last occupation phase (BP I) except that the distribution of burnt rooms does not cluster. Some artifactual evidence may also point to destruction by warfare (Table 1). A large votive standard made of ivory was found broken and thrown into an abandoned tunnel with ash and other materials. A charcoal sample found with a surface leading into the tunnel was recently dated by radiocarbon methods to the BP I abandon-

Fig. 5. Grave with mace head.

Table 1. Shiqmim: Distribution of buildings according to Building Phases and evidence of destruction.

	Building Phase I	Building Phase I Burnt	Building Phase II	Building Phase II Burnt
	1	13	2*	20
	2*	14	3	23
	15	—	4	24
	18	—	5	25
	27	—	6	26
			7	28
			8	29
			10	
			11	
			12	
			16	
			17	
			19	
			21	
Totals	5 (71 %)	2 (29 %)	16 (70 %)	7 (30 %)

ment of this area (RT-1341, 5150 ± 40; 3997 - 3828 B.C.). Taken together, the BP II evidence seems to indicate the remains of a destruction level in one of the central areas of the site, perhaps a result of warfare.

Production and Debt

Recently, C. Gosden (1989) drew together the role of production and debt in relation to social change in preindustrial societies. At the heart of this study is Mauss's (1954) classic work, "Essai sur le don" or "Essay on the gift." By examining a wide range of ethnographic and ethnohistoric sources of pre-industrial societies, Mauss concluded that gifts are given as a means of setting up obligations, with the recipient under the obligation of the giver. Gift giving is organized so that the maximum number of relationships can be created and sustained by placing participants in a situation of debt. In debt-based societies the conditions of production are different from those where value dominates. Personal ownership of land does not exist, garden or feral land are held in common, and clan members have rights of use, not ownership. Craft production is also not usually in private hands, but is carried out by castes or by each individual household (Gosden 1989:359). Whereas in industrial societies commodities are freely interchanged, in debt-based societies gifts are ranked. The production of gifts for debt takes place within the relationships of the kin group and is aimed at producing items that will build lasting relationships between the transactors. For Sahlins (1974:133, 169), the gift is the primitive way of achieving the peace that in civil society is obtained and guaranteed by the state. Seen in the context of the political economy, the relation giver-receiver is the equivalent of leader-follower. As Gosden (1989) points out, the main factor needed to create regular flows of debt, which form the basis of social inequality, is some means of restricting the access to gifts. In the Beersheva valley, those individuals in the higher ranks were probably those responsible for organizing risk management strategies, negotiating over regional resource space such as pasture land, and organizing warfare-related activities.

One way of restricting access to gifts is to retain control over the means of production. The smaller the number of people who have the knowledge, skills, access to raw materials, and time necessary to produce gifts, the higher value these items will have (Gosden 1989). Whereas the household focuses on the subsistence economy, the emergence of craft specialization demonstrates modes of production that go well beyond the household level of social integration and its concern with subsistence. While craft specialization can be organized and controlled by individual households, the fact that production is not evenly distributed in the society highlights the shift away from the household. Thus, gifts can be ranked according to the restrictions involved in the production process. At the lowest end of the scale are agricultural products, which, presumably, every household can produce. Higher up the scale are craft products which use restricted raw materials and some skill, and at the top end of the scale are craft products which require specialized skill, special equipment, and rare raw materials. As shown below, by examining early metal production in this light it is possible to observe socio-economic activities which go beyond the household and played a key role in supporting elites. To fully test this hypothesis, multivariate analyses of each realm of material culture are needed. In the future, by starting along the lines initiated by Rosen (1986), quantitative studies should examine the steps in the production process, source of raw materials used, and the number of objects found.

Metal working and Social Change

Copper ore was used for the first time in Palestine during the 8th–7th millennium B.C., when greenstone, probably native copper, was used for beads and powder for cosmetic purposes at Pre-Pottery Neolithic B (PPNB) sites such as Jericho, Nahal Hemar, Nahal Issaron, and Ain Ghazzal (Garfinkel 1987:80-82; Goring-Morris and Gopher 1983; Bar Yosef 1985; Rollefson and Simmons 1986). While the earliest copper slags known from the Middle East come from the northern part of the region of Çatal Hüyük in Anatolia and date to the 6th millennium B.C., in the southern Levant the earliest evidence for copper metal and metal production comes from the Beersheva valley sites of the Chalcolithic period (Tylecote 1979). By far the most comprehensive evidence for early Levantine metallurgy comes from the Beersheva valley sites of Abu Matar, Bir es Safadi, and Shiqmim (Perrot 1955; Eldar and Baumgarten 1985; Shalev and Northover 1987) and the spectacular Nahal Mishmar Chalcolithic hoard where over 460 copper and other Chalcolithic objects were found in a cave in the Judean desert (Bar Adon 1980; Moorey 1988). The objects found in the hoard demonstrate the remarkably high technological and artistic abilities of Chalcolithic metal workers (Key 1980).

Archaeometallurgical studies of Chalcolithic metal working are beginning to shed some light on the problem of ore sources, production technologies, and regional distribution systems (Key et al. 1980; Shalev and Northover 1987; Levy and Shalev 1989; Hauptman 1989; Tadmor 1989). Analyses of copper objects from the Nahal Mishmar hoard and more recent studies of copper-related objects have demonstrated the existence of two distinct processes of Chalcolithic metal production. While "utilitarian" shaped objects such as axes and chisels were forged from blanks cast in nearly pure copper, elaborately shaped objects, including mace heads and scepters, were defined as being cast in the lost wax method in arsenical copper, many with high arsenic content. Shalev and Northover's (1987) work shows conclusively the major ore source for objects manufactured in the Beersheva valley to be the Wadi Feinan in Transjordan, over 120 km away from Shiqmim. According to Key (1980), the origin of the arsenical ore used for the majority of the elaborately shaped objects in the hoard came from Armenia or Azerbaidjan over 1300 km away. Moorey (1988:185) points out that this was taken to reinforce arguments about cultural diffusion and the foreign production of the hoard. These complex shaped objects have been interpreted as having a cultic/prestige function in the Chalcolithic societies of southern Palestine (Levy and Shalev 1989; Rosen 1986).

In a recent study of a copper mace head from Shiqmim, Shalev et al. (n.d.) have added important evidence showing the local production of cultic/prestige metal work by doing a technological study of this object. In the petrographic study of a stone core found inside the mace head, Goren could identify the stone as a glauconitic chalk fragment from the Matered Formation near Ein Yahav in the Arava valley south of the Dead Sea, indicating that the mace head was locally produced in southern Israel-Transjordan. As pointed out by Shalev et al. (in press), the local source of the stone used in the production of the mace head from Shiqmim lends weight to interpreting the complex group of cultic/prestige metal work as local in origin. Although the production site or sites for this group of objects has not been found yet, it seems likely that it will be in southern Israel-Transjordan.

In Palestine, the emergence of metallurgy is perhaps the clearest archaeological indication of an early form of craft specialization which shifts away from the notion of household production. From the Negev perspective, the production of "utilitarian" metal objects appears to be an almost "informational" monopoly of the Beersheva valley Chalcolithic culture. This is highlighted by the regional distribution pattern of copper production sites in Palestine where virtually all such localities cluster along the Nahal Beersheva-lower Nahal Besor (Fig. 6).

Of importance here is the ore procurement process associated with Beersheva metal-working activities. As pointed out by Shalev and Northover (1987), the origin of the majority of ores used in the production of utilitarian objects found at Shiqmim and other Beersheva valley sites was the Wadi Feinan

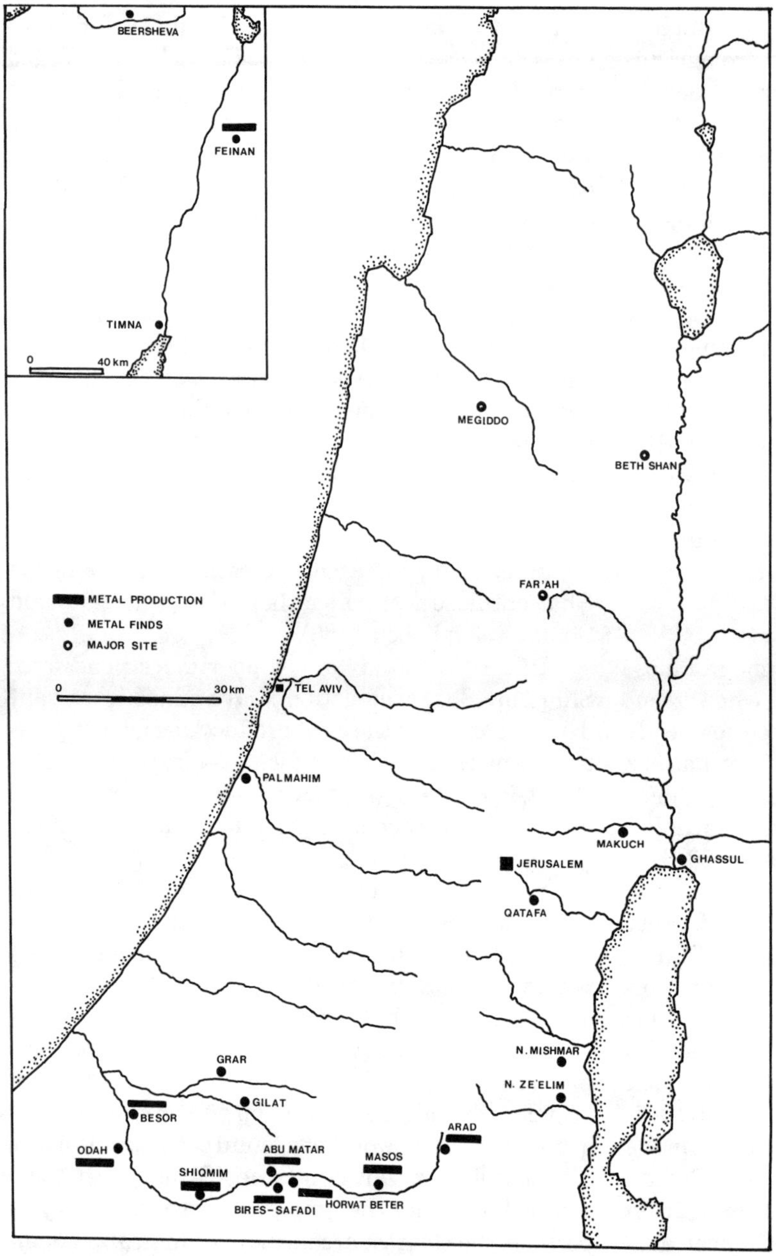

Fig. 6. Distribution map of copper production sites.

in Transjordan over 120 km to the east. Recent archaeological excavations and surveys in the Wadi Feinan (Hauptman 1989:131) have failed to produce substantial evidence of Chalcolithic copper slag and evidence of on-site smelting near these ore sources. This has led Hauptman (1989:132) to suggest that the conspicuous scantiness of copper slags at Feinan may indicate a "slagless metallurgy." While the "slagless metallurgy" production system could be added to the two metal production systems mentioned above, this suggestion may be stretching negative evidence to the limit. The fact that Chalcolithic metal production is represented by thousands of slag fragments at Beersheva valley sites and not near the ore sources may indicate a concern with keeping metallurgical knowledge within the Beersheva valley settlement system. In this context, the intrasite smelting and casting of copper ores suggests that individuals from the Beersheva valley were sent on mining expeditions to bring back the raw materials needed for the production of utilitarian objects at sites such as Abu Matar, Bir es Safadi, and Shiqmim.

The ore extraction pattern changes markedly in the Feinan in the Early Bronze II–III period (ca. 2900–2300 B.C.) when there is the first evidence for extensive mining and smelting of the mixed copper/manganese ores at the mining sites. This exploitation pattern is indicative of an industrial manufacturing

Table 2: Contextual data concerning the distribution of metal objects at Shiqmim.

Copper objects	BP I	BP II	BP III
Awls (11)	Area A (Room 1) Area C (Fill) Area Y (Fill)	Area A (Ashy fill) Area C (mudbrick fill) Area D (3 Room 6) Area D (Mudbrick) Area J (Ash layer) Area J (Subroom 6)	
Blade tools (5)		Area C (Axe in Cache) Area C (chisel in cache) Area C (Axe in Room 4) Area D (Axe in courtyard of Room 6)	Area J (Axe, subroom II fill)
Mace heads (2)		South Trench (Room 4)	Upper village (floor surface ?)
Scepter (2)	Area A (Room 1) (foundation deposit)	South Trench (Room 4)	
Beads (1)		South Trench (Mudbrick debris)	
Miscellaneous (1)			Copper band Area J (Subroom 8)

system where the volume of the Early Bronze Age slag heaps reflects metal production on the scale of 100–200 tons. As shown by Ilan and Sabbane (1989), an intricate copper exploitation system developed by Early Bronze (EB) II, with trade networks between the Sinai and Arad, which seems to have served as a distribution center for copper-related objects in the third millennium. At Feinan 9, 27 Early Bronze smelting furnaces have been excavated to date. Future research will hopefully clarify the relation between Feinan and Arad. However, when this quantity of EB slag is compared to Chalcolithic smelting activities at Beersheva valley sites such as Shiqmim, the contrast in production systems is most apparent. The phase I excavations at Shiqmim (1979, 1982-84) exposed less than 5% of the site and produced less than one kilogram of slag and a similar amount of ore, clearly indicating the non-industrial nature of the Chalcolithic metal-working (Levy and Shalev 1989:363). This suggest that our functionalist definition of Chalcolithic "utilitarian" objects (core tools, i.e. axes, adzes, and chisels) may be incorrect and that the Chalcolithic metal "tools" may have had a higher social value than previously thought.

At Shiqmim, over 200 core tools have been found in the phase I excavations, compared to only 5 copper blade tools, giving a ratio of 40:1 (Table 2). As Rosen (1984) points out, during the Chalcolithic period copper "tools" do not replace stone tools, and the majority of copper objects seem to reflect ceremonial and ritual functions.

The presence of one axe and fifteen chisels in the Nahal Mishmar hoard suggests that these objects may also have had symbolic value (Bar Adon 1980:112-115). This is in contrast to awls, which have been found in clear functional contexts on the floors of domestic structures in both Chalcolithic and Early Bronze Age contexts (Ilan and Sabanne 1989; Levy and Holl 1987). The ratio of stone to copper blade tools and the intrasite distribution of the "utilitarian" group of metal objects at Shiqmim indicate that they are rare and associated with caches or large non-domestic structures suggesting that these objects may also have had symbolic importance.

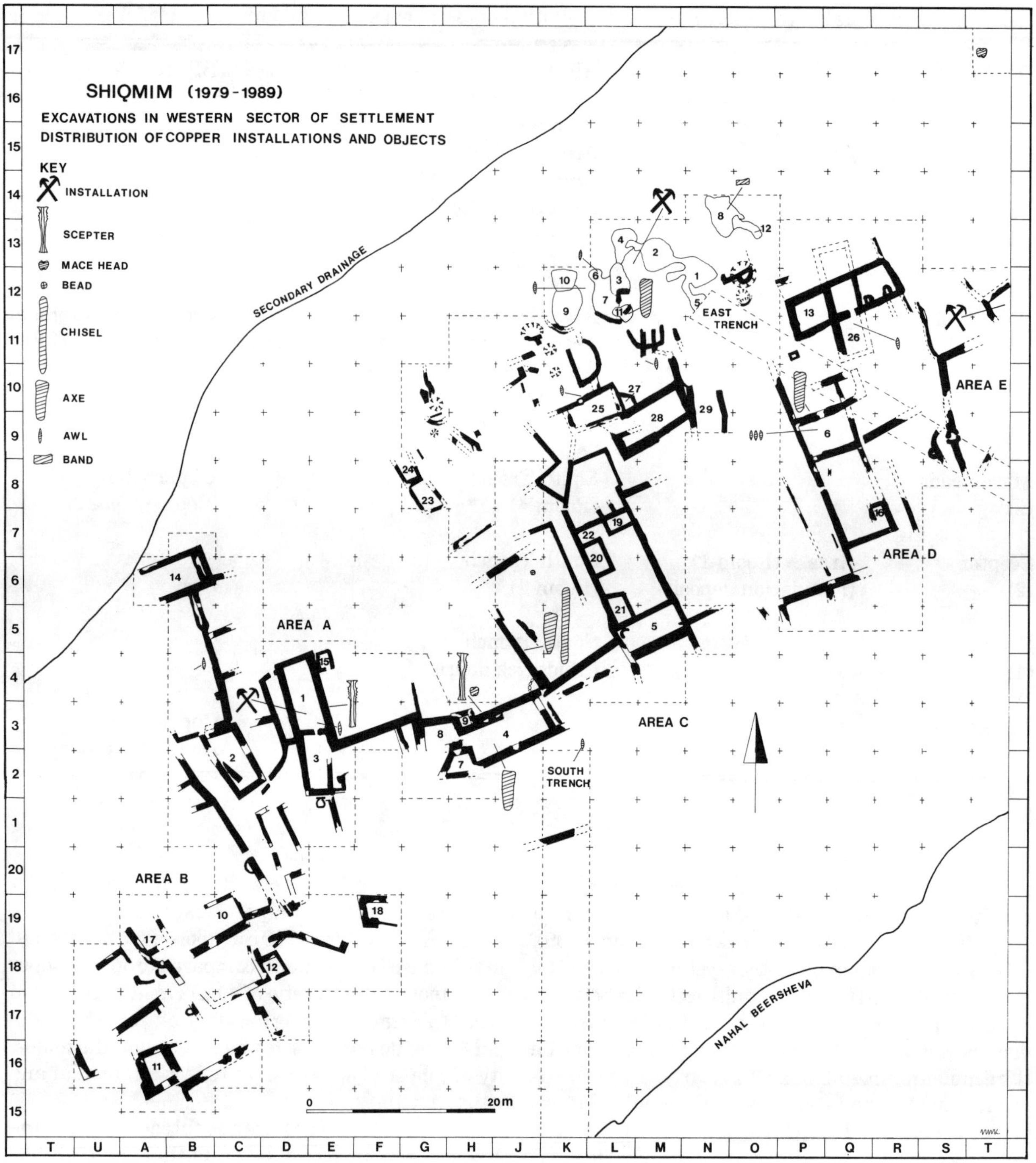

Fig. 7. Map of copper working installations.

The location of metal-working installations at Shiqmim shows them to be present in at least two building phases (BP I and II) and to cluster around non-domestic structures. Although slags have been found washed over many areas of the site, the actual metal-working installations (n = 3) provide the best indication for the location of metal-working activities within the community space. As seen in Figure 7, one series of metal-working installations was located near Building 26 (BP II), a structure which contained a cluster of painted pebbles similar to those found at Abu Matar (Perrot 1955). The third metal-working installation was found in Building 1 (BP I) which opened at its southern end during this occupation phase. The association of the metal-working installations with the large non-domestic structures may be an indication of the restricted access to metal production within the community to individuals or groups which utilized the large buildings.

That metal working may have been an event closely associated with cult activities is highlighted by the discovery of a large fragment of a drilled ivory tusk found near the metal-working installations in Building 1 at Shiqmim. The tusk fragment is identical to complete examples found in the Cave of the Treasure; however, the Shiqmim example shows more signs of decoration, characterized by numerous small holes drilled around the edge of the perforated ivory tusk (Bar Adon 1980:16-22). Bar Adon suggested that these ivory objects were used as standards carried on wooden poles inserted into the central perforation of the tusk. Until now, the relationship between the copper and ivory objects from the treasure has remained unknown. The close association of the Shiqmim tusk with the metal-working activities in Room 1 suggests that the tusk may have been an integral part of the copper production event, or, to use a more subjective term, copper production ceremony. While Bar Adon's suggestion that the drilled ivory tusks were placed on standards seems reasonable, there is a possibility that they were also used as fire drills in a ceremony involved in making fire by friction for use in metal production. There are examples of Egyptian hieroglyphs representing fire drills as well as numerous ethnographic cases which illustrate their use in Africa and South America (Harrison 1954:223). Forbes (1964) points out that among many primitive metal workers a great deal of ceremony and ritual is associated with each step in the production process, from lighting the fire to pouring the metal in a mould. Thus, the contextual evidence from Shiqmim indicates that metal working was a non-industrial craft, closely related to the production of ceremonial items with high social value, and perhaps a reflection of significant socio-religious activities.

Conclusion

The review of Chalcolithic metal production presented here shows this to be a periodic activity closely associated with ritual and the maintenance of a ranked social organization in the Beersheva valley. As pointed out by Rowlands (1971:212), archaeologists such as Childe (1930:4, 10) believed that skilled specialists are not found in societies whose economy remains at a subsistence level, because it is assumed that an economic surplus would be necessary to support their existence. While there is some evidence for centralized storage at sites such as Shiqmim, these facilities seem more closely tied to risk management than the support of full-time specialists. The emphasis on looking for full-time craft specialists in prehistoric Palestine has diverted scholarly attention from the underlying role of metal production in Chalcolithic societies. This line of reasoning lies behind recent interpretations of early Levantine metal working, which minimize the importance of this activity in the social organization of the Beersheva valley culture (Gilead 1988). However, the ethnographic evidence for primitive metal working assembled by Rowlands (1971) shows that only occasionally are full-time specialist smiths found who are supported by privileged minorities. Rather than take Childe's theory at face value, the approach taken here has been to examine the Beersheva valley archaeological record within its specific eastern Mediterranean context and follow what Ucko (1969) calls a "best fit" approach.

Recently, in discussing the social implications of the Nahal Mishmar hoard, Beck (1989:40) emphasized that any homogenous group of ritual objects can provide information about the society which used them. Few scholars would doubt the ritual significance of the objects found in the Nahal Mishmar hoard; the problem lies in interpreting its significance. Following Drennan (1976:347-48), Beck points out that religion "strengthens the bonds unifying the members of a single local group" and that ritual functions to sanctify and insure acceptance of important messages or conventions which are crucial to the orderly operation of society or the sanctification of persons and institutions. In this context, Beck interprets the objects in the Nahal Mishmar hoard as having had a similar function in Chalcolithic society, with the possibility that a social hierarchy may be reflected in the copper standards found in the hoard. According to this intriguing but untested hypothesis, elaborate standards with unique designs would have been carried by the highest elite group in the community, whereas the more common "simple standards" would have been carried by a larger body of functionaries. Clearly, as Beck implies, to fully test this hypothesis a multivariate analysis of the standards, based on quality of execution, time invested in the production of the object, and the uniqueness of design should be made. However, when these insights are coupled with the problem of risk management, competition over natural resource space, and the nature of Chalcolithic copper production outlined here, the social role of copper production in supporting elites in the Beersheva culture seems more plausible.

Chalcolithic metal working can be more closely linked to the production of symbolic objects (including blade tools) that would have played a key role in the establishment and maintenance of debt relationships (Gosden 1989) among Chalcolithic elite groups in the Nahal Beersheva chiefdom system. The non-industrial nature of the Chalcolithic metal-working process (including the need to organize long-distance mining expeditions) is suggestive of activities which go beyond the household level of production. Resent evidence for early metal working in Palestine suggest that this process was closely tied to only one of the four major wadi systems of Chalcolithic settlement (i.e., the Nahal Beersheva) in the Negev and, hence, metal production served as an important element in solidifying links between different peer polities in this valley (Fig. 5). The recent evidence for the local production of cult/prestige items (although limited), coupled with the iconographic similarity of finds from the Beersheva valley suggest that local metallurgists may also have been responsible for the manufacture of cultic/prestige objects. By controlling production or the producers of metal objects, especially standards and mace heads, there was restricted access to these items which probably circulated among elites (such as religious officials and warriors), focused on one spatial unit, the Beersheva valley. Thus, a means of building and reinforcing ties could be established through a system of gift giving which may have involved the presentation of cultic/prestige metal work as well as the ceremonies involved in the on-site smelting and casting of objects. In this context, metal work (in addition to other products manufactured by specialists such as ivory, lambis shell bracelets, stone mace heads, stone fenestrated stands, and other objects) functioned to reinforce the position of elites associated with problems of risk management and competition over natural resource zones in the northern Negev.

Acknowledgments

I would like to thank D. Alon, O. Ilan, M. Sabanne, B. Brendl, and A. Shalev for many useful discussions concerning protohistoric production in Israel. Thanks also to my wife, Alina, for her erudite and always useful comments and M. Kersel for help in preparing the maps for this chapter. Some aspects of this discussion were presented at the 2nd International Congress on Biblical Archaeology, Jerusalem (July, 1990). I also thank A. Jaffe for reading and commenting this article.

References

Aharoni, Y.
1982 *The Archaeology of the land of Israel.* London: SCM Press Ltd.

Alon, D.
1961 Early settlements along the Nahal Garar and Nahal Patish. *M'Befnim* 1:87-96 (Hebrew)

Alon, D. & T. E. Levy
1980 Preliminary note on the distribution of Chalcolithic sites on the Wadi Beersheva and Lower Wadi Besor drainage system. *Israel Exploration Journal* 30:140-147.
1989 The archaeology of cult and the Chalcolithic sanctuary at Gilat. *Journal of Mediterranean Archaeology* 2:163-221.

Amiran, R.
1978 *Early Arad: The Chalcolithic settlement and Early Bronze city.* Jerusalem: Israel Exploration Society.
1986 The fall of the Early Bronze II city of Arad. *Israel Exploration Journal* 36:74-76.

Amiran, R. & R. Gophna
1989 Urban Canaan in the Early Bronze II and III periods-emergence and structure. In *L'urbanisation de la Palestine à l'Age du Bronze ancien,* P. de Miroschedji (ed.), 109-116. Oxford, BAR International Series.

Avner, U.
1989 Eilat -Tumuli. *Hadashot Arkheologiot* 94:64-65.

Bailey, C.
1980 The Negev in the nineteenth century: reconstructing history from Bedouin oral traditions. *Asian and African Studies* 14:35-80.
1985 Dating the arrival of Bedouin tribes in Sinai and the Negev. *Journal of Economic and Social History of the Orient* XXVIII:20-49.

Bar Adon, P.
1980 *The Cave of the Treasure.* Jerusalem: Israel Exploration Society.

Bar Yosef, O.
1980 Prehistory of the Levant. *Annual Review of Anthropology* 9:101-33.

Bar Yosef, O. & D. Alon
1988 Nahal Hemar Cave. *Atiqot* 18.

Beck, P.
1989 Notes on the style and iconography of the Chalcolithic hoard from Nahal Mishmar. In *Essays in Ancient Civilization presented to H.J. Kantor,* A. Leonard and B.B. Will-

iams (eds.), 39-54. Chicago: Studies in Ancient Oriental Civilization N° 47.
Binford, L. R.
1968 Post-Pleistocene adaptations. In *New Perspectives in Archaeology,* S. R. and L. R. Binford (eds.), 313-341. Chicago: Aldine.
Brandl, B.
1989 Observations on the Early Bronze Age Strata of Tel Erani. In *L'urbanisation de la Palestine à l'Age du Bronze Ancien,* P. de Miroschedji (ed.), 357-387. Oxford: BAR International Series.
Carneiro, R. L.
1981 The chiefdom: precursor of the state. In *The Transition to Statehood in the New World,* G. D. Jones and R. R. Kautz (eds.), 37-79. Cambridge: Cambridge University Press.
Childe, V. G.
1930 *The Bronze Age.* Cambridge: Cambridge University Press.
Commenge-Pellerin, C.
1990 *La poterie de Safadi (Beersheva) au IVe millénaire avant l'ère chrétienne.* Paris: Association Paléorient.
Denyer, S.
1978 *African Traditional Architecture: An History and Geographical Perspective.* London: Heinemann.
Drennan, R. D.
1976 Religion and Social Evolution in Formative Mesoamerica. In *The Early Mesoamerican Village,* K. V. Flannery (ed.), 345-368. New York: Academic Press.
Eldar, I. & Y. Baumgarten
1985 Neve Noy : A Chalcolithic site of the Beersheva culture. *Biblical Archaeologist* 48:134-139.
Firth, C. M.
1927 *The Archaeological survey of Nubia: Report for 1910 - 1911.* Cairo: Government Press.
Forbes, R. J.
1964 *Studies in Ancient Technology, Vol. VIII.* Leiden: E.J. Brill.
Garfinkel, Y.
1987 Bead manufacture on the Pre-Pottery Neolithic B site of Yiftael. *Journal of the Israel Prehistoric Society* 20-79-90.
Gilead, I.
1986 The economic basis of Chalcolithic settlements in the northern Negev. *Michmanim* 3:17-30. (Hebrew)
1987 A new look at Chalcolithic Beer-sheba. *Biblical Archaeologist* 50:110-117.
1988 The Chalcolithic period in the Levant. *Journal of World Prehistory* 2:397-443.
Goldberg, P.
1987 The geology and stratigraphy of Shiqmim. In *Shiqmim I,* T.E. Levy (ed.), 35-43. Oxford: BAR International.Series.
Gopher, A., T. Tsuk, S. Shalev & R. Gophna
1990 Earliest gold artifacts discovered in the southern Levant. *Current Anthropology* 31:436-443.
Gophna, R.
1979 The process of settling the northwest Negev during the Chalcolithic period. In *The Land of the Negev: Man and Desert,* A. Shmouli and Y. Gordus (eds.), 203-208. Tel Aviv: Ministry of Defense, (Hebrew).
Goring-Morris, N. & A. Gopher
1983 Nahal Issaron: a Neolithic settlement in the southern Negev. *Israel Exploration Journal* 33:149-162.
Gosden, C.
1989 Debt, Production and Prehistory. *Journal of Anthropological Archaeology* 8:355-387.
Grigson, C.
1987a Shiqmim: Pastoralism and other aspects of animal management in the Chalcolithic of the northern Negev. In *Shiqmim I,* T. E. Levy (ed.), 219-241. Oxford: BAR International Series.
1987b Different herding strategies for sheep and goats in the Chalcolithic of Beersheva. *Archaeozoologia* I:115-126.
Hardin, G.
1968 The tragedy of the commons. *Science* 162:1243-48.
Harris, M.
1979 *Cultural Materialism.* New York: Random House.
1989 *Our Kind.* New York: Harper and Row.
Harrison, H. S.
1954 Fire-making, fuel and lighting. In *A History of Technology,* Vol. I, C. Singer, E. J. Holmyard and A. R. Hall (eds.), 216-237. Oxford: Clarendon Press.
Hauptman, A.
1989 The earliest period of copper metallurgy in Feinan, Jordan. In *Old World Archaeometallurgy,* A. Hauptman, E. Pernicka and G. A. Wagner (eds.), 119-135. Bochum: Selbstverlag des Deutschen Berghau-Museums.
Hauptman, A., G. Weisgerber & E. A. Knauf
1985 Archaometallurgische und bergbau-

archaologische untersungungen im Gebiet von Feinan, Wadi Arabah (Jordanien). *Der Anschnitt* 37:163-175.

Heskel, D. L.
1983 A model for the adoption of metallurgy in the Ancient Middle East. *Current Anthropology* 25:362-366.

Heskel, D. L. & C. C. Lamberg-Karlovsky
1980 An alternative sequence for the development of metallurgy: Tepe Yahya, Iran. In *The Coming of the Iron Age,* T. A. Wertime and J. D. Muhly (eds.), 229-265. New Haven: Yale University Press.

Hoffman, M. A.
1984 *Egypt before the Pharaohs: The Prehistoric Foundations of Egyptian Civilization.* London and Henley: Routledge and Kegan Paul.

Ilan, O. & M. Sabbane
1989 Copper metallurgy, trade and the urbanization of southern Canaan in the Chalcolithic and Early Bronze Age. In *L'urbanisation de la Palestine à l'Age du Bronze Ancien,* P. de Miroschedji (ed), 139-162. Oxford: BAR International Series.

Jacobsen, T.
1976 *Treasure of Darkness: A History of Mesopotamian Religion.* New Haven: Yale University Press.

Johnson, A. W. & T. Earle
1987 *The Evolution of Human Societies: from Foraging groups to agrarian state.* Stanford: Stanford University Press.

Kempinski, A.
1989 Urbanization and metallurgy in southern Canaan. In *L'urbanisation de la Palestine à l'Age du Bronze ancien,* P. de Miroschedji (ed.), 163-168. Oxford: BAR International Series.

Key, C. A.
1980 The trace element composition of the copper and copper alloys artifacts of the Nahal Mishmar hoard. In *The Cave of the Treasure,* P. Bar Adon, 238-243. Jerusalem: Israel Exploration Society.

Levy, T. E.
1983 The emergence of specialized pastoralism in the southern Levant. *World Archaeology* 15:15-36.
1986 The Chalcolithic period. *Biblical Archaeologist* 49:82-108.

Levy, T. E. & D. Alon
1987 Settlement patterns along the Nahal Beersheva-Lower Nahal Besor: models of subsistence in the northern Negev. In *Shiqmim I,* T.E. Levy (ed.), 45-138. Oxford: BAR International Series.

Levy, T. E. & A. Holl
1987 Theory and practice in household archaeology: a case study from the Chalcolithic village at Shiqmim. In *Shiqmim I,* T.E. Levy (ed.), 373-410. Oxford: BAR International Series.
1988 Les Premières chefferies de Palestine. In *La Recherche* 203:1166-74.

Levy, T. E. & S. Shalev
1989 Prehistoric metal working in the southern Levant: archaeometallurgy and social perspectives. *World Archaeology* 20:353-372.

Levy, T. E., D. Alon, P. Goldberg, C. Grigson, P. Smith, J. Buikstra, A. Holl, S. Rosen, S. Shalev, S. Ben Itzhak & A. Ben Yosef
1991 Protohistoric Investigations at the Shiqmim Chalcolithic village and cemetery: an interim report on the 1987 season. *Bulletin of the American School for Archaeological Research*: Supplement 27:29-46.

Marx, E.
1977 Bedouin pilgrimage to holy tombs in southern Sinai. *Notes on the Bedouin* VIII:14-22 (Hebrew).

Mauss, M.
1954 *The gift: forms and function of exchange in Archaic societies.* London: Routledge.

Moorey, P. R. S.
1988 The Chalcolithic hoard from Nahal Mishmar, Israel, in context. *World Archaeology* 20:171-189.

Perrot, J.
1955 The excavations at Tell Abu Matar. *Israel Exploration Journal* 5:17-41.
1984 Structures d'habitat, mode de vie et environnement: les villages souterrains des pasteurs de Beersheva dans le sud d'Israel au IVe millénaire avant l'ère chrétienne. *Paléorient* 10:75-96

Perrot, J. & D. Ladiray
1980 *Tombes à ossuaires de la région cotière Palestinienne au IVe millénaire avant l'ère chrétienne.* Paris: Association Paléorient.

Potaszkin, R. & K. Bar-Avi
1980 A material investigation of metal objects from the Nahal Mishmar Treasure. In *The Cave of the Treasure,* P. Bar Adon, 235-237. Jerusalem: Israel Exploration Society.

Quibell, J. E.
1900 *Hierakonpolis I.* London: Egypt Research

Account, IV.
1902 *Hierakonpolis II*. London: Egypt Research Account, V.

Rappaport, R. A.
1971 Nature, culture and ecological anthropology. In *Man, Culture and Society*, L. Shapiro (ed.), 237-267. New York: Oxford University Press.

Rollefson, G. & A. H. Simmons
1986 The 1985 season at Ain Ghazal: Preliminary report. *Annals of the Department of Antiquities of Jordan* 30: 41-56.

Roper, M. K.
1969 A survey of the evidence for intrahuman killing in the Pleistocene. *Current Anthropology* 10:427 - 59.
1975 Evidence for warfare in the Near East from 10,000 to 4,300 B.C. In *War: Its Causes and Correlates*, W. Nettleship, R. D. Givens and A. Nettleship (eds.), 299-340. The Hague, Paris: Mouton.

Rosen, S.
1984 The adoption of metallurgy in the Levant: a lithic perspective. Current *Anthropology* 25:504-505.
1986 The analysis of trade and craft specialization in the Chalcolithic period: comparisons from different realms of material culture. *Michmanim* 3:21-32.
1987 The potentials of lithic analysis in the Chalcolithic of the northern Negev. In *Shiqmim I*, T.E. Levy (ed.), 295-312. Oxford: BAR International Series.

Rowlands, M. J.
1971 The archaeological interpretation of prehistoric metalworking. *World Archaeology* 3:210-224.

Sabanne, M.
n.d. *Industrial and functional perspectives on Mace heads from the Potohistoric periods in Canaan*. MA Thesis. Jerusalem: the Hebrew University. (in prep.)

Sahlins, M.
1974 *Stone Age economics*. London: Tavistock.

Shalev, S., Y. Goren, T. E. Levy & P. J. Northover
1992 A Chalcolithic mace head from the Negev. Israel: Technological aspects and cultural implications. *Archaeometry* 34:63-71.

Shalev, S. & P. J. Northover
1987 The Chalcolithic metal and metalworking from Shiqmim. In *Shiqmim I*, T. E. Levy (ed.), 357-371. Oxford: BAR International Series.

Stekelis, M.
1935 *Les Monuments mégalithiques de Palestine*. Paris: Archives de l'Institut de Paleontologie Humaine.

Steward, J. H.
1955 *Theory of Culture Change*. Urbana: University of Illinois Press.

Sukenik, E. L.
1937 A Chalcolithic necropolis at Hadera. *Journal of the Palestine Oriental Society* 17:15-30.

Tadmor, M.
1989 The Judean desert Treasure from Nahal Mishmar: a Chalcolithic trader's hoard? In *Essays in Ancient Civilization presented to H.J. Kantor*, A. Leonard and B.B. Williams (eds.), 249-261. Chicago: Studies in Ancient Oriental Civilization 47.

Tosi, M.
1984 The notion of craft specialization and its representation in the archaeological record of early states in the Turanian basin. In *Marxist Perspectives in Archaeology*, M. Spriggs (ed.), 22-52. Cambridge: Cambridge University Press.

Tylecote, F. R.
1979 *A History of Metals*. London: The Metals Society.

Ucko, P. J.
1969 Ethnography and the archaeological interpretation of funerary remains. *World Archaeology* 1:262-280.

Yadin, Y.
1955 The earliest record of Egypt's military penetration into Asia? *Israel Exploration Journal* 5:1-16.
1963 *The Art of Warfare in Biblical Lands*. Jerusalem: International Publishing Company Inc.

6. Traditional Iron Technology and Settlement Patterns in Central Darfur

Ibrahim Musa

Introduction

The development of iron technology and the use of iron objects in central Darfur is an important subject which merits study in its own right. The adoption of iron technology may have played a dynamic social role, since its emergence was associated with archaeological material which indicates the earliest complex societies known there. However, given the paucity of the evidence and the vastness of the region concerned, a detailed study of the subject cannot be accomplished here. Instead, the relationship between iron technology and settlement patterns in the region will be considered. Of special interest is the acceptance of the technology by local groups and its impact on them. To achieve this, ethnographic observations, the historical record, and archaeological evidence will be used.

The Study Area

Darfur, where this research has been undertaken, derives its name from the Arabic, meaning home of the Fur, the proper name of a group of communities speaking the same language. It is the western-most region in the republic of Sudan and has an area of about 182,400 km^2. Its central part, the focus of this paper, is a flat area dotted with a few ranges of hills; the Tagabo Meidob, Furnong, and Marra. The last is the highest, being more than 3000 m above sea level, and is the watershed between the Nile and the Chad basins (Barbour 1961:170).

Annual rainfall is less than 100 mm in the north, increasing southward to more than 400 mm. In the north the vegetational cover is rather sparse, consisting mainly of semi-desert shrubs and a few trees such as *Balanites aegyptiaca*. In the south, and with increasing rainfall and/or altitude, the vegetational cover becomes denser and gradually merges into savannah vegetation of richer grass and taller trees such as *Acacia albida*. The fauna in the region includes hyena, lion, ostrich, and giraffe; and antelopes are found further south.

There is today a diversity of human societies exploiting varied natural resources in this region. In the north, one finds nomadic and semi-nomadic groups who breed camels and have, to a large extent, similar modes of life. These are the Zaghawa, the Meidob, and the Abala Arabic-speaking groups. The center, especially the highlands, is inhabited by sedentary agriculturalists such as the Fur, Maslit, Tama, Tunjur, Berti, and Daju (further south). Most of them have retained their original languages but speak Arabic as a second one. These groups cultivate grain (millet and sorghum). In the south there are cattle nomads, including the Arabic-speaking Rezzigat, Bani Halba, and peoples speaking Fullani and Gimr (Fig. 1).

Iron-producing Settlements of Central Darfur

Although the writer studied several iron-using settlements which had been radiometrically dated between 300 and 1000 A.D., the focus here will be on the three sites where evidence of iron production was found (Musa 1986:177). They comprise the first early iron production sites to be excavated in the Darfur. It seems that the major factor in the development of iron-using settlements in central Darfur was progressive expansion of the desert as result of climatic changes. This must have affected indigenous people living in this marginal area where there were no permanent rivers and may have pushed them to areas of more water, for example the volcanic/Nubian sandstone hills of the Jabal Marra, the Si, the Tagado and the Meidob. These areas provided the crucial advantages of reliable rainfall and variations of climate conducive to the cultivation of wide range of crops. Other advantages were the availability of iron ore and the fuel for working the metal, and the naturally fortified rocky areas of the hills. The movement of people might have been helped by the use of the horse and the camel, the figures of both of which were found depicted on rock surfaces within early settlements and are believed to have been contemporary with the other remains at these sites (Musa 1986:174). All these settlements are located on isolated hilltops amid

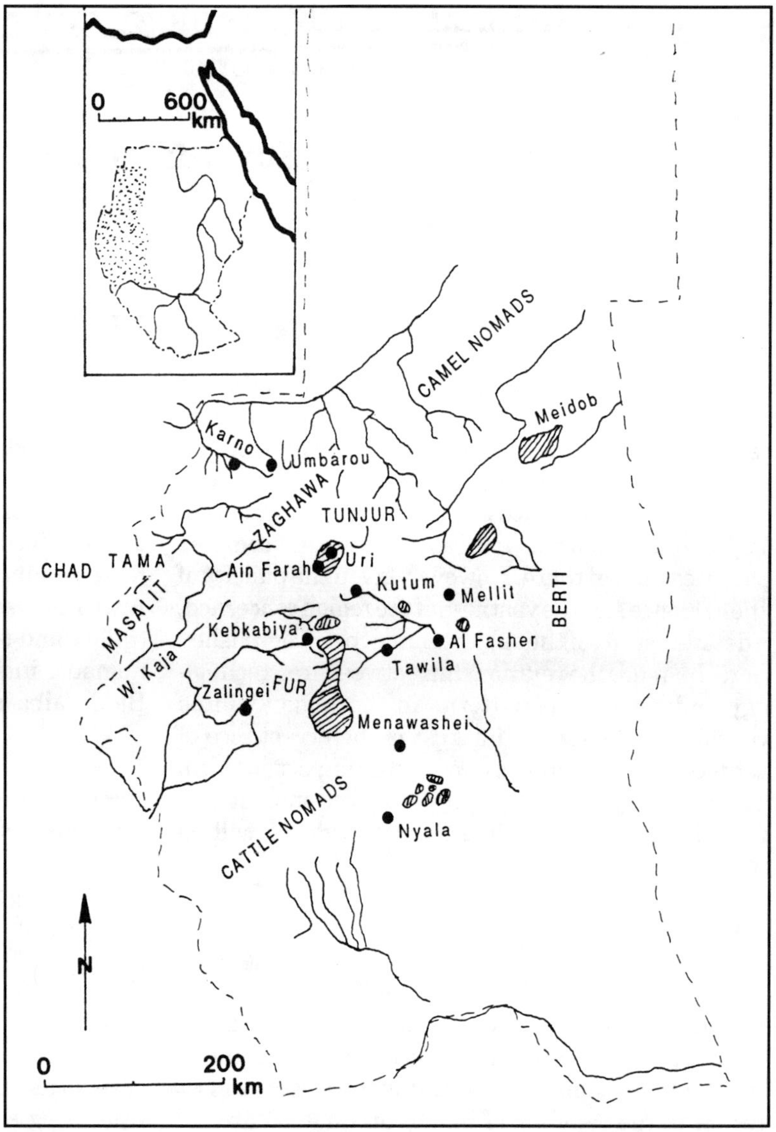

Fig. 1. Central Darfur: location map and distribution of ethnic groups and major settlements.

surrounding plains. They are all naturally defensible, and some have man-made fortifications. The artifacts suggest that the occupants were sedentary agriculturalists.

Structural remains are usually found spread all over the hills from the top to the foot. In each settlement four residential structures were defined in basic units according to size and elaboration, together with structures for communal purposes:

(1) single-room houses without any connection with other structures,

(2) double-room houses directly connected with each other, being with or without enclosures,

(3) compound houses composed of three or more rooms usually having a single enclosing wall,

(4) complex houses (of type 2 or 3) within a single wall, but separated from each other by small walls,

(5) public buildings, irrigation terraces, wells, cemeteries, huge platform granaries, animal pens, and massive defensive walls.

Jabal Mao Settlement

This settlement lies on the northeastern part of the Tagabo hills. In the southwestern part near the foot of the hill is a man-made curving wall about 3 m high and 2 m wide running north-south and joining two small hills together, but there is no wall round the whole settlement (Fig. 2).

Four types of houses were found inside the enclosed area. All, except a group in the iron-working area, were constructed on a double-wall system, with an inner and an outer dry stone wall and the gap between them filled with rubble. The courses of the

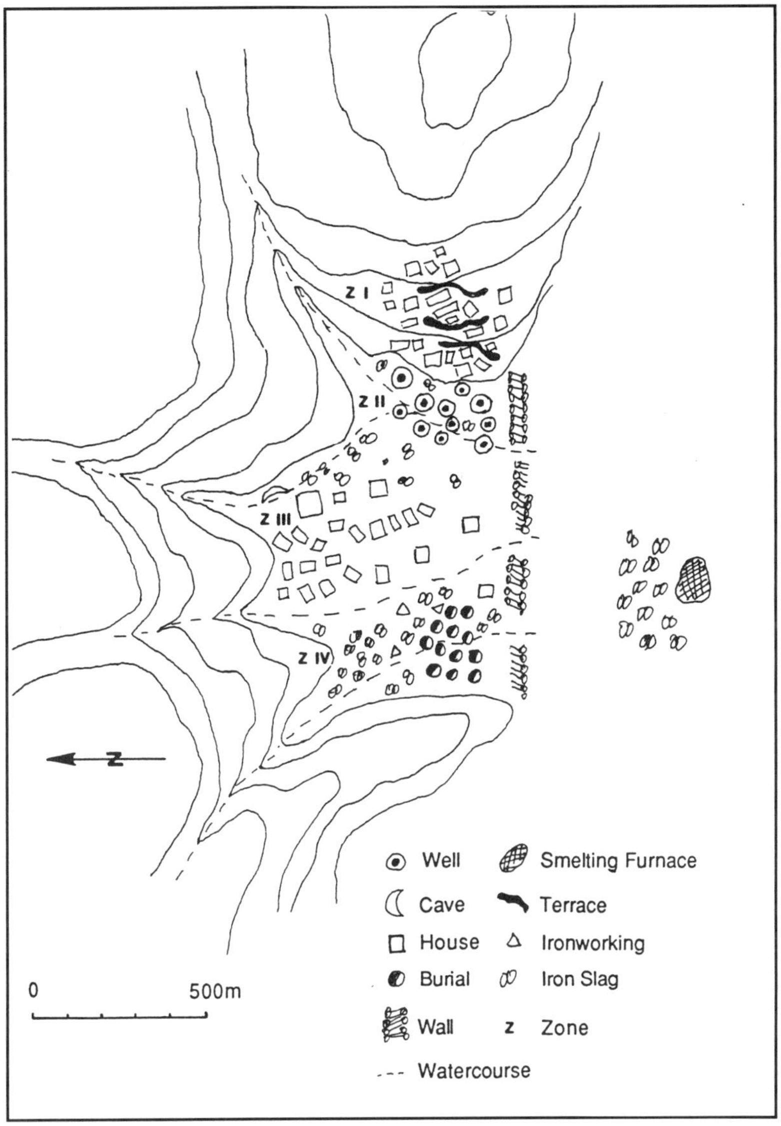

Fig. 2. Jabal Mao: settlement and iron-working area.

walls were held together in horizontal rows by bonding techniques. The walls were constructed without underground foundations. The majority of these houses at least 1200, were of single-unit type. They were spread all over the hill covering an area of about 3 km^2. Some 90 double-room units, 20 compound houses, and 2 complex ones were located. The spatial distribution of the houses does not seem to follow a specific pattern, but it has been noticed that the compound houses were concentrated in the central and the upper part of the settlement. Each complex house had a single-unit house in front of its gate. About ten animal pens of circular shapes, each of less than 2 m diameter were located. Some 25 granaries which had no doorway, being only accessible from the top, were found. A cemetery covering at least 70 x 50 m was located at the southeastern end of the settlement. The excavation of four graves showed that the bodies were laid in contracted position, and some of them had iron objects and bone beads as grave goods. Within this area some iron slag was also uncovered. A group of 17 wells was found in the central part of the settlement. They had been dug in the bed of the wadi; 16 were circular in shape, on average 0.65 m in diameter and 20 m deep. Well 17, which had a rectangular mouth of 2 x 7 m, was 19 m deep.

The characteristic type of Mao pottery is mat-impressed (Farish), with rough untreated surfaces; a few sherds have glossy brown burnishing on the outside and rough inside surfaces. Iron objects uncovered in Moa include: a hoe with a long neck and short socket, two reaping knives, one bracelet and a number of fragments, most probably part of anklets.

Beyond the enclosing wall, 200 m south of the main settlement, 25 iron furnaces were located. All of them were circular in shape and about 70 cm deep.

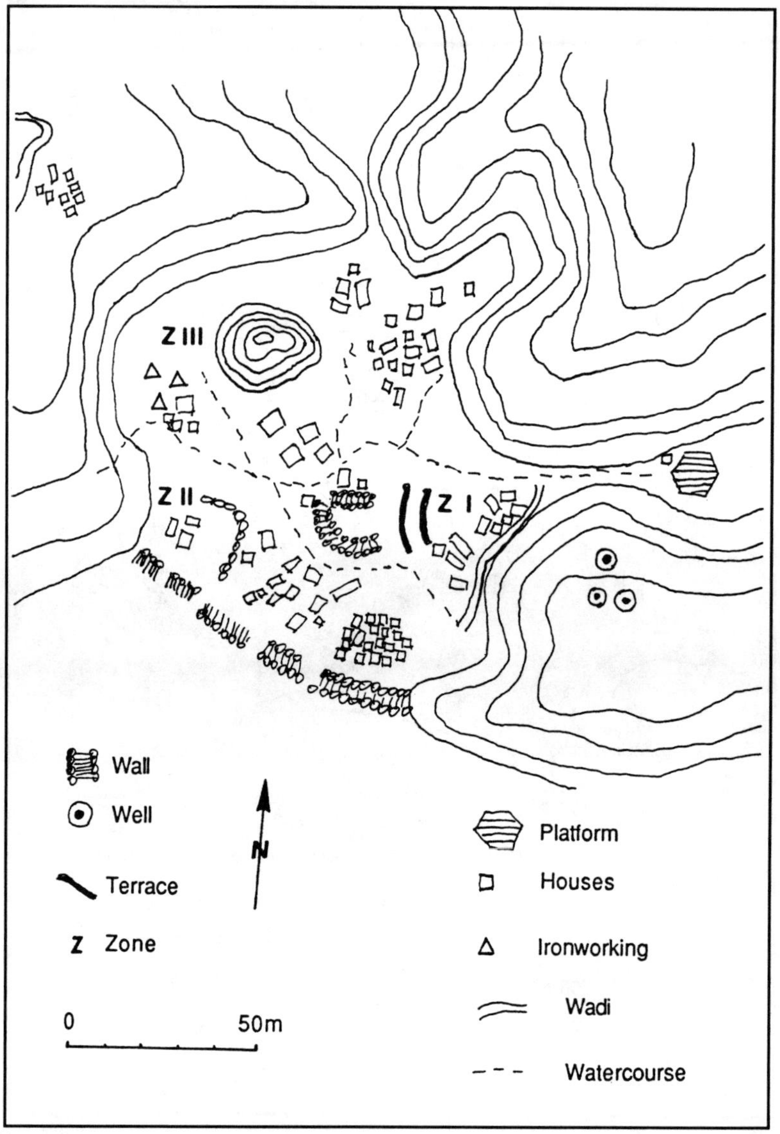

Fig. 3. Jabal Wina: settlement and iron-working area.

Inside the furnaces iron slag was loaded with charcoal in alternate layers; probably they were packed in this manner and then the whole fired with grass. Many small heaps of iron slag were found distributed in an irregular manner. A charcoal sample from one of these furnaces was radiometrically dated to 1050 ± 30 A.D.. More than 200 single-unit houses were found in this iron-producing area, constructed in a completely different way from the other houses at Mao, being made of rows of stone slabs set upright in a foundation trench and with single walls of poorer construction than the double-wall houses of the main settlement.

Jabal Wina Settlement

Jabal Wina was a walled settlement built in the southwestern part of the Simiat hills and dated to the first millennium A.D. (Fig. 3). It comprised the same four types of housing units as Jabal Mao. More than 350 single-unit houses were found scattered within the enclosing walls. Some of them were located in front of the main gates of compounds. About 25 double-room houses were found spread throughout the area. Some 15 compound houses were found, but only one complex house was located. A large circular animal pen to keep goats and cattle, measuring 20 m in diameter was located at the center of the village. At the eastern end of the settlement, at the foot of Jabal Wina, a platform and one single-room house were also located. The platform, isolated without any enclosing wall, was 10 m in diameter and 2 m in height, retained by dry stone masonry walls of seven courses. The lower courses were wider than the upper ones, and the top was levelled to form a circular area. This was constructed in the same manner as that of Mabo in the Tagabo range (Musa 1986:184). Three circular wells were located in a depression to the east of the platform. They were not lined with stone but dug directly through bedrock. Only a few potsherds decorated with mat impressions and tempered with organic matter were found. In an isolated part at the southeastern end of the settlement a group of single-unit houses containing iron slag was found, and numerous pieces of slag were also found scattered around them. They indicated an area of iron production.

Bora Settlement

Bora lies at the northwestern end of the Jabal Si range. This undefended settlement occupies a flat area in a naturally fortified region (Fig. 4). It has been shown by a radiometric date to be 560±30 A.D.. Like the previous two settlements, four types of houses were located here. Some 600 single houses were found distributed all over the settlement area, but the majority were clustered in the west. More than 60 double-room houses with enclosures were found spread all over the area. About 30 compound houses and a single complex house were found only in the western part. A cemetery occupying an area of 40 x 30 m was found at the southwestern edge of the settlement. In two test excavations in this cemetery, the bodies were found to be laid in a contracted position, with iron, bone, and copper objects. The most common pottery found at Bora had rough, untreated internal and external surfaces mostly decorated with mat impressions (Brish). Among the iron objects found, two were reaping knives with right angle bends at each end, an iron rod with a pointed end, three double edge knives, a number of bracelets, two anklets, and more than 300 iron beads. An area where iron working was practised was located in the southern part of the settlement. A number of pieces of slag were found scattered in this isolated area. A test excavation showed a 10 cm deep layer of slag, but no intact furnaces were found. Houses with extensive hearths were found in this area.

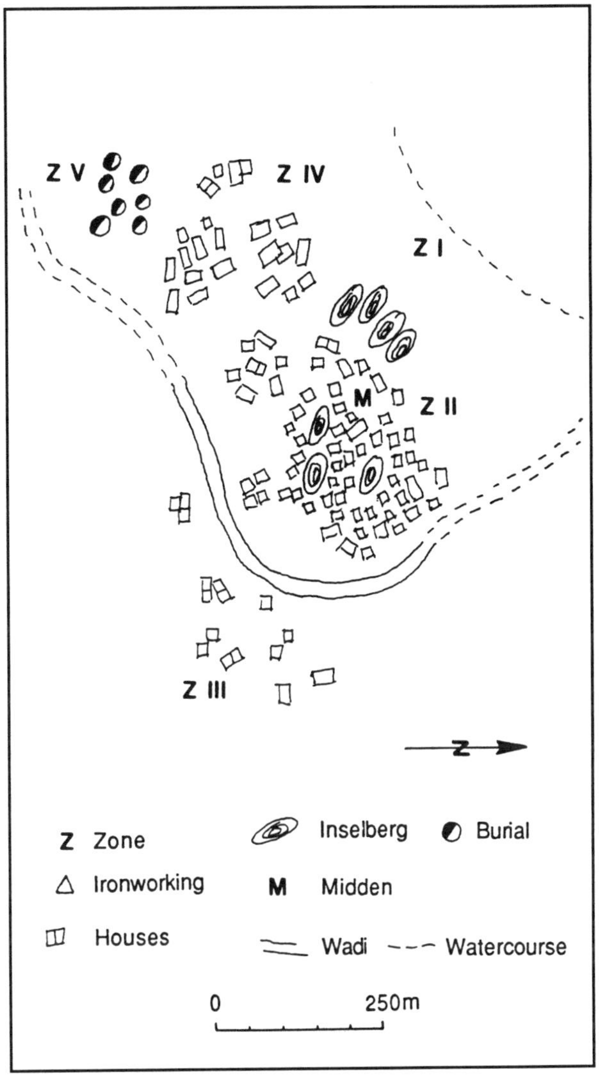

Fig. 4. Jabal Bora: settlement and iron-working area.

The Communities

The location and pattern of distribution of the residential units and communal features in these three generally contemporary settlements show the existence of structured societies. Each had a pyramid of authority culminating in a small elite, around which were different ranks forming the basis of a political unit. Four levels which structured the societies of the occupants, common to all the settlements discussed in this chapter, can be inferred from the structural remains as follows:

(1) Individuals of very high status who were housed in complex structures may be considered as rulers. They were probably responsible for the general organization and distribution of the community.

(2) Individuals of high but subordinate status who may have been officials or soldiers were housed in compound houses.

(3) The general population probably occupied single houses. Some of these houses were apparently

for minor specialists such as guards, as they were located outside the gates for regulating and controlling access to the settlement; others may have been for craft specialists such as bead makers and builders.

(4) An isolated group of perhaps the lowest status of all, if recent evidence is significant, comprised iron workers and potters (since this is usually the craft of their wives). Their houses were of simple construction, built in isolated and separate parts of the settlements.

(5) Cemeteries in two cases are on the southwestern side of the settlement, with the same burial fashion and similar bone beads. This could be taken as a possible indication of similar burial rites.

Discussion

The recurrence of the same pattern of location of iron-production areas and, presumably, the houses of the smiths in isolated parts on these settlements, more than 150 km apart (Fig. 1), raises interesting questions. The most important one concerns the spatial location of the iron industry and the social position of its producers. Such a question may not be readily answerable from archaeological considerations alone, but a study of ethnographic data may be helpful in this regard. This is because many aspects of iron production and other craft specializations closely associated with it—such as pottery—did not change for many centuries in the area, and environmental conditions have remained the same since iron was adopted there.

Technically, it has been revealed that there are striking similarities between the iron furnaces excavated by the writer and the ones in use in the 19th century and early 20th century A.D. before the advent of the industrially produced iron (Haaland 1980:40; Musa 1986:131). Iron objects excavated by the writer and those which were collected from archaeological sites by previous researchers (Arkell 1937:306-307, 1952, 1966; Musa 1986:133-134) are very similar to those described by early travellers (Browne 1799:267; Al Tunisi 1845) and ones currently in use in the area, even though the last group is made of scrap from modern industrially produced iron. Thus, it seems that iron technology in Darfur has remained relatively static for the last few centuries, and may have been so for a longer time.

Socially, there is a general consensus among researchers that smiths were despised by the communities in which they lived. They are an isolated, hereditary caste and did not mix with non-smith members of their societies (Macmichael 1922, Vol. I:89; Nachtigal 1971:175; Al Tunisi 1845:304-305). Moreover, no members of the non-smith families would have marital relations with them (Musa 1986). Thus, iron technology and pottery have been carried out in a traditional way by a stigmatized group isolated from the rest of the population. This social discrimination against smiths has been attributed to their mixed tribal origin and bad social behavior, and sometimes they were feared because of their presumed ability to transform themselves into animals (Haaland 1980; Macmichael 1922).

In 1981, as a part of an archaeological project, the writer reviewed the social position of the smith. His study in the main confirmed and added to earlier evidence. He concluded that smiths are more despised among nomadic pastoral groups than among sedentary agriculturalists. The former regard the smiths as inferior persons, and any contact with them would cause contamination. This is especially so among the Zaghawa nomads, who regarded smiths as polluted from birth and felt that any interaction with them would cause contamination (Tigani 1982:42). However, smiths are less despised and more respected among sedentary agriculturalists such as the Berti and the Fur. These communities do not despise the smith, at least overtly, and have some contacts with them. For example, on social occasions smiths mix with members of these two ethnic groups, e.g., eating together and/or dancing with them.

In general, attitudes towards the smiths and potters are today expressed in two ways: (a) smith houses and iron-producing areas are located at a distance from the main village (usually in the southern part), (b) marriages between smith and non-smith families are very rare. Smiths therefore marry the daughters of smiths within their kin group, who are always potters. It is thus clear from the ethnographic observations that there is a pattern of social behavior towards the smiths and the potters in which the society accepts the technology, while it despises those who produce it. This is not true for the bead makers or weavers who can freely intermarry with other families.

Summary of Archaeological Evidence

The isolation of the smith's residence and working area is very important because it indicates social behavior in a material way. This can be seen as one ethnographic situation which could be tested archaeologically. If isolated smiths' residences and working areas could be identified in peripheral areas, as opposed to a non-smith group in a central area within a single settlement, then a differentiation between the two groups on the basis of social status could presumed. If this is accepted, then the restriction of iron-working remains to specific areas in the archaeological sites described above exemplifies a rather low status for the smith, which has existed in central Darfur since the introduction of iron working. Smiths may have originally belonged to a different ethnic group from the rest of the population. However, since they had no communal structural remains of their own (such as wells and cemeteries), they must have joined with others for matters concerning the community as a whole. Therefore, it could be suggested that, despite apparent social discrimination against the smiths, they were always accepted in a limited way within settlements of sedentary agriculturalists. In the rest of this chapter, further evidence will be considered to see if the ethnographic examples can throw some light on the interpretation of the archaeological record, with special emphasis on the acceptance of iron technology and its impact on communities in central Darfur.

The Beginning of Iron-using

Darfur has often been considered the bridge between the Nile and Chad basins through which iron technology was transmitted from Meroe to West Africa during the Meroitic or Christian eras (Arkell 1951:1962). This postulate is refuted by the recent radiometric dates which suggest that the West African iron technology is as old as that of Meroe and had a different type of smelting technology. Hence, its knowledge cannot be of Meroitic origin (Mauny 1978:27; Posnansky and McIntosh 1976:169; Tylecote 1983:63; Grebenart 1985). Because Darfur shows many archaeological and ethnographic affinities with areas to the west or north, the writer is of the opinion that iron technology came to Darfur from the west or north, and the finding of camel remains in Egypt dating to the 9th century B.C. suggests that such trans-desert connections were possible (Rowley Conwy 1988:93). It should be pointed out that, at this stage of knowledge, there is no evidence to suggest that iron technology was locally invented in Darfur. However, there are many forces which (despite possible constraints) push people to adopt a new technology, such as iron working, which is useful, e.g., for agricultural tools, building equipment, prestige objects, and weapons. These uses may have induced indigenous peoples to use iron and probably to accept immigrant smiths to work among them. This may have happened, hypothetically, through individual contacts in one or more of the ways discussed below. However, it should be remembered that the models used in this paper are based on ethnographic data and that the coming of iron technology and the relationship between smiths and local people in the beginning of their contact might not have been as simple a process as the one illustrated by the ethnographic examples.

Mass Migration

A major factor in the history of the Darfur is the progressive expansion of the Sahara as a result of climatic change. In a marginal area such as the one under discussion, where there are no permanent rivers, there is always the risk that temporary deterioration of climatic regimes may push people to areas of more water. This could have been a factor which pushed some people to the volcanic/Nubian sandstone hills (of more reliable rainfall and arable land) within Darfur such as the Jabal Marra, Jabal Si, the Tagabo and the Meidob hills, as havens of safety from immigrants expanding onto the surrounding plains. Small refugee populations may band together in the hills or be incorporated into existing dominant groups, e.g., the Berti or the Fur. It is therefore possible that large-scale movement of people southwards, due to the deterioration of climatic conditions (Musa 1986:139), had shifted some iron-using nomadic or semi-nomadic people and brought them into contact with indigenous peoples in Darfur. The latter may have learned iron technology from the former (probably mainly by acquiring finished tools through some form of exchange at the initial stage). This hypothetical mass movement should not be seen as a permanent population upheaval, but as a seasonal one, from which most communities would have returned to their original homes whenever the situation permitted in a way similar to the movements caused by the draught of the 1970's and 1985-1986.

Small scale Migration

For the spread of a complex technology such as iron working, skillful craftsmen and local resources are required. Hence, knowledge could have been introduced to the area by small groups or even single families (Trigger 1968:44) of specialized craftsmen moving south looking for fuel and ores for their industry, pasture for their animals, and security for themselves. They might well have been nomadic or semi-nomadic groups (not necessarily from the same ethnic background) familiar with the Sahel area and its surroundings, driven from their original homelands by deteriorating climatic conditions or political factors. They were probably moving from one area to another, working iron for people in their own localities before settling with specific groups. The recipient groups would have been sedentary agriculturalists who may have welcomed smiths because they needed iron tools and weapons. In contrast, nomadic/pastoralist groups, who today have strong negative attitudes towards smiths and their products, are less influenced, needing only weapons, which for many centuries could be obtained, and of better quality, from a distance. Hence, smiths may always have been less welcomed among such groups.

In this model of small scale migration, the economic and cultural values of iron may have resulted in the acceptance of the smith within society (Alexander 1980:327). This suggestion can further be strengthened by ethnographic examples of change and adaptation to different modes of life among groups within this marginal zone when pressed by economic and/or ecological factors. The culture of one group can be affected by members of different groups in varying degrees, sometimes to the extent of completely changing modes of daily life. A good example in this regard is given by some Fur sedentary agriculturalists who abandoned their sedentary occupation in favor of cattle nomadism (Haaland 1979:72; O'Fahey 1980:8). This may have been one of the ways through which semi-nomadic groups (including smiths) in what is now desert north of the Sahel became completely nomadic and moved further south.

However, of more relevance to the model of small scale migration are the following two examples, which illustrate how small nomadic groups settle among sedentary agriculturalists when pushed by climatic factors. The former may have been accepted by the latter because they were useful, and most of them never went back to nomadism, though some may feel some nostalgia for it.

(1) Some Zaghawa people, reported by Tobert (1983) to have given up camel nomadism because of the failure of pasture caused by worsening climatic conditions and who became completely sedentary in the Fur area of Jabal Marra/Si, were interviewed by the writer in 1982. Those who came fifteen years ago first worked as laborers for the Fur, who owned the land, but now they cultivate the land and share the crop with the Fur owners. Although they speak Fur and dress like the members of the Fur communities, no cases of marriage between them and members of the Fur have yet been reported.

(2) A few members of the Meidob camel nomads have given up their original occupation (when they no longer had sufficiently animals for herding) and joined the sedentarized Berti, accepting the latter's modes of life and regulations (Musa 1986:139). They were accepted among the Berti because they are useful agricultural laborers (Holy 1974:83). However, it is very difficult, if not impossible, for a man from the immigrant Meidob to marry a Berti girl. The very rare cases in which such marriage occurs were through the court, without the consent of the women's parents (Holy 1974:77). Because such marriage is never accepted by the local community, the couple usually moves away to towns, where people are less strict about such norms.

These examples show that nomadic smiths may have adopted agriculture, and when they proved to be useful were accepted by the agrarian community. However, it should be noted that the skills of the smiths and the importance of iron may have made them more welcome than ordinary people working as laborers.

If these ethnographic examples are accepted, then they may be taken as possible indications of the process through which iron technology was spread in central Darfur by people whose occupations were different from those of the recipients. These people would have been welcomed because they were needed, even though they may not have been completely assimilated within the host society. They may have found it advantageous to adopt the overt habits of their hosts, such as dress, religion, and language, which would have established good relations between them and their new community, helped them to raise their prestige, and probably provided them with protection.

Ironically, blacksmiths today are not accepted socially by nomadic groups, perhaps because they are not needed greatly and because they they are known to non-smith nomadic groups to come from "inferior" backgrounds. Moreover, it is possible that they are regarded as inferior because they changed their identity, an act which is considered very shameful among the nomads. However, the fact that marriage to smiths is very rare among both pastoral and agricultural societies could, hypothetically, be explained by regarding this as a method of controlling smiths and confining their industries and their wives to a certain group. Because of the great importance of iron technology, it was probably kept secret at the beginning (Trigger 1967:28), under tight control by those who monopolized it. Hence, social constraints may have been imposed deliberately by the elite of the host communities on those who worked iron, in order to isolate them socially by casting doubt on their origin and presenting them as an inferior group, thus stopping them from intermingling with non-smith groups and so preventing the spread of the technology to those who did not possess it. This probably prevented smiths from gaining access to power by being mixed with powerful families (Hodder 1982:90). This could have been effective in impeding the spread of iron technology, as distinct from finished iron objects, which could have been spread through other channels such as trade. Although social constraint confines the flow of technological innovation to a certain group, it ensures the continuation of production within such a group and protects them economically. Probably because of such restriction, iron technology and pottery making have remained unchanged in the area for a long time. All these points suggest that the question the diffusion, as well as invention, of iron using and/or technology is a complicated one which needs to be investigated within its local context, since local conditions and social behavior may have hindered or facilitated these processes (Alexander 1980:328).

Political Actions

Most of the iron-using sites in Darfur, especially the iron-producing ones, are located in a naturally fortified areas, and the settlements associated with them, two of the three studied in this chapter, were defended by man-made fortifications. This has been taken as an indication that there was lack of security, and that could be a factor which induced sedentary communities there to adopt iron technology. Although there is very little archaeological evidence indicating warfare in the region in the first millennium A.D., scenes of warriors armed with what are probably iron weapons are found depicted at several rock art stations in central Darfur. Some of these drawings were found at the same sites as remains of early iron working—in settlements such as Jabal Mao. This suggests that iron weapons were important in central Darfur as early as the first millennium A.D.. It was probably owing to the need for superior weapons that the local groups were induced to adopt iron technology. Smiths may have been recruited peacefully or forcibly by political groups in the area. It has been suggested on the basis of anthropological evidence and linguistic research that smiths were discriminated against among the Zaghawa of Darfur because they were slaves taken by the Zaghawa in their wars (more probably raids) with Bornu further west (Tigani 1982:44). It is known historically that Sultan Ahmed Bkur (in the 18th century) recruited skilled craftsmen from the west to work in Darfur, and this may have been a long standing tradition (Balfour 1956:24).

Currency and Hunting

Iron objects were used in the 18–19th centuries as currency in Darfur. Hoes were used as currency at Jadid Ras al Fil in Darfur in the beginning of the 19th century (Al-Tunisi 1845:320). A curved iron tool very similar to a hoe was used as currency around Lake Chad in the 18th century (Denham et al. 1814:95). In the 18th century in Kordofan, not only iron bars but also miniature hoes were used as a basis for exchange (MacMichael 1911:67). These examples suggest that iron objects were not only trading items to be used but were also valued as a currency. This may have enhanced the spread of iron within the region.

Some of the rock drawings mentioned above show horse riders armed with what may have been iron weapons, hunting giraffe and ostrich. This may be taken as an indication that hunting was one of the major reasons for the adoption of iron weapons, for iron working in this zone, during the last two hundred years has been closely associated with hunting. Both were carried out together in Darfur and Chad by blacksmiths who as professional hunters followed game for long distances (Al-Tunisi 1845:250; Huard 1966). This might be taken as a possible indication of the process through which knowledge of iron came to Darfur from the area further west.

Conclusions: the Impact of Iron Technology

Because of the similarities described above between the remains of early iron objects and those of modern times, it is suggested that they have played similar roles. Consequently, analogy between objects found in excavated contexts and their ethnographic parallels will be used to infer the impact of iron technology. In such a harsh environment as central Darfur, iron must have offered great ecological advantages to its users, especially in the field of agriculture. This is suggested by the excavated iron agricultural tools: the hoes and reaping knives. The evidence of hoes found in settlements in highland areas suggests that the settlers may have also exploited sandy lowland areas, since such hoes are best suited to sandy plains. This suggestion may be strengthened by the fact that agricultural practices and land tenure in Darfur have remained unchanged for at least two hundred years (O'Fahey 1980:180). Iron could have been useful for digging wells in an area where, to many people, water is life itself. Any shortage of water, even for a short period of time, had and still has disastrous consequences. Iron also could have been used for quarrying stones for building such huge structures as the platforms at Mao and Wima. This may indicate that iron using was associated with new trends in building techniques in Darfur. Iron using also may have played a major role in the development of settlements in the area in the following two ways: Firstly, in areas such as Mao, where iron ore was abundant, it attracted settlers to exploit it (Haaland 1980:43). This is shown by the large number of furnaces and the numerous mounds of slag in the area. Secondly, in some cases, when the settlers have exhausted the natural resources for iron working (fuel and ore) in one place, they may move to another, and this may have caused migration, especially in areas where trees are scarce and there is little or no variation in species. This suggestion is strengthened by a recent experimental study carried out in Darfur, which suggests that traditional iron technology requires a great amount of wood and hence causes massive deforestation (Haaland 1985:63).

Iron-using settlements in the area suggest communities with hierarchical social structure, which show signs of urban ways of life and state formation. In Mao, Bora, and Wima there are indications of elites who ruled from large population centers. They were probably responsible for the control and distribution of resources in the area (including iron production). The rock drawings show that those who possessed iron in the area were probably able to subdue their rivals and even to enslave them (Musa 1986:175). In historical times, iron played a significant role in the development of states such as Wadai and the Keira Sultanate of Darfur. They were both able to expand and to annex new groups to their territories because of the superiority of their iron equipment, including chain mail (O'Fahey 1983:92-98). This was very effective when coupled with the use of horses and probably helped considerably in the process of urbanization and state formation.

Iron objects have been used for the last two centuries as symbols of prestige. The Berti who inhabited the area have a reaping knife as a symbol of authority, and such signs have been found drawn in Mao cave associated with figures believed to date to the first millennium A.D. (Musa 1985). Under the Keira Sultans an iron spear was an important item of regalia, and iron throwing knives were used in the Nadinga ceremony, which was one of the most important Keira ceremonies for the installation of new sultans. The throwing knives were carried by senior royal ladies who clashed them to produce a special sound during the ceremony. Until 1916, an iron axe was handed annually to a sultan by the Malik al Hadadin (Chief Smith) to cut a branch of a tree as a symbolic gesture to declare the beginning of the agricultural season in the hope of securing a good harvest. Iron also seems, because it was used for grave goods at Ain Farah and Bora, to have had ritual significance in pre-Islamic times in the area. The use of iron in spiritual contexts can be confirmed by ethnographic as well as historical evidence. Perhaps iron was used for keeping away evil spirits. The writer was informed by Abu Katuring of Bora in 1980 that a few people still use it for this purpose in Jabal Si.

The economic importance of iron production can be seen in the taxes levied by both the Sultanates of Wadai and Darfur, which ranged to about 20 percent of iron production. In the latter sultanate, it is said that taxes were levied not only on finished iron tools but that the iron ore of Jabal Tayu was also taxed (Haaland 1986:54). The amounts of slag suggest that iron working was undertaken on a large scale. Such production may have played a significant role in the economy of Mao and its contemporary Tagabo settlements. The distribution of iron remains suggests that production was carried out in specific areas, perhaps in the first millennium A.D. by organized groups within the communities. Such restriction of iron-working remains to special areas in the surveyed sites suggests a rather low status for the smith and may be taken as the beginning of an endogamous group in central Darfur societies as early as that time.

References

Alexander, J. A.

1980 The spread and the development of iron using in Europe and Africa, In *Proceedings of the 8th Panafrican Congress of Prehistory and Quaternary Sciences*. Leakey, R. E. and B. A. Ogot (eds.), 327-330. Nairobi.

Arkell, A. J.

1937a An extinct Darfur hoe. *Sudan notes and records* XX (I):146-150.

1937b The Tigda or reaping knife in Darfur. *Sudan notes and records* XX(II):306-307.

1952 History of Darfur A.D. 1200-1700 *Sudan notes and records* XXXII-XXXIII.

1966 The Iron Age in the Sudan C*urrent Anthropology* 7:451-2, 469-84.

Barbour, K. M.

1961 *The Republic of Sudan*.London: University of London Press.

Browne, W. G.

1799 *Travels in Egypt, Syria and Africa* (second edition 1806). London: Longman and Rees.

Conwy, R.

1988 Early radiocarbon accelerator dates for

camels from Qasr Ibrim *Sahara* 1:93.

Denham D. Clapperton & Oudney

1826 *Narrative of Travels and Discoveries in Northern and Central Africa in the yaers 1822, 1823 and 1824*. London, 2 vols.

Haaland, G.

1969 Economic determinism in ethnic process. In *Ethnic groups and Boundaries*. Barth, F. (ed.), 58-73. Boston: Little Brown and Company.

Haaland, R.

1978 Ethnographic observation of pottery making in Western Sudan with some reflections on archaeological interpretation *Studies in Scandinavian Prehistory and Early History* 1:47-61.

1980 Man's role in the changing habitat of Mema during the Old kingdom of Ghana *Norwegian Archaeological Review* 13(1):31-46.

1985 Iron production; its socio-cultural context and ecological implications. In *African Iron Working: Ancient and Traditional*, R. Haaland and P. Shinnie (eds.), 50-72. Bergen: Norwegian University Press.

Hodder, I.

1982 *The Present Past: An Introduction to Anthropology for Archaeologists*. London: Batsford Press.

Holy, L.

1974 *Neighbours and Kinsmen: A study of the Berti People of Darfur*. London:Hurst.

Huard, P.

1966 Introdcution et diffusion du fer au Tchad. *Journal de la Société des Africanistes* VII(3):377-404.

MacMichael, H. A.

1912 *The Tribes of Northern and Central Kordofan*. Cambridge: Cambridge University Press.

1922 *The History of the Arabs in the Sudan*. Cambridge: Cambridge University Press.

Mauny, R.

1978 Trans-Saharan contact and the Iron Age in West Africa. In *The Cambridge History of West Africa* Vol. 2, J. D. Fage (ed.), 272-341. Cambridge: Cambridge University Press.

Musa-Mohamed, I.

1986 *The Archaeology of Central Darfur in the first millenium A.D.*. Oxford: B.A.R. International Series.

Nachtigal, G.

1971 *Sahara and Sudan*, Vol. 4. London: Hurst.

O'Fahey, R. S.

1980 *State and Society in Darfur*. London: Hurst.

Tobert, N.

1983 *Fire as fuel: blacksmith and potters of Darfur*. London.

Posnansky, M. & R. J. MacIntosh

1976 New radiocarbon dates for northern and Western Africa. *Journal of African History* XVII(2):161-194.

Trigger, B. G.

1968 *Beyond History: the methods of prehistory*. New York.

1969 The myth of Meroe and the African Iron Age. *African Historical Studies* 2(1):23-50.

Tunisi, al M. O.

1845 *Voyage au Darfur*. Paris.

1851 *Voyage au Ouadday*. Paris.

Tylecote, R. F.

1975 The origin of iron smelting in Africa. *West African Journal of Archaeology* 5:1-9.

7. Late Neolithic Cultural Landscape in Southeastern Mauritania: An Essay in Spatiometrics

Augustin Holl

Prologue

In the Dhar Tichitt-Walata region of southeastern Mauritania, the impressive Neolithic sites characterized by massive dry masonry have become famous in West African archaeology primarily because of the discovery of macro-botanical remains in potsherds by P.J. Munson (1971, 1976). This discovery, later supported by additional findings (Amblard and Pernès 1989), has been used to support the idea of local domestication of bulrush millet (*Pennisetum sp.*), whose cultivation went along with the opportunistic exploitation of wild grains. The Neolithic occupation of this arid area of sandstone cliffs lasted from ca. 4000 B.P. to 2000 B.P., and different competing models have been used to explain the processes which may best explain the nature and characteristics of the archaeological record observed (Amblard 1984; Munson 1981; Holl 1985a, 1986a, 1986b, 1989; 1990). In general, there is a consensus on two elementary issues:

1) The Neolithic communities inhabiting important villages built with dry stone masonry techniques practised mixed farming based on grain cultivation and the animal husbandry of cattle, sheep and goats.

2) Their subsistence was complemented by fishing of nile perch (*Lates niloticus*) and siluridae (*Clarias sp.*), hunting of gazelles, antelopes, hippopotamus, etc., and the gathering of wild grains and fruits. These general statements, derived from the study of material culture items such as stone and bone tools, pottery, rock art, plant and animal remains collected during many field campaigns, are obviously very limited in scope if we wish to understand and explain the diversity and variability of patterns of past behavior which have generated the impressive archaeological record observed in the southwestern Sahara today. In this chapter, I emphasize the fact that the study of larger quantities of material culture data alone will not lead to sophisticated and genuine explanations of Neolithic socioeconomic organization, nor of its settlement dynamics, congruent with what we expect from archaeological research today. As pointed out by Renfrew (1984:3), in studying the human past it is not enough simply to reconstruct what happened. Reconstruction is indeed one of the legitimate concerns of the historian and the archaeologist, and a necessary preliminary to further analysis, but we need to know more. We need to understand in some sense *how* and *why* it happened. We have to discern some pattern, to identify some simplifying principles. We have to decide what is significant for us.

> Without new methods of analysis, archaeological theory could not expand efficiently, since a modern empirical discipline ought to be able to aim at a more rewarding result than the piling up of data and a steady output of imitation history. (Redman et al. 1978:5)

To achieve such an aim, we will have to shift our focus and move from the sole study of special categories of artifacts, e.g., stone tools, pottery, and animal bones, to the study of higher-level components which may give meanings to these more discrete finds. Such components will have to be selected according to what we know about the dynamics of social systems which are congruent with the cases under investigation. The household, the community inhabiting the same village or site, and aggregates of communities sharing the same territory are such units. The study of settlement patterns is thus a better research strategy, which may lead to a deeper understanding of the processes that formed the Neolithic cultural landscape in southeastern Mauritania.

Cultural Landscape in Spatiometric Perspective

Theoretically, any action of man on the natural landscape may produce imprints, but some imprints are more important and irreversible than others. When such imprints are patterned and enter into the archaeological record, they are amenable to systematic study. Settlement patterns belong to this category of human imprints on the natural landscape, and their systematic study reveals what is termed in this chapter the *cultural landscape*. Consequently, cultural landscape may be defined as any system of structural features necessary for human life, built and located in multidimensional space according to actual social rules. Such rules concern issues related to social distance between individuals and/or groups and govern their spatial location relative to each other: e.g., kinship, alliance relations, domination/subordination, man/woman, senior/junior, parents/children, public/private, etc. These rules generate sets of patterned and fluctuating modes of spatial behavior varying in a continuum from tight clustering, preferential aggregation, through loose distribution to total dispersal. In this perspective, at different levels of any social system, individual spatial modules are always integrated into higher-level spatial components, and some of them, such as the domestic, community, district, and regional units, will be considered in this chapter.

The issues discussed can be clarified through the formulation of a number of straightforward questions:

- How is the domestic space organized and why?
- How is the site layout organized and why?
- How are district settlement patterns structured and why?
- How is regional settlement pattern structured and why?

Different approaches are equally relevant for the study of the issues outlined above, and it seems to me obvious that the different aspects of social distance between individuals and groups are less a matter of mere measurements of physical distances than qualitative statements about the spatial location of individuals relative to each other in daily interaction. I consider that an important part of these qualitative statements is amenable to systematic investigation, which may bring to light a hidden dimension of both present-day and past societies. Consequently, I have coined the term *spatiometrics*, combining the idea of semiotics, a hybrid discipline concerning the study of the structures and meanings of signs, and cliometry which is used to characterize a part of scholarship in history based mainly on the use of quantitative methods. In his critique of the quantitative approach in history, Finley (1987:112) points out:

> It is precisely by reducing the number of variables to be considered that cliometry has succeeded in achieving the status of science and has produced its most significant results. but one may add that, by doing this it has payed a high cost, that of omitting the most important part of the human lives so recorded. (*Translation mine*)

This objection warns us about the overemphasis which is always possible when using a particular method and reducing the complexity of the issues being investigated to only few aspects of the problem being investigated. The spatiometric approach devised here is complementary to former research on the Neolithic societies of the Dhar Tichitt published elsewhere. However, it aims to study Neolithic spatial behavior and its links with social dynamics. In simple terms, the research problem in this chapter concerns the social meanings of the spatial distributions of built facilities at both intra- and intersite levels. Technically, the method is based on series of measurements of the size of the different spatial units recorded in the southwestern Sahara, such as compounds, aggregates of compounds, sites, aggregates of sites, and the distances in straight lines between villages at different levels of the settlement system. In terms of quantitative methods, we have chosen to resist the appeal of sophisticated mathematical techniques which are now easily accessible, and use simple statistical methods which are more congruent with our research problems, and in agreement with Whallon (1987:148-9) who states that:

> ...it must be our archaeological ideas, models, or theory that generates expectations, potentially observable consequences for the archaeological record, which we then can examine against available statistical methods to see if adequate and effective approaches exist that will allow us to test for the presence or absence of such expectations or to observe the degree of congruence to, or deviation from, these predicted consequences.

The research strategy outlined above operates within a few constraints, the most important being the degree of resolution of the studied sample, which will condition the pertinence of the measurements and their congruence with the research problems. The problems of the degree of resolution concern the visibility of archaeological features, the adequate assessment of the total extent of sites, and the adequate coverage of the whole landscape under investigation. In other words, adequate information is needed on the size of any single site, on every compound, the areal extent of each site, the number and location of each site in every part of the study area, and the region as a whole. Due to the building material used by the Neolithic peoples of the southwestern Sahara and the preferential location of their settlements on the top of sandstone cliffs, the accumulation of sediments on structural features after their abandonment is minimal. Some small sites and portions of larger sites located at lower elevations are indeed buried under drifting sand. However, in the majority of cases (86 sites out of a total of 90) there are no sediments masking the archaeological features. Thus, the layout of built features in sites is easily accessible through surveys (Mission Préhistorique de Tichitt n.d.) and the use of high-resolution air photos especially made for the Tichitt Prehistoric Mission by the Institut Géographique National (Mission IGN Mau 80). Enlarged versions of these airphotos, each measuring one meter square (i.e., 1:12,500), were used to produce a series of village maps. When needed, these aerial photos were checked and corrected in the field (Amblard 1984).

Research Perspectives

The Neolithic occupation of the southwestern Sahara lasted from ca. 4000 B.P.. to ca. 2000 B.P..(3830 ± 260 B.P., GIF-2884) to 2170 ± 105 B.P. (I-3819), when the area was abandoned due to increasing aridity. During these two thousand years, the whole area was colonized, settled, and dotted with numerous villages of different sizes, generating a cultural landscape which can also be considered as a sociopolitical map. Obviously, the process of expansion of human settlement along the series of sandstone cliffs located in southeastern Mauritania was generated by the combination of many factors which may have amplified some trends while inhibiting others. Some of these factors which are amenable to systematic archaeological investigation will identified and discussed.

The research presented in this chapter concerns the buildup of different spatial modules generated by the dynamics of the subsistence system, the socioeconomic organization, and the political organization and how these different components have shaped the Neolithic cultural landscape fossilized today in the archaeological record. These Neolithic communities practised mixed farming; their subsistence was complemented by hunting, fishing, and gathering of wild grains and fruits. The environment as reconstituted through the use of pollen analysis and fauna (Holl 1986a, 1986b) and geomorphological analysis of sediments accumulated in former fresh water lakes (Hugot 1977), was characterized by an open savanna with a very light tree component inhabited by herds of antelopes and gazelles, with a series of freshwater lakes located in the lowland, in interdunal depressions, with populations of fishes such as nile perch (*Lates niloticus*) and siluridae (*Clarias sp.*), crocodiles, and hippopotamus. During this period, the climate appears to have been dry and characterized by two contrasted seasons: a short wet season lasting three to five months and a long dry season (Servant and Servant 1980; Munson 1981; Maley 1981; Nicholson and Flohn 1980; Lézine 1988, 1989).

The study area, the Dhars Tichitt-Walata, named after two major oases, Tichitt in the west and Walata in the east, is situated at 18°20'–18°30' N. latitude and 8°30'–9°30' W. longitude, in the present southwestern part of the Sahara desert (Fig. 1). It measures 140 by 20 km (2800 km^2). A line of steep sandstone cliffs, standing on the average 50 m above mainly

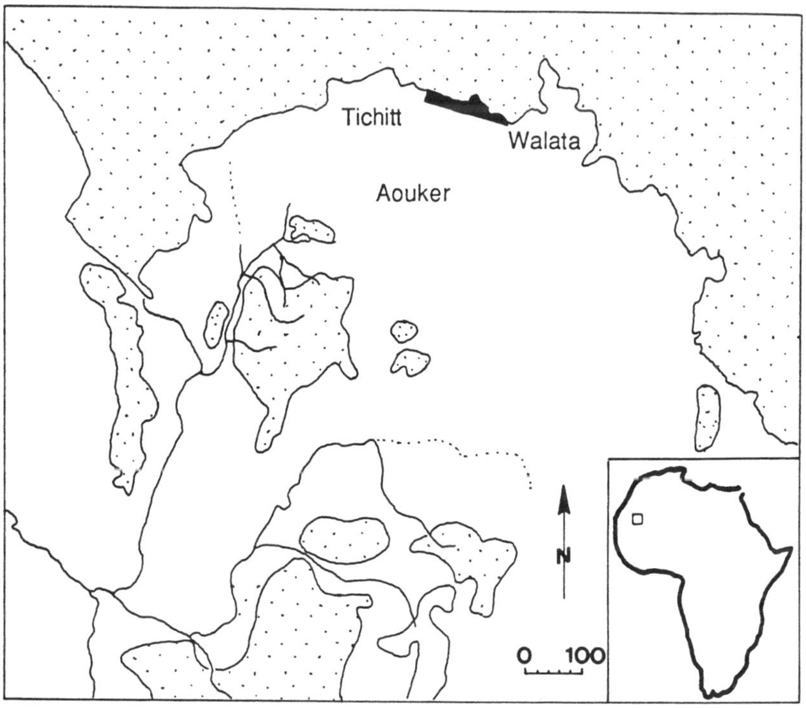

Fig. 1. Location map of the Dhars Tichitt-Walata in southeastern Mauritania.

sandy flats, and a series of interdunal depressions formerly filled with freshwater lakes form its main topographic features. The narrow plateau is dissected by valleys of seasonal streams, or wadis. The hydrographic regime was an endoreic one, the wadis emptying into lakes located in sandy interdunal depressions. This hydrographic network was fed by rains and the water table. Ninety-five archaeological sites have been mapped: 5 are surface sites located in the sandy flats, and 90 are built sites located on the cliff plateau.

The first issue to be discussed concerns the dynamics of the subsistence system devised by the Neolithic societies to counter the environmental risk and threat of food crises due to the overall unpredictability of climatic parameters, mainly rainfall, and their consequences on the distribution of critical resources such as water, pastures, and agricultural land (Halstead and O'Shea 1989). Then, we will move to the analysis of the socioeconomic organization and try to identify the basic social units which articulated the production, distribution, and consumption of resources as well as the biological and social reproduction of the Neolithic societies. The last part of the analysis will focus on the structures linked to sociopolitical organization. As far as this chapter is concerned with the spatial dimension, my discussions will focus on the diversity and variability of archaeological features and their spatial locations relative to each other.

There is little doubt that site structure is patterned in the archaeological record (Oswald 1984), but these patterns may have been altered by both the Neolithic people themselves and by post-depositional processes. Ideally, therefore, depending on the nature of the occupation, its duration, and the activities performed, repeated associations of structures and facilities can often be found. Debris will be clustered in dumps or discrete areas, rather than being scattered evenly and randomly over an entire site. The problem lies in knowing what the observed patterning means. Consequently, our goal as students of past societies is to be able to move from the static patterning of site structure to inferences about the social and technological organization of prehistoric societies.

Archaeologists seek to understand and explain the relations between human behavior and material culture, in the past as well as in the present. All these features of human life are in varying degrees shaped by sets of shared systems of meaning and symbols which may be called cultures (Kent 1984). Even if it remains difficult to trace a neat boundary between culture, behavior, and material culture, which are always intimately interrelated, we may agree that their relations of inclusion are not interchangeable. Behavior is social action which may result in the creation of material objects. The domain of material culture is thus constituted of the tangible products of human behavior. If there are behaviors without material outcome, there can not be creation of material items without behavior. This "isomorphism" (Hoftstadter 1985:57) is of paramount importance in the study of archaeological record. It suggests that the study of material culture can lead to genuine understanding of past cultural systems.

According to Binford (1980), the archaeological record is the product or derivative of a cultural system such that it is symptomatic of the past, and insofar as we cannot hope to understand the causes of these remains through a formal comparative study of the remains themselves, we have to search for a deeper understanding of the relationships between the dynamics of living systems in the past and the material by-products that contribute to the formation of the archaeological record remaining today. Our inferences about past societies must therefore be based upon coherent sets of empirical data, which will be used to evaluate the accuracy of our theoretical models. One of the key concepts in this regard is the archaeological visibility of patterned behaviors; this means the ability to identify a past event or occupation at a site in terms of the physical changes there and, hence, record its observable attributes. This visibility generally increases with time, intensity, length, and permanence of occupation, access to and/or ability to acquire durable and bulky building material and items, and economic and social positions which may generate differential access to material items.

Archaeological investigations are mostly based on the study of sociotechnological variables and their consequences for site structures. A large body of anthropological data (Hill 1982; Kramer 1982; Durrenberger 1984; Ardener 1981; Bohannan and Bohannan 1968; Kent 1984; Evans-Pritchard 1968; Harris 1980) demonstrates the existence of correlations between some types of social and technological organizations and the distributions of the larger and more permanent constituents of settlements' spatial structures. Theoretically, site structure may depend on the specific subsistence and socioeconomic organization of a given society at a given period and the structure of the time-space allocation system devised to face the varying needs of daily life. It may be useful to explore these features in more detail to derive a series of expectations.

Minimally, the subsistence and economic spheres

of any social system may be defined as the combined results of multiple individual and collective decisions regarding the procurement, processing, distribution and consumption of resources, various kinds of goods, and services. In this perspective, subsistence and economic activities are always socially organized; the research problem lies in our ability to identify the structural nodes which articulate any specific subsistence and economic system. Hence, if we consider subsistence and economy as sets of activities through which the consumer population organizes, integrates, and manages various kinds of resources, goods, and services for its own biological as well as social maintenance and reproduction, they appear to be characterized by two major components: 1) the forces of production, that is, land and its potential and effective resources, knowledge or stock of information, and technological skills, and 2) the social relations of production, e.g., division of labor, social distribution of roles, tasks, and products. These two aspects are always intimately interrelated so that it is possible to identify specific modes of production, if this stimulating concept had not been used as a "smoke screen" concept in a part of the Marxist historical and anthropological literature (cf. Godelier n.d., 1980, 1984).

In the context of economic systems based exclusively on man's bare labor force for the procurement and production of plant and animal resources, the concept of mode of exploitation of land, whatever its limitations may be (Testart 1982) is useful. According to Meillassoux (1977), in hunting and gathering economies, land is an "object of labor." The resource procurement system consists of the extraction of natural resources through foraging and collecting. In food-producing economies such as agriculture, pastoralism, and agro-pastoralism, land becomes a "means of labor" to a varying degree. This happens because the labor force is invested in the land, or livestock, or both, with the expectation of a delayed return. These kinds of societies witnessed major changes in their social, political, and ideological structures and in their relation to the natural landscape. With mixed farming economies the management of productive activities and their necessary conditions may be made more explicit by pinpointing some simple principles related to time-space allocation systems which may seem trivial at the first glance but will be shown to be very important in the final analysis.

The first principle is related to the discrete nature of human beings. We can not *yet* be at more than one spatial location at the same time; this may be termed the principle of "non-ubiquity." Faced with the differential distribution of potential resources in space in any given region, human societies have to devise some strategies to cope with this general situation. These strategies depend on the nature of the resources desired and processed.

The second principle is related to the specific nature of time, which can not be stored. Time is irreversible, it is a unidirectional and continuous flow (Bailey 1983; Carlstein 1982). Time can thus be partitioned into three main aspects:

1) "duration," which refers to a block of time during which an event occurs and also the interval of time between two events following each other,

2) "succession," which refers to the sequence of events in a continuum, and

3) "simultaneity," referring to the co-occurrence of two or more events within the same block of time reference.

These two principles have tremendous implications for every socioeconomic system. According to the mechanical properties of facilities needed for the performance of productive activities, their locations in space, the equipment required, logistics, and the labor force needed, some economic tasks may be successive and/or simultaneous, may last for short or long periods of time, and may mobilize a few individuals or large groups. To deal with these fluctuating features, societies create different managing structures among which patterned divisions of labor, specific task groups, and procedures of recruitment and mobilization of labor force. With the emergence of differential skills, various kinds of craft specialization develop. The household may be considered as such a unit. If it is able to face all the organizational problems of the socioeconomic system, it may be in some contexts an autonomous unit of production and consumption. Consequently, within the Neolithic economic system of the southwestern Sahara, with its ecological context characterized by seasonal fluctuations of potential resources, we would expect the development of productive strategies to counter environmental hazards, such as semi-nomadism, fission and fusion of social groups, and mobility of at least a part of communities in the region.

In order to infer social and technological organization from the archaeological record, two sets of problems must be considered in any attempt to analyze site structure, the mechanical properties of activities performed, and their sociotechnological contexts. The first concerns the procedures and materials associated with all activities which cross-cut all social and ethnic affiliations and establish the basic spatial requirements for every task. The second limits the way in which space can be organized to accommodate the mechanical needs of any activity. Hence, any kind of activity has scheduling patterns which depend on basic characteristics such as frequency, periodicity, duration, number of participants, facility requirements, and the relative bulk of associated materials (Oswald 1984; Kent 1987). In this chapter, after a short discussion of the subsistence system we will focus on the structures of units of production and consumption and explore their integration into higher-level social units such as the community, districts, and the region.

Subsistence Patterns

The model presented to account for the subsistence patterns of the Neolithic communities of southwestern Sahara takes into consideration the distribution of sites in the whole area, their morphology, their topographic location, the differential distribution of plant macro-remains, the dynamics of the ecosystem, and relevant ethnographic analogies.

The study of site morphology (size and number of compounds) and topographic location (upland and lowland) allows for the identification of two main sites categories: the first is composed of built sites with dry stone masonry structures, located on the plateau above the cliff, and the second is composed of surface sites without built structures, located in the sandy interdunal depressions on the shores of former freshwater lakes.

If we examine the differential distribution of macro plant remains between these two categories of sites, it appears that wild grains of *Cenchrus biflorus, Panicum laetum, Brachiaria deflexa*, and *Echinochloa sp*. were heavily exploited at surface sites located in the sandy interdunal depressions (more than 90%), and cultivated grains of bulrush millet *(Pennisetum sp.)* were preferentially consumed in sites located on the plateau (from 60 to 70%). Wild plants grow on seasonally flooded sandy soils, and their grains mature during the dry season, the time of the year during which they are easily available for gathering (Holl 1986a:156-7).

During the Neolithic occupation, ecosystem dynamics were characterized by the existence of two contrasting seasons: a short rainy season and a long dry season (Hugot 1977; Munson 1981). The streams were seasonal and emptied into freshwater lakes located in the interdunal depressions. In this endoreic hydrographic network, due to the differential seasonal balance of water between rainfall, evaporation and infiltration, the interdunal depressions were probably flooded during the rainy season, and the plateau was devoid of water during the dry season. The lack of any water control features such as wells and cisterns in the whole area during the Neolithic occupation gives additional support to the hypothesis of a drastic seasonal shortage of water. This variation in the seasonal availability of water may have conditioned the distribution of pasture necessary for livestock herding.

Thus, the southwestern Sahara appears to have been settled during the late Holocene by short-range, semi-nomadic agro-pastoral societies. The main settlements located on the plateau may have been inhabited by a whole community at each individual site during the rainy season, the optimal period of the year for agricultural activities. During the dry season, at least a part of the communities of each village—special task groups such as herders and fishermen—may have settled in temporary camps, the dry season camps, for purposes of animal husbandry and fishing, and may have relied on the gathering of wild grains and fruits as complementary food. Depending on the duration of the dry season (the lean period of the year), shortages of cultivated grain may have led to the gathering of additional wild grains which were included in the diet, and the consumption of larger quantities of fish as attested by the high frequency of fish bones in the archaeological record of lowland sites.

However, there is a large gap in the archaeological record between the number of "upland" sites (90) and that of "lowland" sites (5). This discrepancy results from the combination of two factors and is not a real challenge to the model proposed here. The first factor is the fascination exerted by the unexpected and impressive built villages of the plateau on all the researchers in this area. As a result, many surface scatters of archaeological material were observed and poorly reported without further consideration. The second factor concerns the dynamics of the system itself. I shall argue that in short-range, semi-nomadic societies, there is no direct correlation between the number of permanent villages and the number of dry season camps, and people from different settlements may share the same dry season camps. Overcrowding which may occur around some perennial water sources such as the large 20-hectare surface site of Ngoungou, which is located on the shore of a former freshwater lake (Munson 1971), is not unknown in the ethnographic record, and I have had the opportunity to observe a similar pattern among the Shuwa-Arab pastoralists of the southern Chad basin. Consequently, this numerical discrepancy is almost predictable in the pattern of settlement among semi-nomadic societies.

In terms of the cultural landscape, the subsistence-settlement system was organized and structured in two different and complementary parts of the Neolithic territories:

1) a dry season camping area in the lowland, with its series of freshwater lakes and ponds, settled by a part of the population with temporary features, and

2) the upland with its series of permanent villages, consisting of habitations built of dry masonry structures, located on the plateau.

The sandstone cliff constitutes the demarcation line between these two subsistence zones. Neolithic people coming from different villages probably met in the dry season camps and certainly took that opportunity to create new social relations or reinforce preexisting ones.

Socioeconomic Organization

Subsistence patterns result from the dynamics of socioeconomic organization, which concerns the integration of social units that manage the economic continuum of procurement-processing-distribution-consumption. Our research problem in this regard may be formulated as follows: what are the characteristic units of production and consumption of the Neolithic communities of southwestern Sahara? Are they visible in the archaeological record?

Units of Production

Units of production may be defined as minimal labor communities in which a part or the total range of a production process is accomplished (Digard 1981:170). It is not always possible to translate such a definition into archaeological terms, due to the overlapping of varying and diversified activities in some archaeological features. However, it is often possible to identify an archaeological structure with a specific function or a site with a special purpose. These sites may indicate, e.g., the procurement of raw materials such as flint, clay, or ore, the processing of these raw materials into lithic tools, pottery, or metal objects in workshops, hunting and/or butchering of large animals (butchering sites). These archaeological remains reflect different units of production, even if it remains difficult to know precisely the nature of the social entities responsible for these attested activities.

Units of Consumption

Units of consumption are defined as the minimal social entity in which individuals are in daily interaction and share food and other commodities such as shelter. Analytical differentiation between production and consumption is theoretically valid and is based on the assumption that production is a precondition to consumption; however, there is always a part of one in the other. Situations of shared consumption of food and other commodities may vary from specific and strict social circumstances to more generalized and long-lasting ones. Faced with severe difficulties of definition due the high degree of variability of both units of production and units of consumption, as well as problems of archaeological visibility, we will have to shift our focus and concentrate on another analytical unit: the household.

Modelling Household Dynamics

A functional definition of *household* is difficult because the characteristics of this social unit vary from one society to another (Deetz 1982; Kent 1990; Kramer 1982; Warnier 1985; Wilk and Rathje 1982). However, following Hammel (1980:251), the household may be defined as "the smallest grouping with the maximum corporate function." If the different activities carried out by a household are conceptualized as constituting "activity spheres," it is possible to see that these spheres overlap considerably. Consequently,

> A group that shares a living space (coresidence), a group that shares in the activities of food preparation and consumption and a group that socializes children often overlap completely; they are one and the same. Defining the household in a particular social setting does not require that each household have the same overlapping spheres of activity but that in each case we find...the smallest groupings with the maximum corporate function. (Wilk and Netting 1984:5)

It appears therefore that households perform five primary categories of activities: production, distribution, reproduction, coresidence, and transmission. The first two spheres of activities are directly related to socioeconomic organization, the third to the biological reproduction of individuals, the fourth to the structural features for habitation, and the last to the transmission of wealth and social position from one generation to the next. Concerning the economic sphere of activities, production systems are either diverse, requiring the execution of different tasks simultaneously, or simple, with productive activities executed successively. If the household is considered as a labor group, the yearly fluctuations of workloads will have strong effects on its optimal size. It will have to devise adequate space-time allocation systems which must face variation in productive tasks.

At some times of the year the demand for labor is low, and at other times this demand is very high and may generate activity "bottlenecks." The scheduling mechanisms developed will have to integrate within the yearly cycle both the absolute timing of the productive tasks and their sequencing or ordering :

> From this perspective we can generate some testable hypotheses about the direction and the nature of household adaptation to particular differences in scheduling. We expect that the more simultaneous the labor requirements of major productive tasks, and the more diverse the productive tasks within the yearly cycle, the more tendency we will see for larger households groups. Unless there is some other reason for large households to exist, we expect that linear tasks arranged in a simple yearly cycle favor the small household as a productive group. (Wilk and Netting 1984:7-8)

During the life cycle of households, there are also variations in demographic structure, number of members, social position, and economic status. Chayanov (1966, cf. Durrenberger 1984:39) has shown that there are sets of structural relations between the demographic composition of households, their potential labor force, their farming capacities and agricultural output. In this perspective, according to its position in its life cycle, the same household is a totally different "working machine," with periods of increasing labor force potentials followed by periods of decrease.

At the heart of Chayanov's approach to the analysis of peasant economies is the idea that, technology being constant, there is a natural limit to increasing output, determined by the balance or unstable equilibrium of increasing drudgery of labor and the decreasing marginal return of output. According to Chayanov (1966:5-6), the amount of labor product is determined mainly by the size and the demographic composition of the working household and the number of its members capable of work, then by the productivity of the labor unit, and the degree of self-exploitation through which the working members effect a certain quantity of labor units in the course of the year. Thus, he considers some key variables, and mainly their intersections, to study the dynamics of peasant farm organization, such as the consumer/worker ratio, which varies with the life cycle of the household, and the marginal utility/drudgery ratio which limits the amount of labor input at certain levels:

> Thus every family, depending on its age, is in its different phases of development a completely distinct labor machine as regard labor force, intensity of demand, consumer/worker ratio and the possibility of applying the principle of complex cooperation. (Chayanov 1966:60)

Through what he termed the "natural history" of the household, Chayanov developed the concept of demographic differentiation, according to which the size and internal composition of households vary from the time of marriage of a young couple through the growth of their children to working age and finally marriage of this second generation.

This theory of peasant economy is very stimulating for archaeological research. The fact that there are strong correlations between the demographic structure of a household, its size, its potential labor force, its wealth, its social position, and probably its spatial layout is amenable to archaeological model building. The dynamics of the household outlined above, linked to the process of generational segmentation, may be useful in the understanding of processes of settlement expansion at both intra- and extra-site levels.

A number of anthropologists (Bohannan and Bohannan 1968; Dumas-Champion 1983; Hill 1982; Sahlins 1969) have observed the dynamics of households in some of their case studies. In all these societies, kinship is the base structure of households, since very low proportions of its members are unrelated to the household head, whether by consanguinity, marriage, or adoption. In dealing with regions in India and northern Nigeria which are characterized by dry grain farming, Hill (1982:91-2) observed that married sons find considerable difficulty in establishing independent, viable households that are dependent mainly on farming their own land, unless they receive some help from their father. But fathers generally prefer family labor to hired labor. Thus, they are usually anxious to retain the services of their married sons as much as possible, especially since the heads of large extended households are apt to be well respected by the village community, but at the same time this generates tensions between generations. Bohannan and Bohannan (1968) have found the same feature among the Tiv, where a large compound with many wives and children is the optimal type of maximization for any individual Tiv, leading to prestige and wealth.

The household as social unit can also be considered in spatial terms as a micro-territorial module. Hence, the analysis of the multiple spatial dimensions of human social systems is more productive if we can consider space not as a given, static physical category but as representing sets of specific patterns regarding, for instance, activities, social distance, relations of production, etc. (Agorsah 1988; Ardener 1981; Hillier 1985; Holl 1990; Kent 1984; Levy and Holl 1987). Once space has been bounded and shaped, it is no longer merely a neutral background, it exerts its own influence, it becomes, following Ardener's words (1981:13), a "social map" or, in the terms of this chapter, a cultural landscape.

Archaeology and Household

One of the major problems in the archaeology of households concerns the archaeological visibility and the identification of a household unit. The coresidence factor, while being one of its necessary conditions, does not seem sufficient to some researchers (Kramer 1982a, 1982b) who warn us to be cautious in our process of inference building about households in archaeological contexts. According to Deetz (1982:717), households and houses are not components of an isomorphic relation. Conditions of preservation, the extent of excavation, sampling errors, and punctual analogy can generate serious shortcomings. However, even if we do not deny the complex nature of the relations between households, houses, and families, it seems unquestionable that households are a real socioeconomic microcosm with a necessary spatial dimension:

> Yet a doubt has been frequently raised as to the status of "residence" as a criterion for the analysis of the family, whether comparisons are being made over space or through time. There are nonetheless perfectly sound reasons for considering that the knot of persons who sleep and frequently, if not invariably, take meals together under the same roof constitute a unit for social analysis, and can form a basis for revealing inter-society comparisons, particularly if due attention is given to the means by which that unit has been brought together. (Smith 1984:ix)

Under a set of conditions such as in this research program, given its excavation techniques and the degree of preservation of the archaeological record, the household as an archaeological unit of analysis presents many advantages for the study of past societies:

1) This unit may be spatially circumscribed, especially if the building material and architectural techniques are bulky.

2) The distribution of activity areas in that spatially circumscribed unit may allow an analysis of the social organization of the domestic area.

3) In some situations, when the household is considered as primary unit of social reproduction (Friedman and Rowlands 1977; Sahlins 1968; 1976; Tringham 1983:4), it may allow a discussion of changes in social structures through the study of various dimensions of the structural transformations of its spatial layout.

Thus a research procedure for the study of household organization which bridges the gap between systemic and archaeological contexts can be outlined. Raw materials, resources, goods, or, for short, matter is channelled in social system following a schedule of productive activities. According to their timing and sequencing, these activities take place in specific locations. Daily living activities or maintenance tasks are more often than not executed in the domestic area. Even if this spatial unit is sometimes well structured, we may provisionally consider it as a "generalized activity" area, the core of the household domain. Some specific activity areas may be included in the domestic space, such as storage and working areas, or located immediately outside (Fig. 2). The combination of various activity areas ranging from specific to generalized is the easiest archaeological strategy for reconstructing the household.

Dynamics of an Agro-pastoral Economy

Fully or partially pastoral economic systems have been the subject of intensive anthropological research. In the extensive anthropological literature on these systems, various researchers have outlined a range of recurrent features that are characteristic of this specific mode of exploitation of natural resources (cf. Johnson 1969; Khazanov 1984; Nelson 1973; Spooner 1973; Weissleder 1978). Mixed agro-pastoral economies combine in varying degrees:

1) agricultural activities, the production of plant resources, relatively immobile in space, and

2) pastoral activities, the management of animals, often mobile in space and time.

In the yearly cycle, both sets of productive activities have periods of low and high demands on labor, which may generate serious problems of scheduling. In this regard, one may seek to know what are successive and/or simultaneous productive activities in the yearly cycle, the nature of the scheduling mechanisms and what are the dominant features of division of labor in each set of activities.

I will not attempt to discuss all these issues in details. However, an overview of a number of ethnographic case studies will help to identify some key mechanisms which structure the dynamics of agro-pastoral socioeconomic systems. The selected case studies are the Baxtyari nomads of Iran (Johnson

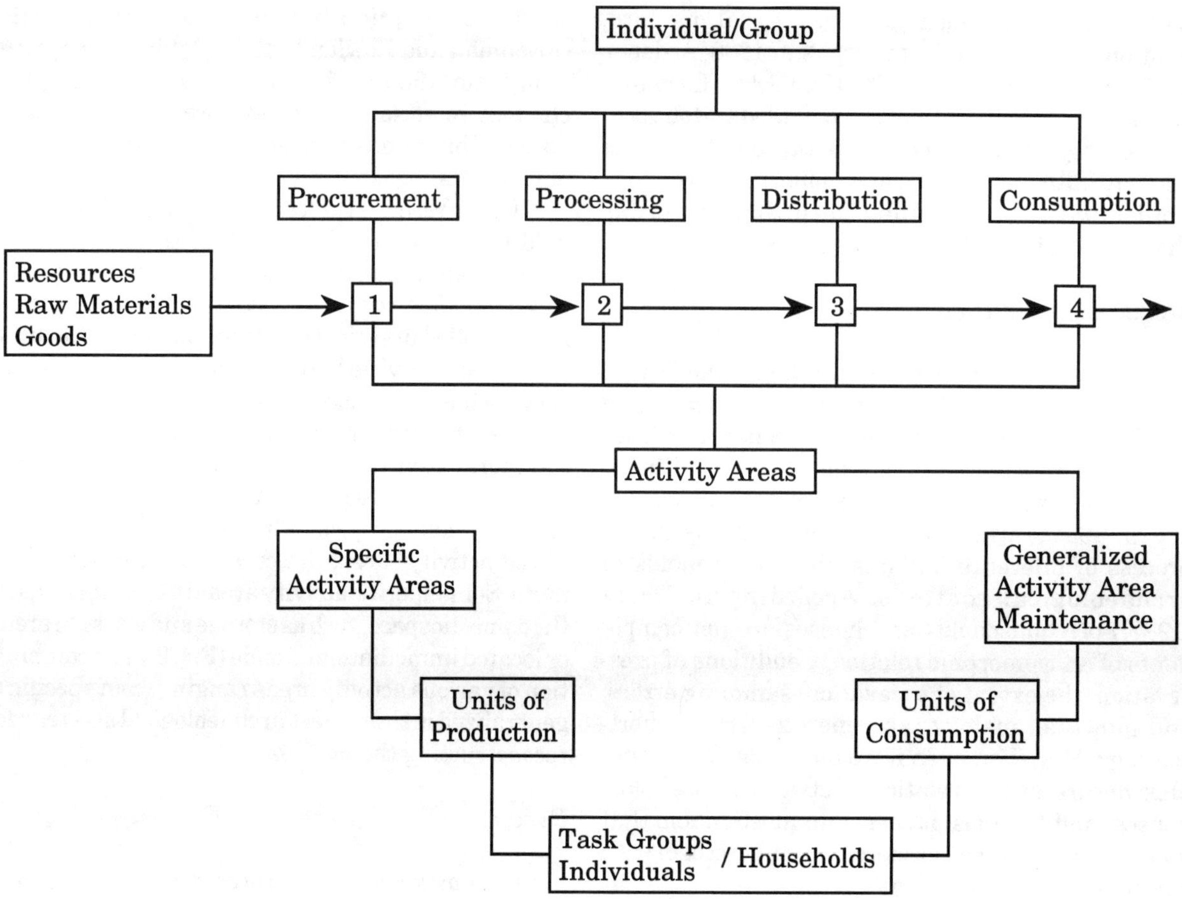

Fig. 2. A simplified model of units of production and consumption.

1969; Digard 1978, 1981), the Massa of Chad (Dumas-Champion 1980, 1983), the Guajiros Indians of Venezuela and Colombia (Picon 1978, 1983), the Nuer of Sudan (Evans-Pritchard 1968) and the Tuareg Ullimiden of Niger and Mali (Bernus 1981; Johnson 1969; Smith 1978). The variability of animal species herded, cattle, camels, equids, sheep and goats, and the wide geographic distribution of the selected case studies in three continents, Western Asia (Baxtyari), Africa (Massa, Nuer and Tuareg) and South America (Guajiros) will certainly allow the search for structural features of agro-pastoral economies which go beyond territorial and cultural contingencies (Frantz 1978; Khazanov 1978; Spooner 1973).

The Baxtyari population amounts to about 600,000 individuals inhabiting a territory of approximately 75,000 km^2 in the southern part of the Zagros mountains in Iran. Their herds are essentially composed of sheep and goats, with a minor component of cattle and equids. Many Baxtyari, mostly the poor, grow wheat. They spend summer in the highlands and winter in the lowlands in order to buffer the consequences of the drastic seasonal variations of pasture in these two complementary ecological zones. The Tuareg of Niger and Mali are camel herders practising a system of long-range nomadism like the Baxtyari. They number about 80,000 in the area studied by Bernus (1981). Agriculture is marginal and is practised by slaves and their descendants. The remaining three groups practice short-range and pulsatory nomadism; their herds are primarily composed of cattle. The Massa are about 150,000 and inhabit the Chad-Cameroon border area in the Logone lowlands; the Nuer are about 200,000 inhabiting a territory of 48,000 km^2 in Central Sudan, and the Guajiros Indians, who adopted cattle husbandry soon after the Spanish conquest of Columbia and Venezuela, live in a territory of 15,000 km^2; their number amounts to 100,000 people.

From these case studies, it appears that agricultural and pastoral activities are complementary in the subsistence of the peoples involved. With the exception of the Massa, the other groups consider pastoral activities to be more prestigious than agricultural ones. Whatever the situation may be, at the level of yearly cycle pastoral activities are constant and impose a rhythm on community life in both the practical and ideological spheres. Agriculture is not a socially valued activity, and work is done as fast as possible (Nuer), done by slaves (Tuareg), by wage workers and the poor (Baxtyari), or by the poor (Guajiros). Nevertheless, in spite of this value hierarchy, agriculture and pastoralism belong to the same annual cycle of activities, and their articulation leads to the specificity of each of the systems examined.

The execution of necessary subsistence tasks, agricultural as well as pastoral, demands the availability of a sufficient labor force. Due to the multiplicity of such tasks, the nuclear family is obviously inadequate as a self-sustaining socioeconomic unit; it is therefore always included in set of social relations or larger social units such as extended families, labor parties, camps or villages, which behave like units of production. This situation is common for matters of animal herding. On the other hand, agricultural activities are often executed at the household level, which may be composed of one or several nuclear families.

During the dry season, the search for water and pasture is the dominant activity, while being the dead season for agriculture. Pastoral activities are carried out by special purpose groups of young boys in the process of initiation (Massa) or "specialized" herders (Guajiros, Tuareg, Baxtyari), who spend the major part of their time out of the main settlement, living in temporary camps moving from place to place. Hunting, fishing, and foraging of wild resources generally complement the daily food intake during this lean period of the year.

In terms of the cultural landscape, each of these ethnic groups has different names for the part of its territory settled during each season, such as *Yeylag* (summer territories) and *Garmasir* (winter territories) for the Baxtyari or *Cieng* (permanent villages) and *Wec* (dry season camps) for the Nuer (Evans-Pritchard 1986). According to Digard (1981:14), *Yeylag* and *Garmasir* finally represent more than simple names of places, they represent authentic Baxtyari ways of life, and the move from one place to the other during the fall appears to be a kind of rite of passage. The move from main settlements to dry season camps or from one part of the territory to the other according to the seasonal variation of water and pasture thus plays an important social role in some of the societies examined here and ensures the passage from childhood to adulthood, supporting the hypothesis of the crucial importance of the cultural landscape.

Neolithic Household: Compounds and Spatial Organization

In the context of built sites with dry stone masonry structures, the inhabited space is divided into compounds of different size, separated from each other by massive walls, pathways, and open places. The compound thus appears to be the primary spatial unit which may be equated with household; it is a coherent and self-contained archaeological unit with clear cut boundaries delineated by dry stone walls. I have excavated such a compound at Akreijit, designated 50E, covering an area of 450 m^2. In this enclosed space with one functional doorway, there are five main dwelling units, structures 501 to 505 (Figs. 3 and 4), and a smaller one in the eastern corner, interpreted as a small storage area. The dwelling units are trapeze-shaped and characterized by three to five rows of sandstone pillars or large blocs and lines of stones (Fig. 3). Their surfaces vary from 12.5 m^2 (505) to 8.4 m^2 (503) (Table 1). As far as dwelling units are concerned, the total built area in this compound measures 55.6 m^2, 12.3% of the available enclosed surface. The relative spacing of dwelling units from each other varies from 10 m between 501 and 503 to 3 m between 504 and 505 (Table 2). There is also one hearth near 502, located at the center of the compound.

The first striking feature of the spatial patterning of archaeological structures in this compound is the central place of the hearth and dwelling unit 502. The remaining dwellings are located at an average distance of 4. 75 m from the hearth, varying from 5.5 m (503) to 4 m (505). This unique hearth seems to represent the focal point of the domestic life in the compound, and it is obvious that the importance of social activities represented by the hearth has generated the relative centrality of its location within the household spatial patterning of activities.

Dwelling unit 502 has three different kinds of grinding stones, while the other dwelling units have only one kind in each. In her ethnoarchaeological study of grinding equipment in the modern oasis of Tichitt, Roux (1983) has shown that different grinding stones are used for processing different materials; the processing of some products such as different grains for food, medicine, or crafts are considered incompatible and are thus processed with different tools. All the households do not have the full range of grinding equipment in their domestic toolkit; consequently there are systems of borrowing and even "part-time specialists," women who are paid to grind different products. In this regard, the case of dwelling 502 suggests that the household members have managed

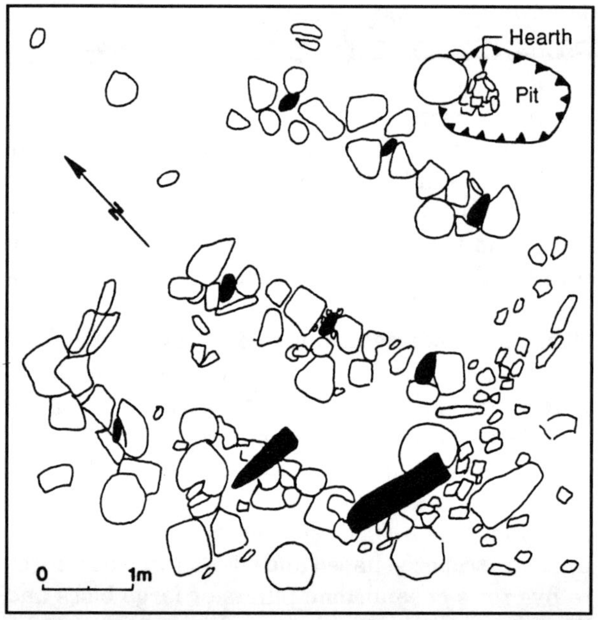

Fig. 3. Dwelling unit 502 in Compound 50E at Akreijit.

Table 1. Measurements of dwelling units from compound 50E.

Dwelling Units	501	502	503	504	505
Length					
Min.	4.5	4.0	3.9	4.5	5.0
Max.	4.7	4.5	4.0	5.0	6.4
Width					
Min	2.7	3.2	2.0	2.0	2.0
Max.	3.0	4.5	2.1	2.2	3.0
Surface (m^2)	8.9	9.9	8.4	11.0	12.4

Table 2. Spacing between dwelling units from compound 50E.

Dwelling Units	501	502	503	504	505
501	–	–	–	–	–
502	4.0	–	–	–	–
503	4.5	5.0	–	–	–
504	10.0	4.0	8.0	–	–
505	7.5	4.0	3.0	4.0	–

to maintain the full range of necessary grinding equipment. The equipment needed for daily food processing was present in all dwelling units, and that needed from time to time was pooled in one dwelling unit, probably that of the household head.

Furthermore, in each dwelling, there is a co-occurrence of grinders/grinding stones and hammerstones/stone anvils (Fig. 4). In this context, grinders and grinding stones are equipment which was used mostly for food processing. Stone anvils and hammerstones may have been used for the manufacture of various tools, in stone as well as in bone. The presence of a large stone polisher located in the western corner of the courtyard, flakes, and lithic waste give additional support to this argument.

If one agrees that sexual division of labor is one of the preeminent characteristics of the "Domestic Mode of Production" (Sahlins 1968, 1976), the inference to be drawn from the distribution of archaeological data presented above seems inescapable. Each dwelling appears to have been inhabited by at least one man and one woman. Therefore, this compound seems to have been inhabited by a large family entity, probably an extended family with a household head and his married sons or daughters. This kind of household clearly appears as an optimal socioeconomic unit in the context of mixed farming, with the capacity of mobilizing labor force to face the diverse productive tasks of the yearly cycle. The pooling of resources is reflected by the presence of a storage area; in Moala, Fiji, Sahlins (1957:449-62) has observed that when food is pooled in an extended family, cooking is shared and there is only one kitchen for all the members of the household. At Akreijit, which was inhabited during the whole Neolithic occupation of the Dhars Tichitt-Walata, from surface inspection, it was observed that each compound has only one hearth; this suggests that the organization identified in compound 50E represents the basic structure of domestic space during the whole Neolithic occupation.

Neolithic Cultural Landscape: Theory and Model

The expansion of inhabited space at both the levels of site and region results from the combined effects of several factors operating at different levels of the

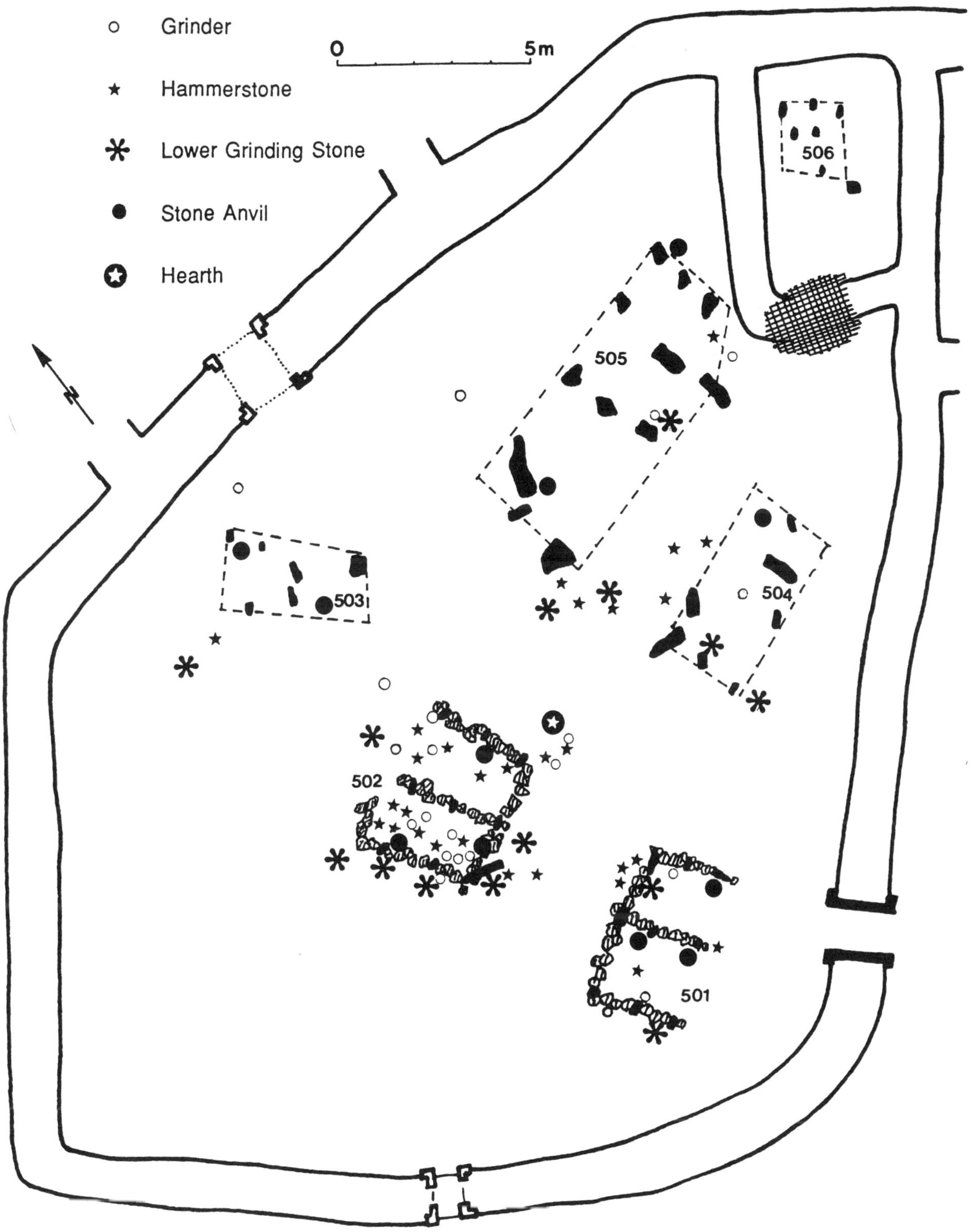

Fig. 4. Plan of Compound 50E at Akreijit.

social systems. It may result from fission after disputes, the search for new agricultural and grazing lands, or as the consequence of warfare or trade. Here, our discussion will focus on some of those factors amenable to systematic archaeological study in the context of the Neolithic societies of southeastern Mauritania. We will first consider the dynamics of the socioeconomic system at the household level and its consequences for the growth of inhabited space. In this discussion, our basic assumption is that of the natural growth of the local population from the earliest period of settlement. If economy is defined as a set of spheres of social activities dealing with the procurement of resources, goods, and services, their processing, distribution and consumption, for the maintenance and biological and social reproduction of the society as a whole, the household appears in many cases to be the primary socioeconomic unit. One of the most critical features of the household economy is the recruitment of labor. From this point of view, in self-sustaining mixed farming societies the forces of production are essentially tools and land. While these are easily accessible to members of the social group, labor force and the skills necessary to achieve diverse and overlapping socioeconomic tasks provide those who possess them with genuine authority over the laymen. This is because the continuation of the group depends on these features (Meillassoux 1980a). The pooling of labor force and knowledge are often acquired with seniority, thus supporting the fundamental senior/junior relationships. The man/woman relationship is not parallel to it but it has its own dynamics which may be complementary or contradictory in the household structure. Considering the overlapping nature of the generational structure in all societies, one may agree that there are always at least three generations present in a living society: the old, the middle-aged, and the young, with each generation playing a role in the maintenance and the reproduction of the whole society:

> Societies need some mechanism which allows individuals to give to the old and have confidence that they in turn will be the recipients of gifts when they are old. Money, ritual knowledge, clubs, land, kinship groups, and a host of others are all social arrangements which help to inspire this confidence and to achieve an optimal allocation of consumption. (Walsh 1983:647)

In this perspective, kinship relations in a household are at the same time relations of production, with two kinds of circulation of resources, goods and services. The seniors receive the juniors' prestations and then supervise the whole group output. In this specific case, the generalized reciprocity model (Sahlins 1968, 1972) is inaccurate and the concept of delayed reciprocity seems more appropriate. According to Bouju (1984:19), the prestation/redistribution cycle is the expression of an asymmetrical and complementary social relationship. In that relation every transfer of goods or services is a response to the simple obligation included in the set of rights and duties implied by kinship status. A household head may therefore try to have a large number of people dependent on him in order to secure a labor force, a large amount of output, authority, and prestige. The qualitative link between household structure and the community and regional levels is based upon these features. In the anthropological literature, surplus production is sometimes considered to be the key variable in vertical social differentiation. In a review of theories of social stratification in sociology and anthropology, Cancian (1976:230-1) persuasively argued that the idea that stratification resulted from the creation of a material surplus is not only a simplistic view, but also has little support, since its definition in absolute terms is not workable. However, in relative terms this concept may be useful as an indication of an increased output beyond the subsistence requirements of a production unit. Economic differentiation based on the control of people and consequently their productive and reproductive capacities is not operative in terms of so-called "surplus" production but mainly in terms of prestige and social influence arising from a large and "wealthy" household.

At the household level, kinship relations, recruitment of labor force, the senior/junior relationship with its corollary, delayed reciprocity, output intensification, and circulation of prestige items are in a state of punctuated equilibrium and generate different and overlapping social networks which link this primary socioeconomic unit to community, regional, and even extraregional networks. Population increase and generational segmentation allow territorial expansion (Bohannan and Bohannan 1968; Bouju 1984; Pollet and Winter 1980; Sahlins 1961, 1969) through the search for new agricultural and grazing lands. Given enough time, one would expect a wide distribution of socially and historically related communities in a given region, a cumulative growth process of a cultural landscape which may be slowed down or accelerated according to actual demographic and environmental circumstances. Household heads, having a large following and large production output, may therefore be in a position to achieve greater distributive capacities, prestige, and elite goods, incentives to vertical differentiation among households.

We may thus expect larger households to have inhabited larger compounds.

At the community level, cooperation and competition are both present. Household heads with the greatest distributive capacities and prestige have better opportunities to reach, directly or indirectly, positions of authority as community elders or decision-makers, organizing communal works for the benefit of the entire community (Harris 1879:98). Due to community dynamics, land availability, population increase, and environmental conditions, given enough time, daughter communities may develop in the surroundings. In mixed farming economies these new settlements may depend, at least in their pioneer stage, on the accumulation and storage of foods and seeds from their former communities (Meillassoux 1980b). These relations may be of a various, political, economic, ideological nature, or all of these, and may create regional networks. In this regard, the very existence of technology, subsistence activities, and social relations affects societies as they are symbolically mediated (Coe 1981; Freidel 1981; Keatinge 1981; Sahlins 1980). Ideologies and religious practices are more than simple epiphenomena of the techno-environmental-political realm. The difficulties of studying them in the material record of prehistoric societies does not mean that they are not significant:

> In the absence of naked coercive force, religious sanctions provided a path toward the development of political centralization. The amount of resources both human and natural, expended on religion in the form of temple construction and tribute must have a profound effect on the configuration of early state economies as well as on the forms of political organization developed to organize and direct the exploitation of these resources. (Keatinge 1981:187)

In this regard, the senior/junior relationship previously examined in our discussion of household socioeconomic dynamics may provide one possibility for understanding the lineage system's ideology. For example, land allocation systems, or, more generally, the access to means of production, is strongly controlled by a segmentary society's ideology, particularly in the cases of communal ownership of land (Bouju 1984:104).

At the regional level, communities are horizontally and/or vertically differentiated. To ensure their social and biological reproduction, communities are involved in multiple exchange networks of people, goods and services. The nodes of differential concentration of people and habitation facilities in the continuum of population distribution over the landscape of a region may generate segregation. This concept refers to the extent to which households or groups of households are independent of each other. We may thus expect the emergence of patterns of distinct and changing social networks with preferential exchange partners. Exchange of people, goods, services, prestige items, and tribute may be channeled through the networks thus created

> ...Linkages between specialized subsystems may take the form of transactions in the context of central institutions. Chieftainships, governments and markets are such examples of such central institutions. (Blanton 1976:251)

Differential concentration of people and historical factors such as "anteriority" (e.g., historically earlier settlers) may lead to a hierarchy of settlements, which may have been reinforced by tribute flow from lower to higher centers, and prestige goods flow in the inverse direction (Friedman and Rowlands 1977; Steponaitis 1978, 1981). In general, information needed for the operation of the system is not available everywhere in the same quantity and quality but is spatially variable. The influence of distance as a frictional force in attenuating information flows, suggests that settlement hierarchy plays a critical role in channelling information flows. The geographic location of main centers is therefore an important variable in determining the form and extent of different levels of a society's cultural landscape (Lloyd and Dicken 1977:317). These features have relatively clear archaeological correlates, which can be partly revealed by locational analysis.

In the model presented here, I have derived some expectations which will help make sense of the southeastern Mauritanian archaeological record. The model has fragments of a deterministic approach to social systems. Following Harris (1979:108), it is argued that it is not by denying the existence of a deterministic component in social processes that one will improve that situation, and, for the sake of intelligibility, it is necessary to delineate such a component. The empirical test implications of this model involve the archaeological analysis of the spatial distribution of compounds in different sites and of the settlement patterns at the district and regional levels. Four sites have been selected for detailed analysis, according to their size, location, and position in the hierarchy of settlement which is composed of four ranks: regional center, large village or district center, small village and hamlet.

Chronology and Settlement Expansion

The chronology of settlement expansion of the Neolithic societies of southeastern Mauritania is based exclusively on the research carried out in the Dhar Tichitt region, situated in the westernmost part of the study area, where more intensive fieldwork has been undertaken (Amblard 1984, 1986; Holl 1985a, 1985b, 1986a, 1986b, 1989; Munson 1971; Vernet 1984, 1986). My chronological ordering of the Dhar Tichitt settlement dynamics is not yet universally accepted by students of the Neolithic societies of southwestern Sahara (Vernet 1988; Munson 1989), partly because of basic differences in the research perspectives adopted and also because of the relative small number of radiocarbon dates and their uneven distribution between sites. However, it seems to me that that chronological ordering is the most congruent with the data base available today for the Neolithic societies of southeastern Mauritania. It appears that the surface sites or dry season camps studied by Munson (1971) and located on the shores of former freshwater lakes in sandy interdunal depression were settled during the whole Neolithic sequence and date from ca. 4000 B.P. (3830 ± 120 B.P., Gif-2884) to ca. 2000 B.P. (2290 ± 110 B.P., Gif-4110). Sites built with dry stone features and located on the plateau of the sandstone cliff, which are considered to have been permanent villages, were settled over the same length of time and have been dated from 3850 ± 250 B.P. to 2170 ± 105 B.P., (I-3819) (Table 3). This first chronological ordering suggests that the exploitation of different but complementary ecological zones was a permanent feature of the Neolithic socioeconomic system.

According to their size and location, the permanent villages in the Dhar Tichitt archaeological record can be partitioned into three classes of what appears to be a hierarchy of settlements. There are four rank 1 sites. Their surface extents vary from 3.5 ha with 120 compounds at Chebka to 17.5 ha and 180 compounds at Khimiya. All of them are located near or on the edge of the cliff escarpment, in what appears to have been an optimal location considering the dynamics of the mixed farming system—on the demarcation line between the lowland and the upland. In general, these sites are the earliest Neolithic sites of the study area (Table 3, Fig. 5a).

Tentatively, it may be argued that from these pioneer sites settlements were created in the whole region. It appears that rank 2 sites, characterized by the presence of 21 to 50 compounds, were settled from ca. 3000 B.P. (2780 ± 140 B.P., GX-1325) and lasted up to the end of the Neolithic occupation at ca. 2000 B.P. (2170 ± 105 B.P., I-3819). These rank 2 sites are distributed in two clusters, one with four sites in the surroundings of Akreijit and the other with six sites in the vicinity of Chebka (Fig. 5b), and are located along the edges of the main wadis and isolated sandstone massifs. The 28 rank 3 sites, containing less than twenty compounds each, were settled from ca. 2500 B.P. (2600 ± 105 B.P., Gx-1326) to ca. 2000 B.P. (2330 ± 105 B.P., I-3566), and most of them are located along the edges of secondary valleys (Fig 5c). It appears that settlement expansion, which certainly results from the dynamics of the socioeconomic system, started very slowly and accelerated through time. From four sites during the pioneer sequence, we have 14 in the middle sequence and 42 in the late and final sequence. The number of sites was multiplied by 3.5 (from 4 to 14) in a period of 1,000 years, with the appearance of rank 1 and 2 sites, and then multiplied by 3 (from 14 to 42) over a period of 500 years, with the addition of rank 3 sites.

This chronological model from the Dhar Tichitt region will be expanded and used to study the buildup of the Neolithic cultural landscape at a larger territorial scale, that of the Dhars Tichitt-Walata archaeological record. Thus, in this chapter, the largest sites will be considered as the earliest settlements, which have witnessed sequences of expansion during the whole Neolithic occupation of the study area. This pioneer settlement stage was followed by the emergence of small villages during the middle sequence and hamlets during the late sequence. It is the buildup of this larger Neolithic cultural landscape which will now be discussed.

Cultural Landscape I: the Early Settlement Sequence (ca. 4000–3000 B.P.)

The early settlement sequence lasted for one thousand radiocarbon years and started around 4000 B.P. Six sites belong to this sequence, from the west to the east: Chebka, Tijot, Khimiya, Akreijit, Dakhlet el Atrous, and Imdel el Abiod. Three are located on or near the main escarpment of the cliff and the three others on isolated sandstone massifs in what appears to be the demarcation zone between two complementary ecological areas, the sandy interdunal lowland and the sandstone plateau upland (Fig. 6). In terms of the dynamics of mixed farming systems, this site location strategy appears optimal, allowing direct access to both ecological zones. The cultural landscape was actually characterized by a linear pattern of settlements. Distances between nearest-neighbor

Table 3. Chronology of settlements and radiocarbon dates from Dhar Tichitt (B.P.).

Location:	*Upland*	*Lowland*
Nature:	Permanent villages	Dry season camps
Rank 2 sites		
	Akreijit	Ngoungou
	3850 ± 250 (?)	3465 ± 160 (Gx-1421)
	3776 ± 120 (DAK-32)	3425 ± 130 (Gx-1889)
	3490 ± 50 (MC-427)	3350 ± 110 (I-3561)
	3400 (TL. CRIAA)	3205 ± 95 (Gx-1323)
	3122 ± 120 (DAK-203)	3190 ± 110 (I-3562)
	2975 ± 110 (DAK-187)	2950 ± 100 (I-3563)
	2760 ± 160 (DAK-190)	
	2680 ± 90 (Gif-3406)	
	2430 ± 80 (Gif-6083)	
	Tijot	Site 46
	3205 ± 105 (I-3564)	3830 ± 120 (Gif-2884)
	2885 ± 140 (Gx-1888)	
	2700 ± 115 (Gx-1324)	
Rank 3 sites (Chebka district)		
	Site 14	NI* Neolithic hearth
	2780 ± 140 (Gx-1325)	2610 ± 110 (Gif-4110)
	Site 9	
	2170 ± 105 (I-3819)	
Rank 4 sites (Chebka district)		
	NI*	NI* Neolithic hearth
	2600 ± 105 (Gx-1326)	2290 ± 110 (Gif-4112)
	Site 1	
	2330 ± 105 (I-3566)	

*NI = Non-Identified site.

sites vary from 4 km between Tijot and Akreijit, Khimiya and Akreijit, 5 km between Tijot and Khimiya, 11.5 km between Chebka and Tijot, 41 km between Akreijit and Dakhlet el Atrous and 48 km between Dakhlet el Atrous and Imdel el Abiod. Three of the settlements (Akreijit, Khimiya, and Tijot) among the six recorded are clustered, and their respective site catchment areas (Vita Finzi and Higgs 1970) have an average radius of 2.5 km, while other sites (Chebka, Dakhlet el Atrous, and Imdel el Abiod) have relatively extensive catchment areas. On the average, the total land available for each site was 466.7 km^2. It is axiomatic that the surface extent of these sites was basically time-dependent. Consequently, the settlements certainly started with a small number of habitation units, and, with the increase of population, site layouts were progressively filled with new compounds, as will be shown later, even if the lack of fine-grained chronological study of each site does not allow us to go very far in understanding this specific issue. Two sites, Dakhlet el Atrous I, the largest site, considered as the regional center, and Akreijit, a district center or large village, will be considered in more detail, to highlight their spatial patterning.

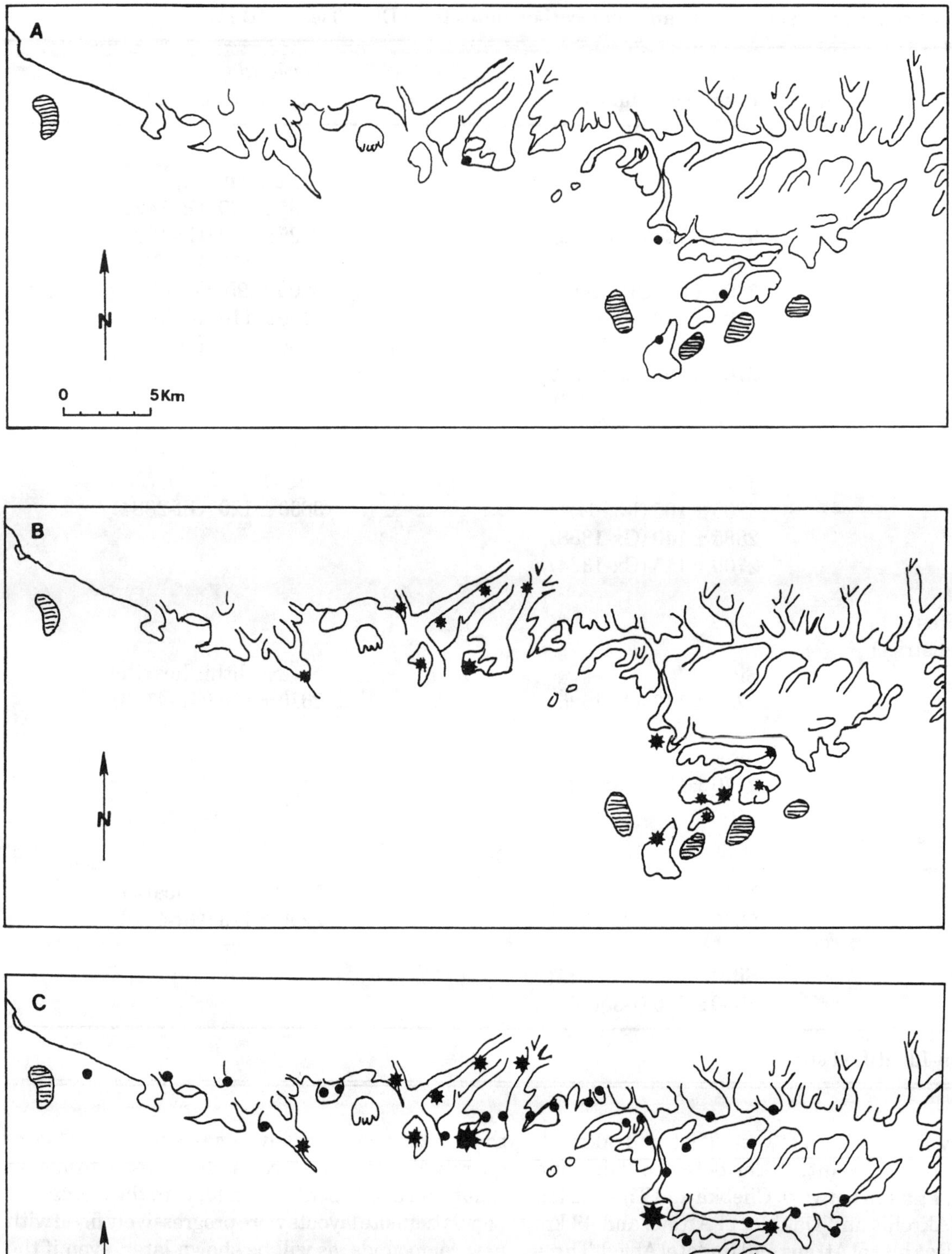

Fig. 5. Sequences of settlement expansion in the Dhar Tichitt region.

Fig. 6. Early settlement sequence: distribution of pioneer sites.

Dakhlet el Atrous I: the Regional Center

Dakhlet el Atrous I, which became the major regional center, is located exactly at the center of gravity of the study area, 65 km from the western "boundary" and 75 km from the eastern one. This extensive settlement measures 92.75 ha, with 590 compounds distributed in two parts: the Main site measuring 80.5 ha with 540 compounds and the Satellite site measuring 12.25 ha with 50 compounds. There is also an extensive field system measuring one kilometer in radius and located to the south of the site, with about 100 parcels delimited by lines of stones and sometimes dry stone walls (Fig. 7). Burial mounds built with stone blocks are distributed around the site, located on the periphery. It thus appears that there was a spatial segregation between the space of the living and that of the dead, with the exception of two large stone tumuli integrated within the site layout. The settlement layout is characterized by the presence of clusters of compounds of varying size: 26 clusters in the Main site, with 12 isolated compounds, and 11 clusters in the Satellite site, with 10 isolated compounds. The density of compounds varies respectively from 6.7/ha to 4.08/ha (Tables 4 and 5). These clusters are separated by networks of pathways and open places. A cluster of compounds is thus defined as a series of interconnected habitation units sharing common dry stone walls, separated by pathways and open places.

In the main site, the number of compounds in each cluster varies from 2 (four occurrences) to 179 (one occurrence), with a mean of 20.26 (n= 540, R= 177, SD= 36.9, CV= 1.82), and their surface extent from 100 m^2 to 3150 m^2, with a mean of 526.5 m^2 (R= 3050, SD= 501.87, CV= 0.95) (Table 4). Concerning clusters of compounds, their surface extent varies from 425 m^2 to 109,177 m^2. It also appears that, with the exception of smaller clusters, which consist of two to four compounds that are more or less of equal size, there are always a few large compounds situated near each other in each cluster (Fig. 7). The location of both large stone tumuli in such large compounds may suggest that these units have played a specific social role, and if these tumuli are burials, they may have been those of important individuals who had the privilege of being buried within the space of the living instead of the site periphery. Tentatively, these features may be interpreted as symbolic devices to perpetuate the link between the living and the ancestors who founded the settlement. On such large and packed settlements, relations of neighborhood are not always based on kinship and alliances, the space allocation system depending on the spatial distribu-

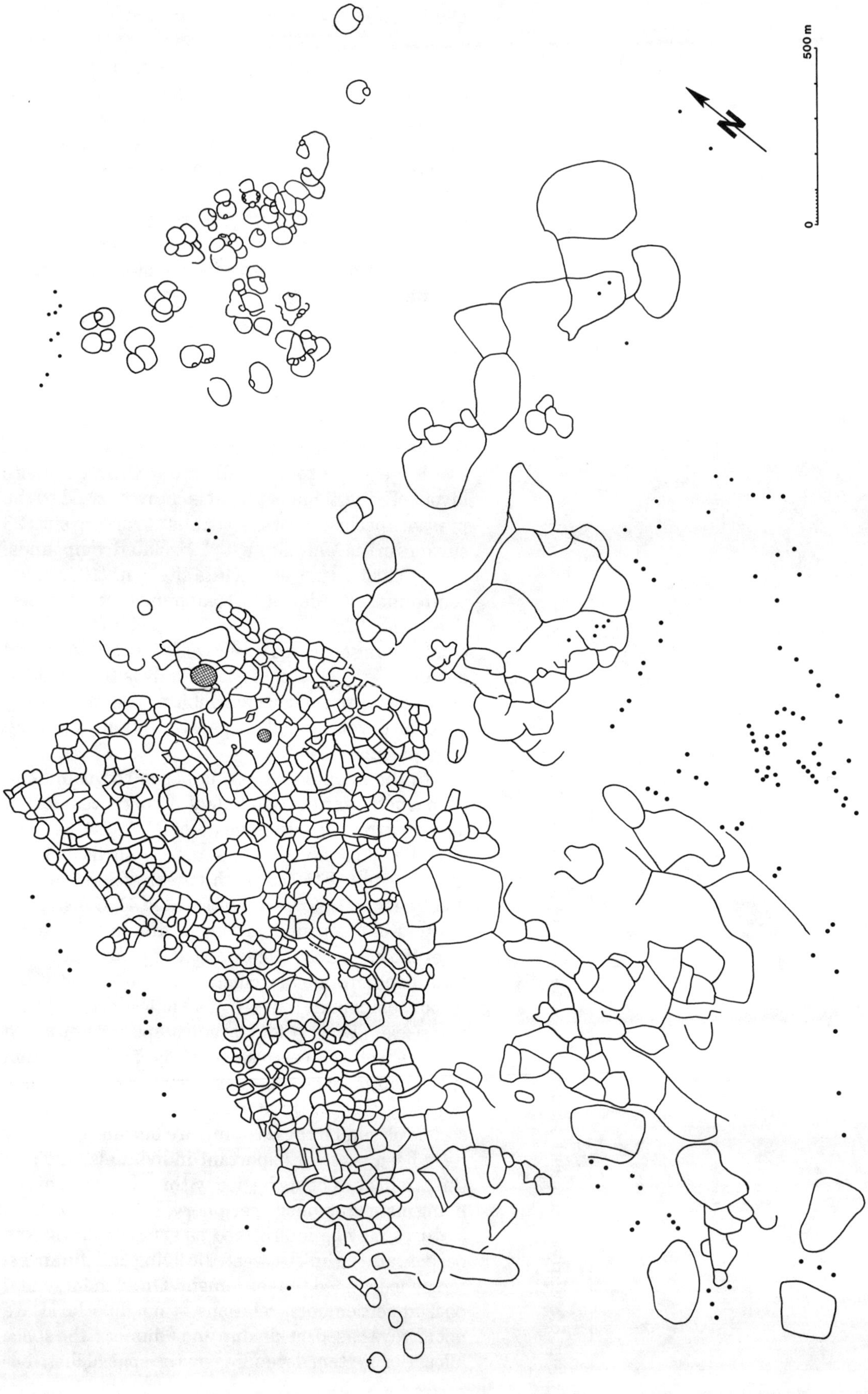

Fig. 7. Map of the regional center Dakhlet el Atrouss I: Main and Satellite sites, + = Burial.

Table 4. Dakhlet el Atrous I: Main Site: size and distribution of compounds in clusters.

Cluster	n	Min. (m^2)	Max. (m^2)	Range (m^2)	Mean	Standard deviation	Coefficient of variation	Total (m^2)
1	2	500	600	100	550	50	0.09	1100
2	179	100	3150	3050	640.91	498.78	0.77	109,177
3	7	200	314	114	259.14	51.42	0.19	1814
4	12	150	2025	1875	562.50	529.39	0.94	7750
5	12	225	750	525	448.75	165.29	0.36	5385
6	18	126	1600	1474	506.16	429.93	0.84	9211
7	71	144	2125	1981	586.92	383.96	0.65	44,572
8	9	100	625	525	338.88	169.60	0.50	3050
9	2	375	525	150	450	75	0.16	900
10	26	150	1250	1100	415.57	243.75	0.58	10,805
11	4	400	500	200	475	82.91	0.17	1900
12	3	300	400	100	333.33	47.14	0.14	1000
13	8	400	2600	2200	1014.37	666.43	0.65	8115
14	13	150	875	725	363.46	273.76	0.75	5525
15	12	250	1350	1100	570	315.11	0.55	6840
16	14	100	1350	1250	407.14	317.69	0.78	5600
17	10	150	800	650	458	198.05	0.43	4580
18	3	475	500	25	491.66	11.78	0.02	1475
19	4	100	375	275	156.25	137.35	0.87	925
20	4	195	700	505	442.50	222.44	0.50	1770
21	24	144	1000	866	507.66	288.68	0.56	12,384
22	79	130	2600	2470	580.94	434.09	0.74	43,695
23	4	100	300	200	175	75	0.42	700
24	2	150	875	725	512.50	362.50	0.70	1025
25	2	200	225	25	212.50	12.50	0.05	425
26	3	200	400	200	300	81.64	0.27	900
Single	12	200	1050	850	483.91	245.93	0.50	5807
Corral	1	–	–	–	–	–	–	5850
Total	540	100	3150	3050	526.87	501.87	0.95	302,280

tion of empty places at the time of the creation of a new habitation. It is thus possible to argue that, at the beginning of the settlement, habitation units of close kin may have been located near each other and had common walls, a system which results in an economy of scale in the workload necessary for the procurement of raw material and building of living facilities.

In the Satellite site there are 11 clusters, and the number of compounds in them varies from 2 (four occurrences) to 8 (one occurrence), with a mean of 3.9 (n= 50, R= 6, SD= 1.92, CV= 0.49) (Table 5). Their size varies from 177 m^2 to 2925 m^2 with a mean of 898.74 m^2 (R= 2748, SD= 532.91, CV= 0.59). Clusters of compounds are more dispersed than in the Main site and there is much more empty space in the site layout. This spatial patterning suggests that kin groups may have located their habitation compounds in preferential units. As will be shown later, this Satellite site seems to have been an offshoot of the Main site when its habitable space became packed. The foundation of the Satellite site thus mimics the processes of clustering which were operating in large and packed settlements.

Akreijit: a District Center

Like Dakhlet el Atrous I, Akreijit, the most intensively studied site of the study area, is located on the escarpment of the sandstone cliff, measuring 15 ha, with 177 compounds distributed in eleven clusters (Fig. 8 and Table 6), and a density of compounds of 11.80/ha. This settlement is closed on its northern side by a dry stone wall beyond which there are three

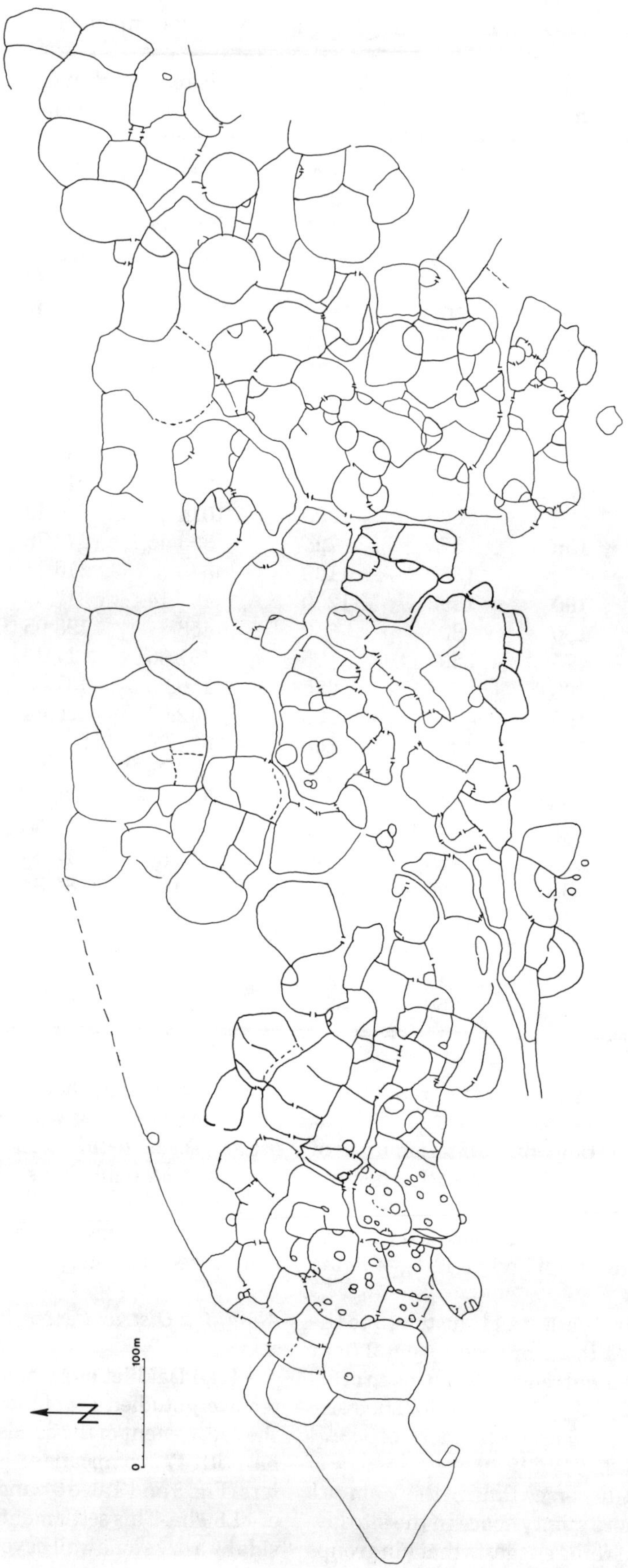

Fig. 8. Map of a district center: the large village of Akreijit.

Table 5. Dakhlet el Atrous I: Sattelite Site: size and distribution of compounds in clusters.

Cluster	n	Min. (m^2)	Max. (m^2)	Range (m^2)	Mean	Standard deviation	Coefficient of variation	Total (m^2)
1	2	1250	2925	1675	2087.5	837.5	0.40	4175
2	8	314	2000	1686	777.62	481.64	0.61	6221
3	5	177	875	691	548.60	225.04	0.41	2743
4	5	450	875	425	690	182.07	0.26	3450
5	2	750	875	125	812.5	62.5	0.07	1625
6	3	177	707	530	399.33	224.62	0.56	1198
7	3	600	1125	525	808.33	227.60	0.28	2425
8	2	600	1050	450	825	225	0.27	1650
9	3	491	1250	759	913.66	315.81	0.34	2741
10	2	750	875	125	812.5	62.5	0.07	1625
11	5	491	1125	634	828.20	247.08	0.29	4141
Single	10	491	2250	1759	1294.30	575.86	0.44	12,943
Total	50	177	2925	2748	898.74	532.91	0.59	44,937

Table 6. Akreijit: Size and distribution of compounds in clusters.

Cluster	n	Min. (m^2)	Max. (m^2)	Range (m^2)	Mean	Standard deviation	Coefficient of variation	Total (m^2)
1	19	75	1575	1500	596.05	377.48	0.63	11,325
2	37	80	1600	1520	461.91	324.01	0.70	17,094
3	21	240	2394	2154	884.47	551.78	0.62	18,574
4	8	360	2200	1840	846.25	669.35	0.79	6770
5	17	170	1650	1480	678.47	353.67	0.52	11,334
6	3	480	1500	1020	1040	422.37	0.40	3120
7	3	306	1176	870	684	364.20	0.53	2052
8	4	91	1200	1109	758.50	427.12	0.56	3034
9	24	180	2280	2100	829.50	487.09	0.58	19,908
10	29	70	1386	1316	495.79	302.49	0.61	14,378
11	11	81	910	829	442.27	261.19	0.59	4865
Single	1	96	96	0	96	0	0	96
Total	177	70	2394	2324	625.14	451.86	0.72	112,550

large stone-lined enclosures interpreted as livestock corrals. The number of compounds in clusters varies from 3 (two occurrences) to 37 (one occurrence) with a mean of 16.27 (R= 34, SD= 10.48, CV= 0.64) and their size from 70 m^2 to 2394 m^2, with a mean of 625.14 (R= 2324, SD= 451.86, CV= 0.72). In terms of spatial extent, the range of the number of compounds in each cluster is larger than in Dakhlet el Atrous I. The clusters of compounds are separated by pathways and open places, but a closer examination of the spatial patterning of the site shows that there were modifications in some compounds, mostly located in the western part of the settlement. As shown in Figure 8, former wall courses (broken lines) were destroyed to allow the enlargement of some compounds, to combine two distinct habitation units, or to reduce the size of a formerly larger unit (in the northeast). In the southeast, former pathways were closed. It is also possible to observe that some compounds communicated with each other with doorways, and some

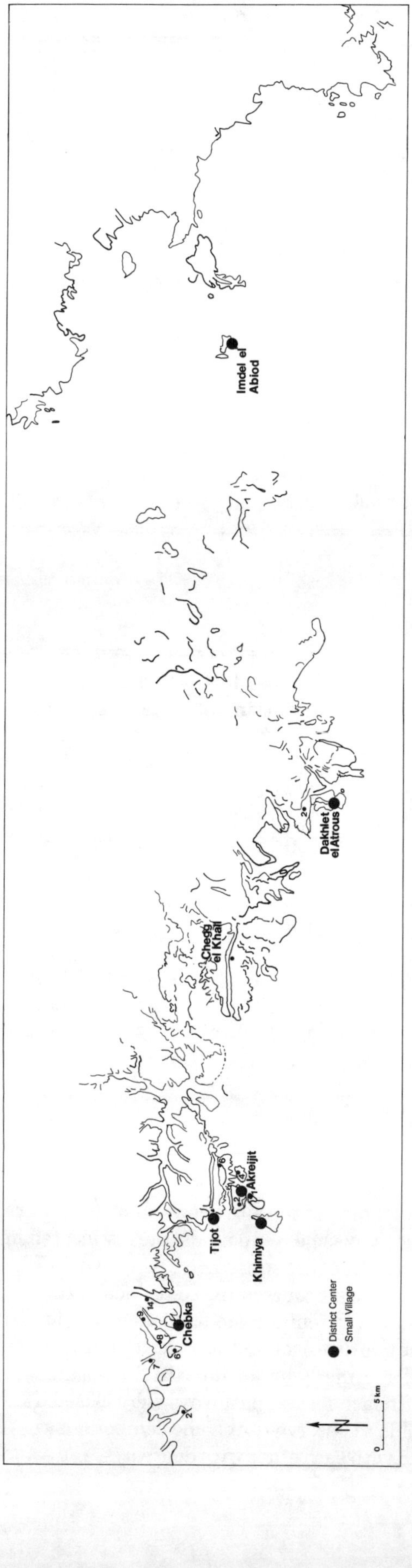

Fig. 9. Middle settlement sequence: distribution of sites.

of them were closed, as attested in compound 50E. The enlargement of compounds is certainly related to the larger number of household members, while intercommunicating compounds suggest the existence of preferential groupings of people according to their kinship relations and/or alliances. The closure of former doorways may have been generated by changing relations between neighbors. Open places distributed all over the settlement may have played the role of meeting and feasting places.

These two examples of pioneer settlements show that community space was shaped through successive stages which finally led to a kind of planning in which an important part of the available space was devoted to public activities, e.g., pathways, places of meeting, feasting, and other kinds of activities. There are, however, striking differences between the two sites. At Dakhlet el Atrous I, Main Site, the "future" regional center, 30.22 ha (37.54%) were devoted to compounds or private domains and 50.28 ha (62.45%) to open or public space. The opposite is true at Akreijit: the community space was not only closed by a dry stone wall, but less space was allocated to public activities (3.75 ha or 25%) while more was allocated to private use in compounds (11. 25 ha or 75%). These variations suggest that the range of public activities in the central settlement generated a specific pattern of space allocation with relatively high packing of compounds per hectare to generate more space for public and communal activities, congruent with its function as a major political center. With the increasing packing of the space within pioneer settlements due to population growth and the resulting relative pressure on productive land in their respective catchment areas, the process of generational segmentation may have generated the creation of new settlements in virgin land.

Cultural Landscape II: the Middle Settlement Sequence (ca. 3000–2500 B.P.)

The middle settlement sequence started with the emergence of twelve small villages located several kilometers from the large pioneer settlements: six in the Chebka district in the westernmost part of the study area, four in the Akreijit district, one near the regional center of Dakhlet el Atrous I, and a new settlement (which later became a new district center) at Chegg el Khail, midway between Akreijit and Dakhlet el Atrous I (Fig. 9). Areas located on the edges of wadis and isolated massifs were settled for the first time. This process is much more spectacular in the Chebka district, in which the narrow plateau generated a wider expansion of settlements in comparison with the other districts. Distances between district centers and small villages vary from 2.5 km to 9 km, with a mean of 4.66 km (n = 6, R = 6.5, SD = 2.11, CV = 0.45), for the Chebka district and from 1 km to 3.5 km, with a mean of 2 km (n = 4, R = 2.5, SD = 1.06, CV = 0.53), for the Akreijit district, and in the Dakhlet el Atrous district the one new village, named Dakhlet el Atrous II, is located four kilometers to the north of the regional center (Tables 7 and 8). There was no change in the easternmost district of Imdel el Abiod. The pattern which emerged suggests the buildup of a political landscape with clusters of settlements of unequal weight. If power is equated with the number of dependent villages, the Chebka district, with seven settlements, was certainly the most powerful district during the middle settlement sequence, followed by Akreijit with five villages, Dakhlet el Atrous with two villages, and Imdel el Abiod and Chegg el Khail with one village each.

In terms of land available for each village, there was an average of 155.55 km^2 of land per site during the middle settlement sequence. It also appears that trends already noted for the early sequence continued unchanged. In this regard, it is not surprising that districts located in the west experienced the highest increase in the number of settlements, from four to fourteen. Consequently, while subregional political networks were emerging in the west, the major part of the study area situated in the east, was still doted with four dispersed settlements that were in varying degrees autonomous.

Table 7. Distances between large and small villages in each cluster of settlements.

Chebka site	Chebka km	Akreijit site	Akreijit km	Dakhlet el Atrous I site	Dakhlet el Atrous I km
2	9	1	1	2	4
6	2.5	2	1		
7	4.5	4	2.5		
8	3	6	3.5		
9	4				
14	5				

Spatial Patterning of a Small Village: Dakhlet el Atrous II

Dakhlet el Atrous II is a small village located four kilometers to the north of the regional center, measuring 10.17 ha with 49 compounds, a density of 4.81/ha. In this settlement, with a subcircular shape, there are 8 isolated compounds; the others are distributed in nine clusters, and the number of units in each varies from 2 (four occurrences) to 15 (one occurrence), with a mean of 4.88 (n = 49, R = 13, SD = 4.09, CV = 0.83). The surface extent of compounds varies from 100 m^2 to 3600 m^2, with a mean size of 763.04 (R = 3500, SD = 661.65, CV = 0.86) (Table 9 and Fig. 10). One of the largest compounds, located at the middle of the settlement, does not seem to have been a habitation unit but more probably a livestock enclosure. Within the site, 3.73 ha, 36.67% of the available space, is devoted to built features and 6.44 ha (63.32%) is empty space.

A closer look at the site map shows that isolated compounds and smaller clusters with two habitation units are located on the periphery of the settlement. This patterning suggests that the compounds of the first settlers of Dakhlet el Atrous II, clustered according to their kinship and/or alliance relations, determined the basic spatial organization of the site, and new settlers or junior households were obliged to build their habitation structures on the periphery of the village. The relatively high standard deviation and coefficient of variation of the surface area of compounds suggest that there were important differences

Table 8. Variation in distance between large and small villages.

District	n	Min. (km)	Max. (km)	Range (km)	Mean	Standard deviation	Coefficient of variation
Chebka	6	2.5	9	6.5	4.66	2.11	0.45
Akreijit	4	1	3.5	2.5	2.00	1.06	0.53
Dakhlet el Atrous	1	4	4	0	4	0	0
Total	11	1	9	8	4.18	2.12	0.50

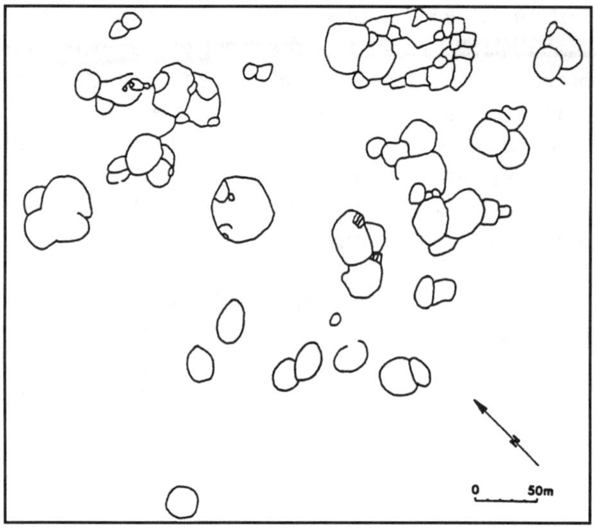

Fig. 10. Map of a small village: Dakhlet el Atrous II.

in the number of members of the different households inhabiting the village. In addition, the large proportion of empty space is not linked to the performance of very important public activities but mostly to the relatively small number of inhabitants, as seen in the low degree of packing of the site layout.

During the middle settlement sequence, the spatial distribution of small villages was still confined within the boundaries of earlier pioneer sites, which led to the emergence of a two-level settlement hierarchy. The districts located in the western part of the study area, Chebka and Akreijit and to a lesser degree Dakhlet el Atrous I, saw the development of incipient forms of subregional polities, while there was no observable change at Tijot, Khimiya, and Imdel el Abiod. The cultural landscape was consequently composed of three incipient subregional centers, the most important being situated in the west with fourteen sites out of a total of eighteen, and three large and relatively autonomous villages.

Cultural Landscape III: the Late Settlement Sequence (ca. 2500–2000 B.P.)

The late settlement sequence started around ca. 2500 B.P. with the emergence of 72 hamlets which were distributed all over the landscape. The colonization process was directed towards wadi valleys of the "hinterland." With the exception of the Chebka district, in which the distribution of virgin land was restricted, settlements expanded in areas distant from previous villages (Fig. 11). This stage of settlement expansion led to the development of structured polities, termed districts and on the average, the amount of land available for each site shrank to 31.11 km^2. A radical shift in settlement distribution occurred during this sequence. The most spectacular growth took place in the eastern part of the study area, in the Chegg el Khail district with 19 new hamlets, in the Dakhlet el Atrous I district with 14, and Imdel el Abiod with 12. In the west, the increase in the number of settlements, even if it appears less spectacular, was important, with 10 new hamlets in the Chebka district, eight in Tijot district, six in Akreijit district, and two in Khimiya. This change in the distribution of population was accompanied by an equally important shift in the balance of power, with the displacement of the most important political center from the

Table 9. Dakhlet el Atrous II: Size and distribution of compounds in clusters.

Cluster	n	Min. (m^2)	Max. (m^2)	Range (m^2)	Mean	Standard deviation	Coefficient of variation	Total (m^2)
1	2	314	491	177	402.5	88.5	0.21	805
2	2	375	707	332	541	166	0.30	1082
3	2	314	525	211	419.5	105.5	0.25	839
4	3	375	1200	825	858.33	351.38	0.40	2575
5	4	1000	2000	1000	1593.75	427.33	0.26	6375
6	2	491	700	209	595.5	104.5	0.17	1191
7	3	500	707	207	602.33	84.52	0.14	1807
8	8	176	1200	1024	691.62	422.28	0.61	5533
9	15	100	1800	1700	448.66	546.05	1.21	8030
Single	8	375	3600	3225	1144	1037.35	0.90	9152
Total	49	100	3600	3500	763.04	661.65	0.86	37,389

Fig. 11. Late settlement sequence: distribution of sites.

west to the central area, and it is certainly during this sequence that Dakhlet el Atrous I, located at the center of gravity of the whole region, became the dominant regional center.

Thiessen polygons have been used to determine the theoretical spatial extent of districts. The number of settlements in each varies from 3 in the Khimiya district, which is the smallest, to 20 in the district of Chegg el Khail.

Distances between district centers and other sites in each district vary from 1 to 11 km in the Chebka district, with a mean of 5.32 (n = 17, R = 10, SD = 2.64, CV = 0.49), 3.5 to 8.5 km in the Tijot district, with a mean of 5.37 (n = 8, R = 5, SD = 1.45, CV = 0.27), 1 to 9.5 km in the Akreijit district, with a mean of 3.5 (n = 10, R = 8.5, SD = 3.01, CV = 0.86), 2 to 14 km in the Chegg el Khail district, with a mean of 7.02 (n = 19, R = 12, SD = 3.23, CV = 0.46), 1 to 24 km in the Dakhlet el Atrous district, with a mean of 9.56 (n = 18, R = 23, SD = 7.82, CV = 0.81), and 13 to 28 km in the Imdel el Abiod district, with a mean of 19.12 (n = 12, R = 15, SD = 4.61, CV = 0.24) (Tables 10 and 11). The constraints of the topography on site location strategies is unquestionable, the best example being found in the district of Imdel el Abiod (Fig. 11 and Table 12), where the nearest hamlet is at a distance of 13 kilometers. In general, however, most of the sites are located between 1 and 12.5 km from the district center, about a two-hour walk (Table 12).

Spatial Patterning of a Hamlet: Rachim I and II

Hamlets are small settlements having less than 20 compounds each. Rachim, a hamlet from the Chegg el Khail district, situated 11.5 km to the northwest of the district center, on the edge of a wadi, is a good example of the different kinds of spatial organization which developed in such settlements (Fig. 12). The settlement is divided into two parts, named Rachim I in the east and II in the west, separated by 200 m. Rachim I measures 1.5 ha, with 9 tightly clustered compounds organized in a circular shape, with three groups of two habitation units each, and three relatively isolated ones. Rachim II measures 1.2 ha, with 7 compounds arranged in a loose east-west linear pattern. One habitation unit is isolated, while the others are organized into three aggregates of two units. Consequently, we may consider that this hamlet all together measures 2.7 ha with 16 compounds.

There are six clusters of two habitation units each and four isolated compounds, the density of compounds being 5.92/ha. Private space devoted to

Table 10. List of distance between centers and other sites in each district.

Site	Chebka	Tijot	Khimiya	Akreijit	Chegg el Khail	Dakhlet el Atrous	Imdel el Abiod
1	11	5.5	Khimiya	1	14	6	18
2	9	5	1.5	1	11.5	4	I.el Abiod
3	8	4	1.5	2	11.5	1	18
4	7	3.5		2.5	9	D.e.A. I	16
5	5.5	4.5		3.5	9	3	15.5
6	3.5	6		3.5	9	5	13
7	5.5	6		5	9.5	5.5	16.5
8	2.5	8.5		6.5	8	5.5	16.5
9	4	Tijot		7.5	5.5	6.5	16
10	1			9.5	C.e.K.	8	22.5
11	Chebka			Akreijit	5	12	27.5
12	4				4.5	16	28
13	2.5				3.5	16.5	22
14	5.5				2	20	
15	2				4	21.5	
16	5.5				2.5	24	
17	7				3		
18	8				3.5		
19					4		
20					6.5		

Table 11. Variations in distance between central and peripheral sites in each district.

District	n	Min. (km)	Max. (km)	Range (km)	Mean	Standard deviation	Coefficient of variation	Total (km)
Chebka	17	1	11	10	5.32	2.64	0.49	18
Tijot	8	3.5	8.5	5	5.37	1.45	0.27	9
Khimiya	2	1.5	1.5	0	1.5	0	0	3
Akreijit	10	1	9.5	8.5	3.5	3.01	0.86	11
Chegg el Khail	19	2	14	12	7.02	3.23	0.46	20
Dakhlet el Atrous	15	1	24	23	9.56	7.82	0.81	16
Imdel el Abiod	12	13	28	15	19.12	4.61	0.24	13
Total	83	1	28	27	8.31	6.44	0.77	90

Table 12. Number of sites by classes of distance between central and peripheral sites in each district.

Distance (km)	1–4.5	5–8.5	9–12.5	13–18	18.5–25	25–30
Chebka	8	7	2	–	–	–
Tijot	3	5	–	–	–	–
Khimiya	2	–	–	–	–	–
Akreijit	7	2	1	–	–	–
Chegg el Khail	7	5	6	1	–	–
Dakhlet el Atrous	3	6	1	2	3	–
Imdel el Abiod	–	–	–	8	2	2
Total	30	25	10	11	5	2

habitation units covers 2.12 ha (78.51%), and what may be called public space only 0.58 ha (21.48%). The size of compounds varies from 314 m^2 to 4050 m^2, with a mean of 1325.06 (n = 16, R = 3736, SD = 991.41, CV = 0.74) (Table 13). The clustering of habitation units into aggregates, measuring 1198 m^2 for the smallest and 5306 m^2 for the largest, does not result from the lack of empty space, as was certainly the case in largest settlements, but was more probably generated by kinship and/or alliance relationships. This kind of frontier settlement seems to have been created almost exclusively for economic purposes, with its characteristic dispersed distribution of habitation facilities.

Districts and Settlement Hierarchy

With the emergence of hamlets, the late sequence of settlement expansion in the Dhar Tichitt-Walata was completed, between ca. 2500 and 2000 B.P. The pattern which appears is that of a settlement hierarchy with four ranks: rank 1 consisting of the regional center at Dakhlet el Atrous I measuring 92.75 ha with 590 compounds in both the Main and Satellite site; rank 2 consisting of large villages, here considered as district centers, such as Chebka (3.5 ha with 120 compounds), Tijot (4 ha with 140 compounds), Khimiya (17.5 ha with 180 compounds), Akreijit (15 ha with 177 compounds), and Imdel el Abiod I and II (32 ha with 198 compounds); twelve rank 3 sites, small villages with twenty to fifty compounds, such as Chegg el Khail, which, although a small village, emerged as a district center in the late settlement sequence; and 72 rank 4 sites, hamlets with less than twenty compounds each (Table 14).

The rate of increase in the number of settlements is exponential. We begin with 6 settlements during the early sequence which lasted 1000 years; twelve new settlements were founded during the middle sequence which lasted 500 years; and 72 were created during the 500 years of the late sequence. Thus, the rate of growth was 1:2:6 (Fig. 13). The cultural landscape which resulted from this long-term process of expansion is a pattern of settlement which is congruent with a paramount chiefdom level of sociopolitical organization with a four-tiered hierar-

Table 13. Rachim I and II: size and distribution of compounds in clusters.

Cluster	n	Min. (m^2)	Max. (m^2)	Range (m^2)	Mean	Standard deviation	Coefficient of variation	Total (m^2)
1	2	1575	3150	1575	2362.5	787.5	0.33	4725
2	2	814	2200	1886	1257	943	0.75	2514
3	2	1256	4050	2794	2653	1397	0.52	5306
4	2	707	1256	549	981.5	274.5	0.27	1963
5	2	962	1256	294	1109	147	0.13	2218
6	2	491	707	216	599	108	0.18	1198
Single	4	314	1256	942	819.25	350.46	0.42	3277
Total	16	314	4050	3736	1325.06	991.41	0.74	21,201

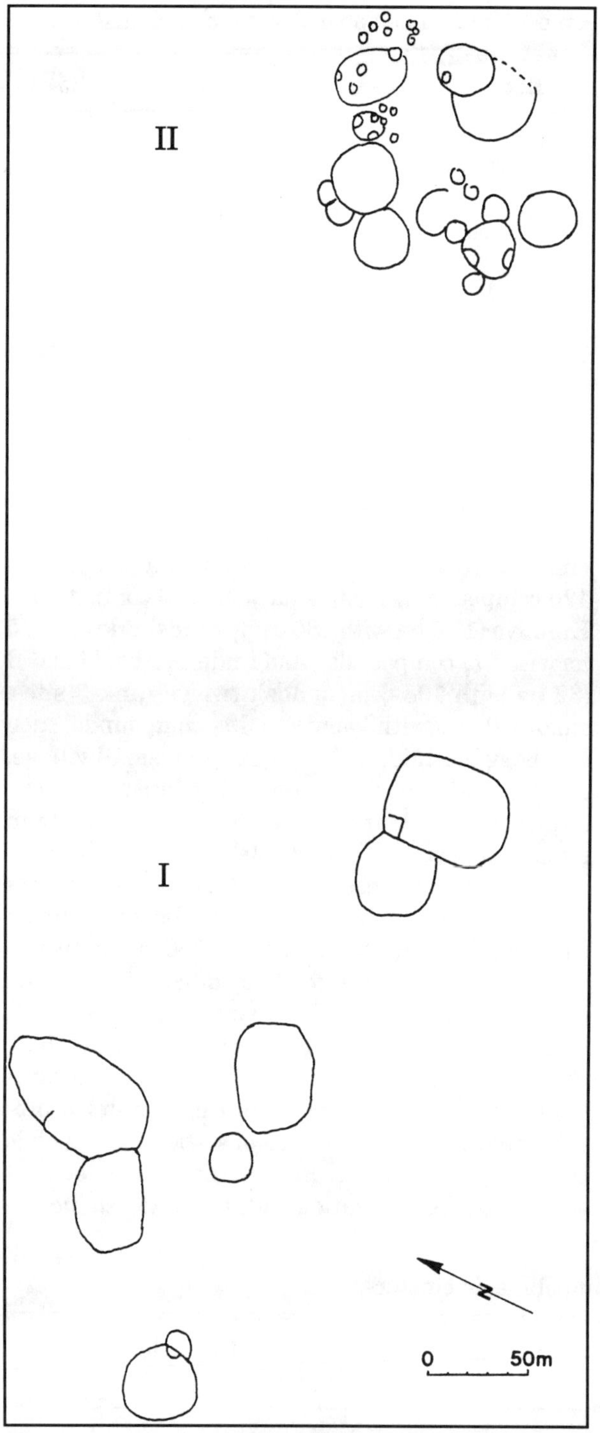

Fig. 12. Map of a hamlet: Rachim I and II.

chy of settlements (Fig. 14) The territorial extent of districts varied from ca. 33 km^2 for Khimiya to ca. 1410 km^2 for Imdel el Abiod (Table 15). The presence of unsettled territory along some major wadis between neighboring districts in the central and eastern part of the study area was probably a device for boundary maintenance. On the other hand, the absence of such features in the west may also explain the existence of defensive walls enclosing district centers. In this regard, the walled villages from the western part of the study area, such as Chebka, Khimiya, Akreijit, and Site 2 (Chebka district), may reflect sociopolitical competition and dispute over land and pastures in this relatively crowded area (cf. Levy, this volume). The fact that district centers located in the eastern part of the region, where large tracts of land are available, are not walled gives additional support to this hypothesis. This relative pressure on land in the western portion of the settled territory can also be seen in the average extent of space per site in each district, which varies from 9.45 km^2 (Akreijit) to 20 km^2 (Tijot) in the west, and from 15.6 km^2 (Chegg el Khail) to 108.46 km^2 (Imdel el Abiod) in the east (Table 15).

Space and Polities

During the late settlement sequence, the Neolithic cultural landscape was composed of 90 settlements distributed over the whole study area. These settlements were structured into a hierarchical pattern with four ranks: one regional center, five large villages or district centers, twelve small villages (one of which, Chegg el Khail, appears to have functioned as a district center), and 72 hamlets. The rank 1 and 2 settlements were located in what is considered an optimal area, at the intersection of two subsistence zones: the lowland, used as a dry season camping area, and the upland, the plateau above the sandstone cliff, where permanent sites were situated. Small villages were located along major wadis, mostly in the optimal area, while hamlets which may be termed "frontier" settlements, were located far in the "hinterland" and on the periphery of the Neolithic landscape. It is thus possible to consider that any single district included three portions of the landscape: the sandy lowland with its potential for dry season socioeconomic activities, the optimal zone of the cliff escarpment, and the hinterland, or periphery, for agricultural activities.

In terms of the spatial organization of the sites at the different levels of the settlement hierarchy, some interesting patterns emerge. The average size of compounds increases from the regional center (526.05

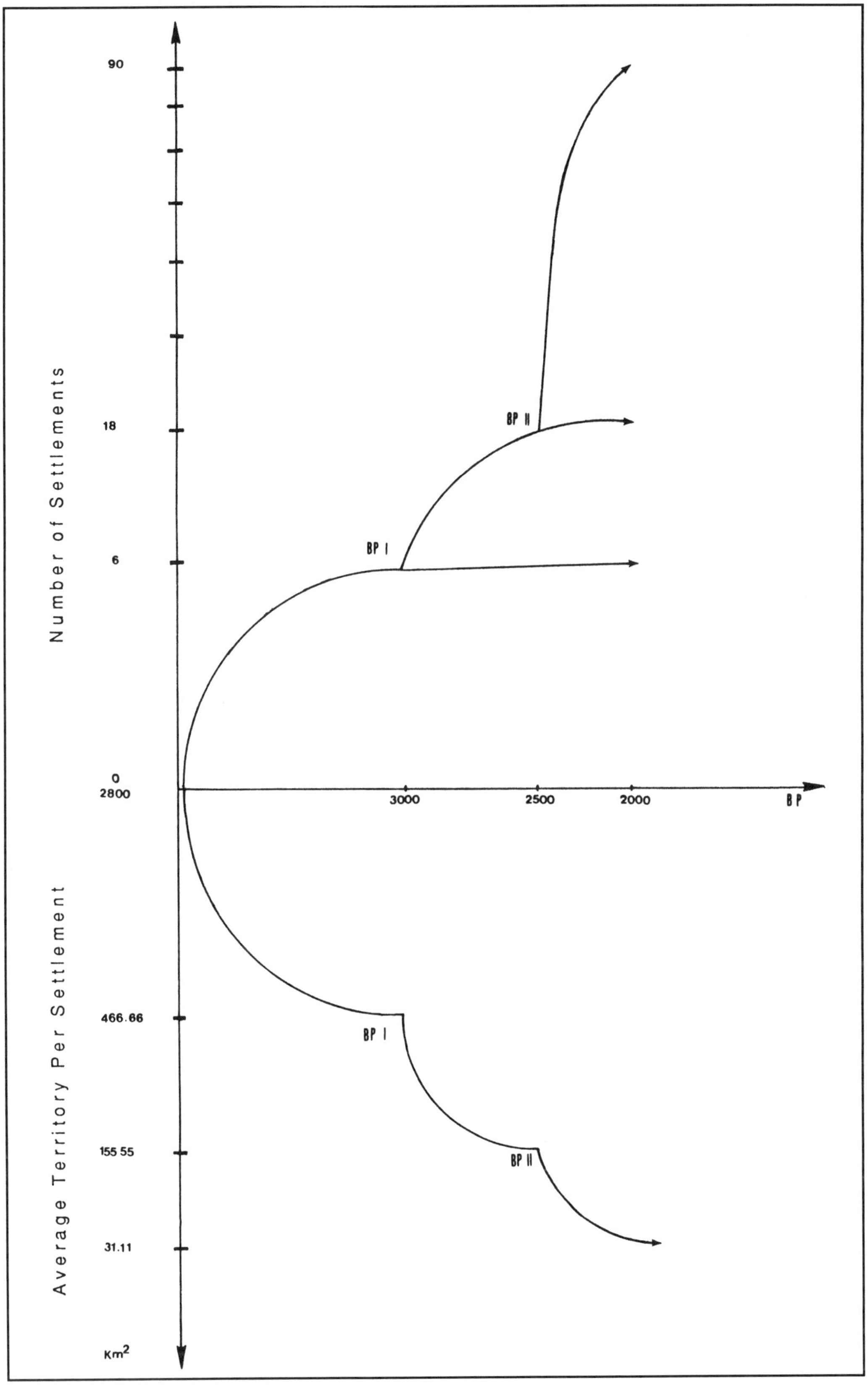

Fig. 13. Logistic curves summarizing the expansion of settlements with bifurcation points.

Table 14. Distribution of sites by settlement hierarchy.

District	Regional center	Large village	Small village	Hamlet	Total
Chebka	–	1	6	11	18
Tijot	–	1	–	8	9
Khimiya	–	1	–	2	3
Akreijit	–	1	4	6	11
Chegg el Khail	–	–	1	19	20
Dakhlet el Atrous	1	–	1	14	16
Imdel el Abiod	–	1	–	12	13
Total	1	5	12	72	90

Table 15. Territorial extent of districts.

District	Length (km)	Width (km)	Surface (km^2)	%	Number of sites	Land/site (km^2)	Number of ranks
Chebka	21.5	10	215	7.67	18	11.94	3(2-4)
Tijot	15	12	180	6.42	9	20	2(2,4)
Khimiya	6	5.5	33	1.17	3	11	2(2,4)
Akreijit	16	6.5	104	3.71	11	9.45	3(2-4)
Chegg el Khail	24	13	312	11.14	20	15.60	2(3-4)
Dakhlet el Atrous	27	15	405	14.46	16	25.31	2(1,4)
Imdel el Abiod	47	30	1410	50.35	13	108.46	2(2,4)
Total	140	20	2800	–	90	31.11	4

m^2) to hamlets (1325.06 m^2) (Table 16), but coefficients of variation (0.95 and 0.74 respectively), standard deviations, and ranges do not follow the same pattern, suggesting that the number of members of households was not dependent on the size of the settlement. In other words, the differences in size among households are comparable in all kinds of settlements. The process of nucleation is low in hamlets and high in larger settlements. The number of clusters of compounds (i.e., interconnected habitation units) vary from 26 at Dakhlet el Atrous I: Main site to 6 at Rachim (Table 17) and the mean number of clustered compounds decreases from 19.69 to 2 respectively. The spatial patterning of Dakhlet el Atrous I: Satellite site, which is considered an off-shoot of the Main site, is similar to that of small villages.

As shown by standard deviations and coefficients of variation (Table 17), the degree of nucleation is thus dependent on the size, and consequently the length of occupation, of a settlement: the longer the occupation, the higher the degree of nucleation. An analysis of the spatial extent of clusters of compounds shows similar patterns (Table 18), and indexes of dispersal, calculated by dividing the number of clusters of compounds by the total number of compounds in each site, show the dispersal of compounds to be minimal in the regional center (0.07) and maximal at Rachim (0.62), a hamlet (Table 19).

If private space is defined as that devoted to habitation units and public space as that dedicated to pathways and open places, the space allocation system may be represented as a ratio. It thus appears that the ratio of private/public space varies from 3.65 at Rachim to 0.57 at Dakhlet el Atrous I: Satellite site and Dakhlet el Atrous II, being 3.0 at Akreijit and 0.6 at Dakhlet el Atrous I: Main site.

Hamlets are frontier settlements settled almost exclusively for subsistence purposes. The ratio of private to public space for small villages (0.57) is generated by the subcircular shape of the studied settlements, which include in their layout large tracts of empty space. At first glance, the figure for Akreijit

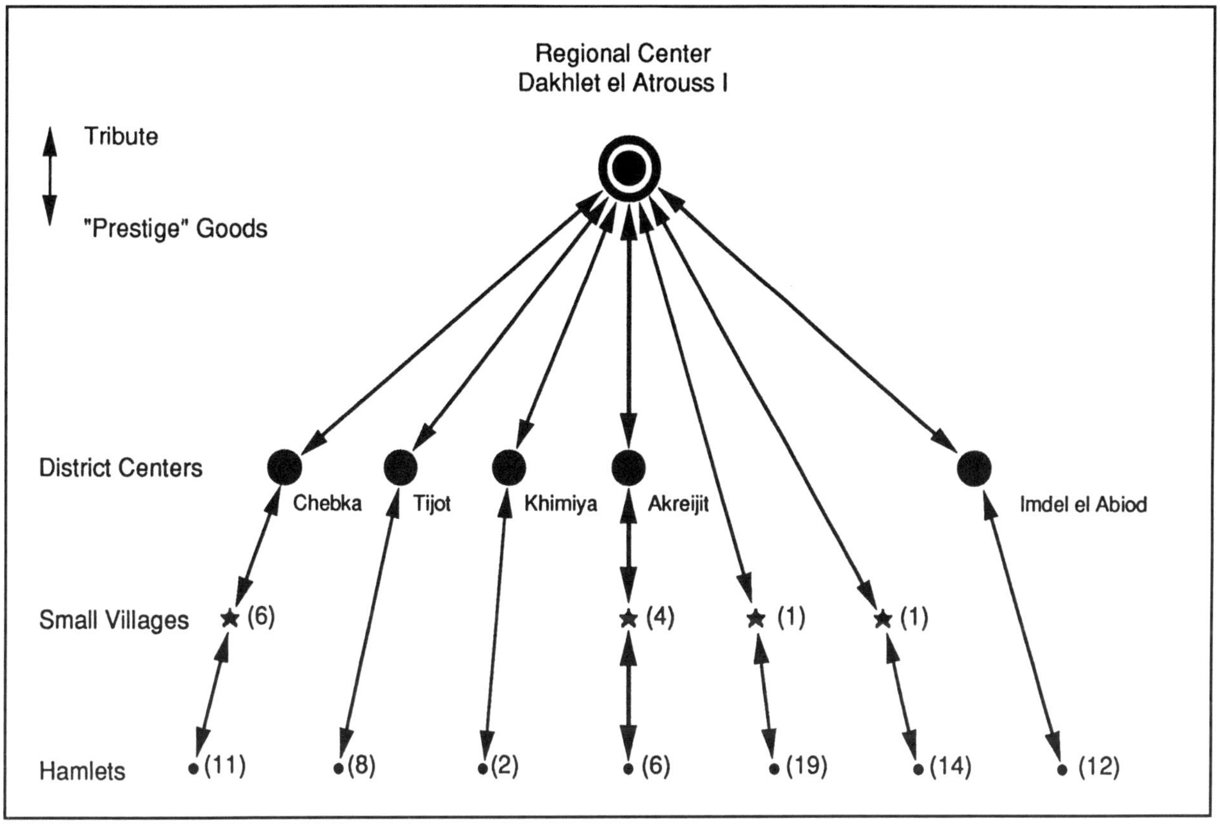

Fig. 14. Simplified model of the settlement hierarchy with the directions for the flows of tribute and prestige goods.

Table 16. Variation in compound size by settlement hierarchy.

	Regional center Dakhlet el Atrous I Main	Satellite	*District center* Akreijit	*Small village* Dakhlet el Atrous II	*Hamlet* Rachim
n	540	50	177	49	16
Minimum (m^2)	100	177	70	100	314
Maximum (m^2)	3150	2925	2394	3600	4050
Range	3050	2748	2324	3500	3736
Mean (m^2)	526.05	898.74	625.14	763.04	1325.06
Standard deviation	501.87	532.91	451.86	661.65	991.41
Coefficient of variation	0.95	0.59	0.72	0.86	0.74

Table 17. Distribution of compounds in clusters by settlement hierarchy.

	Regional center Dakhlet el Atrous I Main	Satellite	*District center* Akreijit	*Small village* Dakhlet el Atrous II	*Hamlet* Rachim
n	26	11	11	9	6
Minimum	2	2	3	2	2
Maximum	179	8	37	15	2
Range	177	6	34	13	0
Mean	19.69	3.63	16	4.77	2
Standard deviation	36.91	1.82	10.78	4.18	0
Coefficient of variation	1.87	0.50	0.67	0.87	0
Total	540	50	177	49	16

Table 18. Areal extents of compound clusters by settlement hierarchy.

	Regional center Dakhlet el Atrous I Main	Satellite	*District center* Akreijit	*Small village* Dakhlet el Atrous II	*Hamlet* Rachim
n	26	11	11	9	6
Minimum (m^2)	425	1198	2052	805	1198
Maximum (m^2)	109,177	6221	19,908	8030	4725
Range	108,752	5023	17,856	7225	8527
Mean (m^2)	11,117.80	2908.54	10,223.09	3137.44	2987.33
Standard deviation	22,561.40	1429.63	6324.50	2603	1497.92
Coefficient of variation	2.02	0.49	0.61	0.82	0.50

(3.0) is surprising at the regional level. This is because we would expect a larger part of the community space to be devoted to public activities in such an important district center. It is sufficient, though, if we consider that, in absolute terms, 3.75 ha concern the public domain. At Dakhlet el Atrous I: Main site, however, the portion of community space allocated to public activities is congruent with its function as the dominant regional center (Table 19).

The different patterns discussed above bring to light a part of the "hidden dimension" of the spatial behavior of the Neolithic societies of the Dhars Tichitt-Walata and suggest issues for future research.

Epilogue

The theories, models, and discussions of empirical data presented in this chapter on the spatial behavior of the Neolithic societies of the Dhars Tichitt-Walata show that all realms of data are useful but must be selected according to their importance for the research problem at hand. The Neolithic cultural landscape we observe today in the archaeological record resulted from successive sequences of settlement expansion which went along with the development of sociopolitical structures congruent with each new situation (Fig. 13).

If we first consider the subsistence-settlement system, the Neolithic cultural landscape was consti-

Table 19. Major characteristics of site spatial organization by settlement hierarchy.

	Regional center Dakhlet el Atrous I Main	Satellite	*District center* Akreijit	*Small village* Dakhlet el Atrous II	*Hamlet* Rachim
Surface (ha)	80.50	12.25	15	10.17	2.70
Private (Pr)	30.22	4.49	11.25	3.73	2.12
Public (Ps)	50.28	7.76	3.75	6.44	0.58
Ratio Pr/Ps	0.60	0.57	3.00	0.57	3.65
Number of compounds	540	50	177	49	16
Number of clusters	26	11	11	9	6
Isolated	12	10	1	8	4
Density /ha	6.70	4.08	11.80	4.81	5.92
Index of dispersal	0.07	0.42	0.06	0.34	0.62

tuted of two basic territorial components: the flat sandy lowland and the upland plateau, with the cliff escarpment as their zone of intersection. The former was used as a dry season camping area and the latter as the main settlement area. In terms of the dynamics of the socioeconomic systems and their corollary overlapping spheres of activities, individual activity space modules were integrated into higher level constructs, the compounds, which were the habitation units of households characterized as extended families. These households were integrated into a higher level of social organization, the community or the settlement, where differences in the size of households was certainly translated into spatial terms, with larger units often inhabiting larger compounds (cf. Agorsah, this volume). At the inter-settlement level, different communities were components of a larger sociopolitical organization, the district, characterized in the archaeological record by a settlement hierarchy. Finally, at the regional level, these different districts were sociopolitical subdivisions of the cultural landscape. We can thus consider that the dynamics of the sociopolitical organization which emerged during the late settlement sequence generated patterned and preferential networks of people, goods and services. In this regard, if the settlement hierarchy is considered as a sociopolitical framework, we may infer that tribute may have flowed from hamlets to the regional center, through small villages and district centers, and prestige goods, such as amazonite and carnelian beads, may have flowed in the opposite direction (Fig. 14).

The spatiometric approach outlined in this chapter gives strong support to a previous study of the Dhar Tichitt sociopolitical organization (Holl 1985b), where conservative statements concerning the political status of those social systems must be reconsidered. In light of the larger regional approach taken here, it now seems that the Neolithic societies of the Dhars Tichitt-Walata had a four-tiered hierarchy of settlement, not simply a two-tiered one, as was concluded from the study of the Dhar Tichitt archaeological record alone. The reevaluation of the social dynamics of the southeastern Mauritanian settlement pattern shows clearly that it was dominated by the regional center of Dakhlet el Atrous I, measuring 92.75 ha with 590 compounds, which may be characterized as a city. Consequently, the skepticism of some scholars concerning the later prehistory of West Africa now seems ill-founded. Their attitude may have been a result of unfamiliarity with the southeastern Sahara archaeological record presented here and certain preconceptions concerning the processes and timing of social change in West Africa.

References

Agorsah, K. A.

1988 Evaluating spatial behavior of pre-historic societies. *Journal of Anthropological Archaeology* 7:231-47.

Amblard, S.

1984 *Tichitt-Walata: Civilisation et Industrie Lithique.* Paris, Editions Recherhces sur les civilisations.

1986 Les villages néolithiques des Dhars Tichitt et Walata: approche et méthodes d'étude.

In *Actes du Symposium Archéologie Africaine et Sciences de la Nature Appliquée à l'Archéologie*, pp. 61-97. Bordeaux.

Amblard, S. & J. Pernès
1989 The identification of cultivated pearl millet (*Pennisetum*) amongst plant impressions on pottery from Oued Chebbi (Dhar Oualata, Mauritania). *The African Archaeological Review* 7:117 126.

Ardener, S.
1981 Ground rules and social maps for women: an introduction. In *Women and Space: Ground Rules and Social Maps*, S. Ardener (ed.), 11-34. London: Croom Helm.

Bailey, G.
1983 Concepts of time in quaternary prehistory. *Annual Review of Anthropology* 12:165-92.

Bernus, E.
1981 *Touaregs nigériens: unité culturelle et diversité régionale d'un peiple pasteur*. Paris: Editions de l'Office de la Recherche Scientifique et Technique d'Outre-Mer.

Binford, L. R.
1980 Willow smoke and dogs' tails: hunter-gatherer settlement systems and archaeological site formation. *American Antiquity* 45:4-20.

Blanton, R. E.
1976 Anthropological studies of cities. *Annual Review of Anthropology* 5:249-64.

Bohannan, P. & L. Bohannan.
1968 *Tiv Economy*. London, Longmans.

Bouju, J.
1984 *Graine de l'Homme, Enfant du Mil*. Paris: Société d'ethnographie.

Cancian, F.
1976 Social stratification. *Annual Review of Anthropology* 5:227-48.

Carlstein, T.
1982 *Time Resources, Society and Ecology*. London: Allen and Unwin.

Chayanov, A. V.
1966 *The Theory of Peasant Economy*. D. Thorner, B. Kerblay and R. E. F. Smith (eds.). Homewood: R. D. Irwin Inc.

Coe, M. D
1981 Religion and the rise of the Mesoamerican state. In *The Transition to Statehood in the New World*. G. D. Jones and R. R. Kautz (eds.),157-171. Cambridge: Cambridge University Press.

Deetz, J. F.
1982 Households: A structural key to archaeological explanation. *American Behavioral Scientist* 25:717-24.

Digard, J. P.
1978 The segmental system: nature model or anthropological construction? Discussion of an Iranian example. In *The Nomadic Alternative*, W. Weissleder (ed.), 315-17. The Hague, Paris: Mouton.
1981 *Techniques des Nomades Baxtyari d'Iran*. London, Paris: Cambridge University Press, Maison des sciences de l'Homme.

Dumas-Champion, Fr.
1980 Le rôle social et rituel du bétail chez les Massa du Tchad. *Africa* 50:161-81.
1983 *Les Massa du Tchad: Bétail et Société*. London, Paris: Cambridge University Press, Maison des sciences de l'Homme.

Durrenberger, E. P.
1984 Operationalizing Chayanov. In *Chayanov, Peasants and Economic Anthropology*, E. P. Durrenberger (ed.), 39-50. London: Academic Press.

Evans-Pritchard, E. E.
1968 *Les Nuer*. Paris: Gallimard.

Finley, M.
1987 *Sur l'Histoire Ancienne: la Matière, la Forme et la Méthode*. Paris: La Découverte.

Frantz, Ch.
1978 Ecology and social organization among nigerian fulbe (Fulani). In *The Nomadic Alternative*. W. Weissleder (ed.) 97-118, The Hague, Paris: Mouton.

Freidel, D.A.
1981 Civilization as a state of mind: the cultural evolution of the Lowland Maya. In *The Transition to Statehood in the New World*, G. D. Jones and R. R. Kautz (eds.), 188-227. Cambridge: Cambridge University Press.

Friedman, J. & M. J. Rowlands.
1977 Notes towards an epigenetic model of the evolution of "civilisation". In *The Evolution of Social Systems*, J. Friedman and M.J. Rowlands (eds.), 201-76. London: Duckworth.

Godelier, M
n.d. La notion de formation sociale économique.
1980 The concept of "Asiatic Mode of Production" and Marxist models of social evolution. In *Relations of Production*, D. Seddon (ed.), 209-57. London: Frank Cass.
1984 *L'Idéel et le Matériel*. Paris: Fayard.

Halstead, P. & J. O'Shea.
1989 Introduction: cultural responses to risk and

uncertainty. In *Bad year Economics: Cultural Responses to Risk and Uncertainty*, P. Halstead and J. O'Shea (eds.), 1-7. Cambridge: Cambridge University Press.

Harris, M.
1979 *Cultural Materialism*. New York: Random House.

Hill, P.
1982 *Dry Grain Farming Families: Hausaland (Nigeria) and Karnataka (India) Compared*. London: Cambridge University Press.

Hillier, B.
1985 Discovering house genotypes. Paper presented at the Annual Conference of the Theoretical Archaeology Group, Glasgow.

Hoftstadter, D.
1985 *Gödel Escher Bach: les Brins d'une Guirlande Eternelle*. Paris: Intereditions.

Holl, A.
1985a Subsistence patterns of the Dhar Tichitt Neolithic (Mauritania). *The African Archaeological Review* 3:150-162.
1985b Background to the Ghana empire: archaeological investigations on the transition to statehood in the Dhar Tichitt region (Mauritania). *Journal of Anthropological Archaeology* 4:73-115.
1986a *Economie et Société Néolithique du Dhar Tichitt (Mauritanie)*. Paris: Editions Recherches sur les civilisations.
1986b Vues divergentes sur le néolithique du Dhar Tichitt. *Journal de la Société des Africanistes* 56:5-19.
1989 Habitat et sociétés préhistoriques du Dhar Tichitt. *Sahara* 2:49-60.
1990 Unité de production et unité de consommation dans le néolithique du Dhar Tichitt. *L'Anthropologie* 94:535-558.

Hugot, G.
1977 *Un Secteur du Quaternaire Lacustre Mauritanien: Tichitt*. Chambery.

Johnson, D. L.
1969 *The Nature of Nomadism*. Research Paper N° 118, The University of Chicago.

Keatinge, R. W.
1981 The nature and role of religious diffusion in the early stages of state formation: an example from peruvian prehistory. In *The Transition to Statehood in the New World*, G. D. Jones and R. R. Kautz (eds.), 172-187. Cambridge: Cambridge University Press.

Kent, S.
1984 *Analysing Activity Areas: an Ethnoarchaeological Study of the Use of Space*. Albuquerque: University of New Mexico Press.
1987 Understanding the use of space: an ethnoarchaeological appraoch. In *Method and Theory for Activity Area Research: An Ethnoarchaeological Approach*, S. Kent (ed.), 1-60. New York: Columbia University Press.

Kent, S. (ed.)
1990 *Domestic Architecture and the Use of Space*. Cambridge: Cambridge University Press.

Khazanov, A. M.
1978 Characteristic features of nomadic communities in the Eurasian steppes. In *The Nomadic Alternative*, W. Weissleder (ed.), 119-26. The Hague, Paris: Mouton.
1984 *Nomads and the outside world*. London: Cambridge University Press.

Kramer, C.
1982a Ethnographic households and archaeological interpretation: a case study from Iranian Kurdistan. *American Behavioral Scientists*, 25:663-75.
1982b *Village Ethnoarchaeology: Rural Iran in Archaeological Perspective*. New York: Academic Press.

Levy, T. E. & A. Holl.
1987 Theory and practice in household archaeology: A case study from the Chalcolithic village at Shiqmim. In *Shiqmim I*, T. E. Levy (ed.), 373-410. Oxford: British Archaeological Reports.

Lézine, A. M.
1988 New pollen data from the Sahel. *Review of Palaeobotany and Palynology* 55:141-54.
1989 Le Sahel: 20 000 ans d'histoire de la végétation. *Bulletin de la Société Géologique de France* V(1):35-42.

Lloyd, P. E. & P. Dicken
1977 *Location in Space: A Theoretical Approach to Economic Geography*. New York: Harper & Row.

Maley, J.
1981 *Etudes palynologiques dans le bassin du Tchad et paléoclimatologie de l'Afrique nord-tropicale de 30 000 ans à l'époque actuelle*. Paris: ORSTOM.

McIntosh, S. K. & R. J. McIntosh
1988 From stone to metal: new perspectives on the later prehistory of West Africa. *Journal of World Prehistory* 2:89-133.

Meillassoux, Cl.
1977 *Terrains et Théories*. Paris: Anthropos.
1980a "The economy" in agricultural self-sustaining societies: a preliminary analysis. In *Relations of Production*, D. Seddon (ed.), 127-57. London: Frank Cass.
1980b The social organization of the peasantry: the economic basis of kinship. In *Relations of Production*, D. Seddon (ed.), 159-169. London: Frank Cass.

Mission Préhistorique de Tichitt
n.d. *Rapport Préliminaire*, (1980). unpubl.

Munson, P. J.
1971 *Tichitt Tradition: A Late Prehistoric Occupation in Southwestern Sahara*. PhD dissertation, Urbana Champaign: University of Illinois.
1976 Archaeological data on the origins of cultivation in southwestern Sahara and their implication for West Africa. In *Origins of African Plant Domestication*. J. R. Harlan, J. M. J. de Wet and A. M. B. Stemler (eds.), 187-209. The Hague, Paris: Mouton.
1981 A late Holocene (4500–2300 B.P.) climate chronology for the southwestern Sahara. *Paleoecology of Africa* 13:53-60.
1989 About "*Economie et société néolithique du Dhar Tichitt*". *Sahara* 2:106-8.

Nelson, C. (ed.)
1973 *The Desert and the Sown: Nomads in the wider Society*. Berkeley: University of California.

Nicholson, S. & H. Flohn.
1980 African environmental and climate changes and the general atmospheric circulation in late Pleistocene and Holocene. *Climatic Change* 2:313-48.

Oswald, D.
1984 The use of site structure to infer social and technological organization from the archaeological record. In *Frontiers: Southern African Archaeology Today*, M. Hall et al. (eds.), 297-309. Oxford: British Archaeological Reports.

Picon, Fr.
1978 L'adoption de l'élevage chez les Indiens Guajiros. *Techniques et Culture* 3:5-45.
1983 *Pasteurs du Nouveau Monde: Adoption de l'Elevage chez les Indiens Guajiros*. Paris: Editions de la Maison des sciences de l'Homme.

Pollet, E. & G. Winter
1980 The social organization of agricultural labor among the Soninke (Diahunu, Mali). In *Relations of Production*, D. Seddon (ed.), 331-356. London: Frank Cass.

Redman, Ch., W. T. Langhorne, M. J. Berman, N. Versagi, E. V. Curtin & J. C. Wanser.
1978 *Social Archaeology: Beyond Subsistence and Dating*. London: Academic Press.

Renfrew, C. A.
1984 *Appraoches to Social Archaeology*. Edinburgh: Edinburgh University Press.

Roux, V.
1983 *Etude Ethnoarchéologique du Matériel de Broyage (Tichitt, Mauritanie)*. PhD thesis, Nanterre: Université de Paris X.

Sahlins, M.
1961 The segmentary lineage: an organization of predatory expansion. *American Anthropologist* 63:322-45.
1968 *Tribesmen*. New Jersey: Prentice Hall.
1969 Land use and extended family in Moala, Fiji. In *Environment and Cultural Behavior*, A.P. Vayda (ed.), 395-415. New York: The Natural History Press.
1976 *Age de Pierre, âge d'Abondance: l'Economie des Sociétés Primitives*. Paris: Gallimard.
1980 *Au Coeur des Sociétés: Raison Utilitaire et Raison Culturelle*. Paris: Gallimard.

Servant, M. & Servant-Vildary, S.
1980 L'environnement quaternaire du bassin du lac Tchad. In *The Sahara and the Nile*, M. A. J. Williams and H. Faure (eds.), 132-162. Rotterdam: A. A. Balkema.

Smith, S. E.
1980 The environmental adaptations of nomads in the West African Sahel: A key to understand prehistoric pastoralists. In *The Sahara and the Nile*, M. A. J. Williams and H. Faure (eds.), 467-488. Rotterdam: A. A. Balkema.

Smith, R.
1984 Preface. In *Land, Kinship and Life-cycle*, R. Smith (ed), ix-xiii. London: Cambridge University Press.

Spooner, B.
1973 *The Cultural Ecology of Pastoral Nomads*. Addison-Wesley Module in Anthropology. N° 45.

Steponaitis, V. P.
1978 Location theory and complex chiefdoms: A Mississipian example. In *Mississipian Settlement Patterns*, B. D. Smith (ed.), 417-453. New York, London: Academic Press.
1981 Settlement hierarchies and political complexity in nonmarket societies: the Forma-

tive period of the valley of Mexico. *American Anthropologist* 83:320-363.
Testart, A.
1982 *Les Chasseurs-cueilleurs ou l'Origine des Inégalités*. Paris: Société d'Ethnographie.
Tringham, R.
1983 The development of the household as the primary unit of production in neolithic and eneolithic south-east Europe. Paper presented at the Annual meeting of the Society for American Archaeology, Pittsburgh, PA.
Vernet, R.
1984 *La préhistoire de la Mauritanie: Etat de la Question*. PhD thesis, Paris: Université de Paris I.
1986 Le néolithique mauritanien; essai de synthèse. *Actes du Symposium Archéologie Africaine et Sciences de la Nature appliquée à l'Archéologie*, 71-85. Bordeaux.
1988 A propos de "Vues divergentes sur le néolithique du Dhar Tichitt". *Journal de la Société des Africanistes* 57(1-2):296-299.
Vita-Finzi, Cl. & E. S. Higgs.
1970 Site catchment analysis. *Proceedings of the Prehistoric Society* 36:1-37
Walsh, C.E.
1983 Saving in primitive economies. *American Anthropologist* 85:643-49.
Warnier, J. P.
1985 *Echanges, Developpement et Hiérarchies dans le Bamenda Pré-colonial (Cameroun)*. Stuttgart: F. Steiner Verlag.
Weissleder, W. (ed.)
1978 *The Nomadic Aternative*. The Hague, Paris: Mouton.
Whallon, R.
1987 Simple statistics. In *Quantitative Research in Archaeology: Progress and Prospects*, M. S. Aldenderfer (ed.), 135-150. London: Sage Publications.
Wilk, R. R. & W. L. Rathje.
1982 Household archaeology. *American Behavioral Scientist* 25:617-39.
Wilk, R. R. & R. McC. Netting.
1984 Households: Changing forms and functions. In *Households: Comparative and Historical Studies of the Domestic Group*, R. McC. Netting, R. R. Wilk and E. J. Arnould (eds.), 1-28. Berkeley: University of California Press.